NEARER MY DOG TO THEE

NEARER MY DOG TO THEE

A Summer in Baja's Sky Island

GRAHAM MACKINTOSH

BAJA DETOUR PRESS

SAN DIEGO, CALIFORNIA

Nearer My Dog To Thee   ISBN 0-9626109-1-7
Library of Congress Control Number 2003095405

First published in the United States of America by Baja Detour Press

Cover design by Tom Klare: tomklare@tomklare.com
Cover photos by Bonni Mackintosh
Interior design and layout by Ellen Goodwin: ellengoodwin@cox.net

First Edition

Address all Correspondence to:

Baja Detour Press
P.O. Box 1982
Lemon Grove, CA 91946
E-mail: bajadetour@aol.com

Dedication

To the Memory of my Mother and Father

And to my wife, Bonni.

Other Books
by
Graham Mackintosh

Into a Desert Place –
(A 3000 Mile Walk Around the Coast of Baja California)

Journey With a Baja Burro

For ordering information go to: grahammackintosh.com

Reviews of *Into a Desert Place*

Mackintosh... makes a great traveling companion.

— *New York Times Book Review*

Always vastly entertaining, this is one of the finest pieces of travel writing to appear in years and certainly one of the best books on Baja ever published. Don't miss this title; it's that good.

— *Coast Book Review Service*

Mackintosh...is an intrepid writer who not only details his very exciting journey but also puts Baja California into historical perspective...An impressive collection of lore, adventure. Mackintosh has a very exceptional ability to involve the reader in his plights and his joys.

— *Book Reader*

Mackintosh is the...fair skinned, flame-headed Brit who, with no money to speak of, walked—read my lips—walked 3,000 miles solo down one Baja coast and up the other, carrying a 60-pound pack and surviving on cactus, rattlesnakes and the fish caught from shore on a small, telescoping Daiwa rod. In searing, killing heat, he painstakingly distilled minuscule quantities of life-sustaining water as he went, and he frazzled seven pairs of boots during the Odyssey...the book is, quite simply, the best Baja book ever published—a sprint-paced, harrowing adventure yarn that has all the elements of a classic film.

— *Western Outdoor News*

A truly uplifting account of what one person alone against the world can accomplish. It is also one of the finest pieces of travel writing of recent times.

— *Irish Independent*

Before the trip, Mackintosh didn't consider himself a writer or an outdoorsman, for that matter. Most of his exercise consisted of knocking back a few beers in a pub or in front of a television set. With Into a Desert Place, Mackintosh proves he is both. In an uncluttered and sincere writing style, he takes the reader along on all legs of the journey, from the slow days of trudging up and down dusty hillsides to lively marine expeditions with Mexican fishermen...As he treks the miles with sore feet, Mackintosh changes from a clumsy, chubby city boy into a competent wilderness explorer, gaining endurance and a self confidence that comes only from pushing internal limits.

— *Albuquerque Journal*

Exciting, colorful, imaginative, amusing, instructive, this is a quirky, highly individualistic account of derring-do...Beyond recounting his travails, victories, hopes and set backs, Mackintosh introduces dozens of cameos of earlier visitors to Baja—John Steinbeck to name one—and a plethora of historical vignettes. Many colorful photographs help put you right in the experience—you'll feel you've participated in every one of the 3000 tortuous and fatiguing miles...reading about it is a glorious experience, a demonstration of the sheer will requisite to conquer an unforgiving area of our planet.

— *Times (New Jersey)*

Reviews of *Journey With a Baja Burro*

Mackintosh has the uncanny ability to take you with him step by step...mixing history with daily recollections. It is a wonderful book, even better than his first...a joyful read.

— Fred Hoctor, *Western Outdoor News*

You'll love this wonderful text because it's full of humorous, colorful historical vignettes and spiritual insights. Mackintosh...is an engaging and enchanting storyteller.

— *Palo Alto Daily News*

In *Journey With A Baja Burro*, adventure traveler Graham Mackintosh returns to the remote desert setting of his previous book in his expedition a thousand miles from the U.S. border south to Loreto. He and his burro follow the trail which leads to most of the mission sites along the way; his humorous first-person account will intrigue a wide audience.

— *Internet Book Watch*

This wonderful adventure held this sentimental "ass" spellbound and joyfully teary-eyed from start to finish. We defy any reader to remain dry eyed while the author struggles manfully himself to keep too much sentiment from the closing pages as he has to bid his beloved burro farewell. As we travel with Mackintosh and Misión, we realize there is a lot more to a donkey than we could have ever known. If you haven't already, you absolutely must read this incredible story. Mackintosh is a spiritual person in the best sense.

— *The Gringo Gazette*

After writing *Into a Desert Place*…Mackintosh returns with this account of his 1000-mile journey by burro from the California border to the oldest established mission in Loreto, located in the southern part of the Baja peninsula. Along the way, he describes the land, the people he meets, the missions he visits, and his travails with the burro. The book is well written and generally keeps the reader's interest.

— *Library Journal*

…a fascinating historical account of the establishment of Baja California's missions, and…the record of one man's quest to challenge himself physically and spiritually.

— *The Journal of San Diego History*

Reviews of *Nearer My Dog To Thee*

Mackintosh goes to the mountain! Baja's peripatetic author at his best.

— Gene Kira, Author of *The Baja Catch* and *King of the Moon.*

The book is much like Mackintosh himself—engaging, candid, and impulsive…chapter by chapter, and sometimes line by line, it swings from the poetic to the practical. I loved both his dogs, but even more so his beautifully drawn San Pedro Mártir.

— Jennifer Redmond, *Sea of Cortez Review*

Funny and full of fascinating information, Graham Mackintosh has beautifully brought to life another area of Baja California.

— Ann O'Neil, Author of *Loreto, Baja California: First Mission and Capital of Spanish California.*

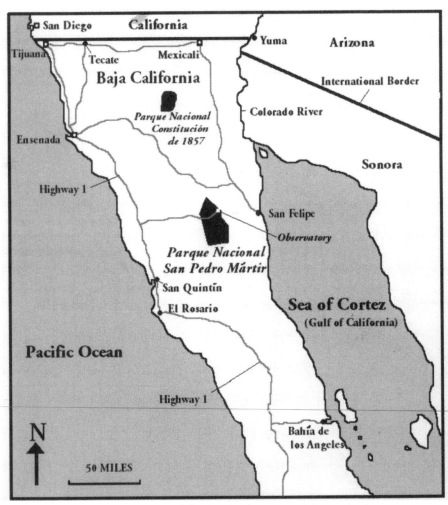

Map 1: Location of the San Pedro Mártir Mountains in
Northern Baja California

CONTENTS

All comments by the author, not otherwise described,
were spoken into a small cassette recorder.

Chapter 1

Flaming Sky Island

Those who picture Baja California as an unrelieved desert would be surprised to discover the highest part of the backbone of the peninsula covered by conifer forests, with winter snows and summer-flowered meadows. This is the Sierra de San Pedro Mártir, an island of rugged forested ridges and broad meadows, standing high above the coastal slopes to the west and dropping sharply to the San Felipe desert on the east. An adventurer who arrives at the top will find...beautiful isolated camp sites surrounded by giant old growth Jeffrey and lodgepole pines, and extensive groves of quaking aspens.

— Dick Schwenkmeyer

When I was thirty-one and could with little hyperbole safely describe myself as the least adventurous person in the world, I decided to set out alone to walk around the entire coastline of Baja California, surviving off the sea and the desert. Through some miracle I didn't chuck in the towel in the first week; I completed the journey in a little less than two years and went on to win the "Adventurous Traveller of the Year Award" in Britain for 1986. I described the trip in my book *Into a Desert Place*. Then at age forty-six, I walked a donkey down through Baja visiting many of the old Spanish missions from the border to Loreto—the site of the first permanent European settlement in "The Californias." That experience led to a second book, *Journey With a Baja Burro*.

Both these journeys involved covering a lot of miles—3000 and 1000 respectively—which meant keeping up a forced pace, making and breaking camp scores if not hundreds of times. Too often, having found a special spot where I would have loved to stay longer, I found myself reluctantly moving on, searching for food or water, or trying to meet some deadline.

Many a time I fantasized that my next protracted Baja trip would involve setting up a base camp in some remote location from where I could explore, be lazy, relax, become part of the scenery, catch up on some reading, listen to all the great radio reception I could get at night, enjoy a few beers, meditate, and ponder the universe. Balanced against whatever I would lose by not constantly being on the move, I could more intimately experience the wilderness and the wildlife and the spiritual nature of the rugged peninsula.

By the spring of 2001, having finished promoting *Journey With a Baja Burro*, I felt in need of a break. Fast rushing up on fifty, I thought I'd better get on my boots and indulge in a further Baja adventure while I could. For that purpose I had four months free between June and September. So where can you go in Baja and camp for the summer and not bake and fry in the sun?

There were places on the Pacific coast where cool currents, sea breezes, and lingering fogs can make for pleasant, sometimes almost frigid temperatures. And I'd be very happy to Robinson Crusoe-like hide myself away in some beautiful, remote sandy cove or up some little valley draining to a rocky shore. But the place that most called me was inland, atop the highest mountain range on the peninsula, the Sierra San Pedro Mártir.

> The heart of the Sierra San Pedro Mártir is a veritable fairyland, contrasted to its barren surroundings. It consists of a vast, gently-sloping plateau, 6000 to 9000 feet in elevation, about forty miles long and ten miles across. This sprawling tableland...encompasses a series of wide, nearly-flat valleys separated by low rocky ridges. Huge granite boulders are piled high throughout the whole country. Rich pine forests dominate the broad valleys and sprinkle the surrounding ridges. In contrast to the dense, nearly-impenetrable thickets of chaparral that blanket the western foothills, underbrush on the plateau is sparse, giving the pine forests the appearance of a well-kept, spacious park.
>
> —*John W. Robinson—Camping and Climbing in Baja*

My wife Bonni and I had spent several weeks there in previous summers and the climate was near perfect. The highest peak stands at 10,154 feet. Another crowning feature, this one manmade, is Mexico's National Observatory, its three white domes rising on a stark pine and fir "sprinkled" ridge—the eastern scarp of the plateau—at over 9,000 feet.

The forest of the San Pedro Mártir Mountains is one of the least known, least visited, least logged, conifer forests in North America. It is a classic ecological "sky island" like those of southeastern Arizona—an "elevational" oasis surrounded by chaparral and desert. There are healthy populations of deer, big horn sheep, and mountain lions. It is home to at least nine species of conifers—including white fir, Jeffrey, ponderosa, lodgepole, and sugar pines, and endemic San Pedro Mártir cypresses. Indeed, the San Pedro Mártir range hosts a plethora of endemic species and subspecies of plants, birds, and other animals.

Not only has it been protected by its own isolation, since 1947 its largely unsullied natural beauty has been assured through the granting of National Park status in Mexico—the first location so honored in Baja California. Hunting, off-road vehicles, and motorcycles are banned in the park.

To get there I would need to drive about 170 miles from San Diego on Baja's Highway One, then a further 60 miles into the mountains on a sometimes rough, unpaved, dirt road. Its dusty, washboardy stretches and endless twists and turns can be off-putting to the casual visitor and downright destructive for a regular passenger car, but I planned to head up in my 4WD truck and camp there all summer.

The trip should cost not much more than 600 dollars, and I wouldn't have any income for that period; but happily, I wasn't born to privilege—a lifetime of tireless industry and answering the call without counting the cost or worrying about tomorrow had left me always refreshingly close to a saintly poverty. A state my good wife Bonni has been wonderfully tolerant of.

She labored hard not to kick me in the bollocks when I related my conviction that taking off on a true spiritual adventure should not be seen as an abandonment of one's responsibilities, but rather should be held as every man's sacred duty, and every responsible life should be so organized and planned as to make it possible.

Even on your knees, gasping for breath, the San Pedro Mártir is a delightful place to see nature at its pristine best. There has been in recent years a heightened interest in the region because its old growth forests have never known the scream and buzz of widespread commercial logging. And thanks to its historical inaccessibility it is, in the words of Melissa Savage of UCLA, "the last landscape-scale mixed conifer forest in North America with an unmanaged fire regime."

Every summer scores of lightning-started fires occur in areas so remote that vehicular access is impossible, and Mexico has never had the trained manpower or aerial resources to adequately fight these wildfires. Fire suppression rarely comes before the mountains and Mother Nature are ready. From the higher ridges and peaks, a discerning eye can often make out a patchwork of previous burn sites. When fires occur they tend to meet these former burn areas and lose their power, or simply sweep through a portion of the forest taking out smaller trees, fallen branches, and brush, but leaving the larger trees intact, protected by their thick bark.

With so many destructive wildfires of late in the United States— more than $500 million a year in nationwide losses and millions of acres going up in smoke—the forests of the Sierra San Pedro Mártir have taken on a special interest to those studying the effects of fire suppression north of the border.

Dr. Richard Minnich of the University of California, Riverside, has, for more than thirty years, been comparing data on fires in Southern California with data from the San Pedro Mártir. In Baja, Minnich noted, fires occur more often but do far less damage. "We found that fires burned under the trees without burning the trees...The big trees survive and the little ones get burned out, creating perfectly managed open forests."

Melissa Savage, comparing the San Pedro Mártir with two similar sites in Southern California that have experienced fire suppression since 1905, points out that, "Tree-ring scars in the Sierra San Pedro Mártir show an average fire return interval of 13.5 years unchanged over the past 200 years," whereas in the Southern California sites, average fire occurrence went from about 12 to 30 years.

She also noted the greater age and grandeur of the San Pedro Mártir trees. The oldest Jeffrey pines encountered in the Southern California mountains were about 300 years, the oldest at the San Pedro Mártir site was 448 years.

Such studies suggest that frequent fires have not damaged the forest ecosystem, but rather have proved completely beneficial. In the park-like openness of the Sierra San Pedro Mártir there is little evidence of widespread insect or pathogenic fungal infestations. Only the most decadent and weakened trees are affected.

As a consequence of fire suppression in the U.S., shrubs and saplings have proliferated in many pine stands while thick accumulations of fuel have built up on the forest floor. Stands become dense and choked. The trees then become stressed and susceptible to attacks by pine beetles and other insects, pathogenic fungi, and dwarf mistletoe. And this leads to more tree mortality and the build up of ever more extensive amounts of fuel. When a fire occurs under these conditions, it is likely to destroy vast stands of forest.

Will Moir, of the USFS Rocky Mountain Research Station, in Flagstaff, Arizona, recently wrote, "Prior to fire suppression, the fires in the pine forests of the region behaved in a somewhat predictable manner determined by years of evolution and natural processes. The forest ecosystem of today, in contrast, has possibly reached a point of unstable criticality. A lightning strike may lead to a few trees burning, a few acres burning, or a catastrophic stand-replacing fire sweeping over thousands of acres of forest. Land managers and scientists are no longer able to predict with much confidence what direction fires…in the Southwest might take."

Indeed, looking at the vigorous old growth forests of the San Pedro Mártir, one could argue that of all human influences in Western forests—air pollution, managed logging, cattle grazing, introduction of exotic plant species, etc.—well-intentioned fire suppression has been the most destructive. Considering the increasing number of disastrous fire seasons in the West in recent years, it might be claimed that, "The chickens are coming home to roast." And so might be a bigger bird.

The range of the California condor has been subjected to a long, slow decline since the Pleistocene era, over 40,000 years ago, when "California" condors were found from British Columbia to Baja California, across the southern United States to Florida, and even up the east coast as far as New York. By the time the existence of the giant scavenger was made known to Europeans in 1603, the birds' range had become limited to the Pacific coastal regions from Baja California to British Columbia.

European colonization had a disastrous effect on the already contracting California condor population. Their numbers plummeted as many were poisoned, shot, and trapped in the mistaken belief that they were preying on livestock…and others were shot simply for sport or target practice.

Even over-eager scientists and museum collectors added to the pressure on the dwindling population. The stuffed specimen on display in the Smithsonian Institute in Washington, D.C. was captured in the San Pedro Mártir Mountains.

The rugged plateau of the San Pedro Mártir was one of the final strongholds of the condor. Its surrounding steep canyons, towering peaks, and abundant deer, cattle, and bighorn sheep provided ideal habitat and feeding opportunities. One scientific report mentioned encountering three condors in July 1937 in the Encantada meadow area. The last credible sighting was in 1947.

Soon after, the condor was only found in the wild in California and was fast heading for extinction. Some U.S. conservationists argued that the condors' only hope was to be granted rigorous legal protection and left undisturbed in the wild; others urged that most if not all condors should be captured and bred in zoos or special facilities. The debate continued until 1985, when 6 of the remaining 15 wild condors disappeared. Only one was ever found. It had died from lead poisoning. It seemed likely that most if not all of the others had ingested lead shot or bullet fragments left by hunters in animal and bird carcasses.

By 1987 the remaining wild California condors had all been brought into captivity. The eggs and birds were taken to either the Los Angeles Zoo or the San Diego Wild Animal Park. The total world population numbered only 27.

Efforts were made to increase the birds' numbers as quickly as possible. Normally, adult females lay one egg every other year but if the egg breaks or the chick dies, they often lay another egg. Using that knowledge, researchers and zookeepers removed the first and sometimes the second egg and began artificially incubating them. When the chicks hatched, they were raised by keepers with the aid of hand puppets to mimic adult birds.

Such was the success of the technique, that in 1992 an attempt was made to release several young condors into the wilds of the Los Padres' National Forest northwest of Los Angeles. But the captive reared condors had through pleasant familiarity lost all fear of man. They landed on buildings, hung out on roads, and begged food from picnickers. One died after drinking antifreeze dumped along a highway, and four others were killed by collisions with power lines. Consequently, the remaining birds were all returned to captivity in 1994.

Zookeepers began teaching the condors to avoid humans by harassing the birds at every opportunity. At first, the condors did not react much when their keepers ran at them yelling and waving their arms, but soon the young condors became frightened and sought to avoid the keepers. In the end most were so well conditioned that they vomited at the mere sight of a person. Power lines and poles were put into the condor pens and rigged to deliver a mild shock every time a condor landed on one. Not surprisingly, when released these birds did much better avoiding humans and power lines.

The areas for release were gradually extended in the U.S., and came to include the Grand Canyon. But releasing the condors back to the wild remained problematic and expensive. Birds have been lost to coyotes, golden eagles, and trigger-happy individuals. Of the 35 condors so far released in the Grand Canyon, 14 have died. The most heartbreaking loss occurred in the spring of 2000 when 5 mature birds died of lead poisoning, again probably from eating carrion contaminated with shotgun pellets or bullet fragments. All the Arizona condors were brought in for testing, and most were treated for various degrees of lead poisoning.

Such tragic mortality in the U.S. brought the Sierra San Pedro Mártir into serious contention as a location for releasing "cóndor californiano." There are no power lines, hunting is strictly prohibited, and the human impact is insignificant.

Any condor released in the San Pedro Mártir would be able to range over much of Northern Baja California and even into the United States. Conceivably, one might even glide down to the Pacific or the Sea of Cortez for a little seafood as its ancestors were inclined to do. Under favorable conditions a condor can easily cover a hundred miles a day.

Perusing a map and taking a "bird's eye view" of the Sierra San Pedro Mártir, my attention hovered over several points of interest. Towards the southwest was the site of the old Dominican mission of San Pedro Mártir. It was a short-lived mission, initially founded April 1794 at 7,000 feet in one of the meadows on the plateau, then because of the prospect of severe winter frosts moved shortly after to a lower location in a valley draining west. Even there, at 5,500 feet, it was the most elevated of all the California missions, and the one with the least cultivated land. It was abandoned around 1806.

To the south was *Botella Azul*, or Blue Bottle peak, at around 9,500 feet the highest point on the plateau. And to the east, across a long chasm of a canyon, stood famed *Picacho del Diablo*, at 10,154 feet:

> …the jagged summit of all Baja California, the unchallenged retreat of lions and mountain sheep, the unscaled lookout of eagles and mighty condors. The glittering granite slopes of this majestic peak glisten in the sun as though robed in purest snow, and even from the banks of the Colorado, a hundred miles away, its jagged white pinnacle juts boldly above the skyline.
>
> — *Arthur North (1906)—Camp and Camino in Lower California.*

I have long wanted to stand atop of Baja's highest mountain. From the plateau the favored approach route was to descend 3,000 feet into the canyon before battling straight up to the peak. The descent and ascent are steep and challenging, but if one can follow the correct route it need not be a technical climb.

The more I perused that map, the more my imagination delighted at the possibilities. Baja was again singing its siren song, calling me down. The San Pedro Mártir would be my destination.

Yet, as I'd found with my previous journeys, no matter how much I plan, they have a tendency to take on a direction and a life of their own. I have learned to keep my mind and heart open to a little Godly guidance.

Chapter 2

Penny From Heaven

When I talked to pilgrims walking with dogs I was surprised to hear that their companions were often not pets brought from home but animals who had at some point joined them on the road and then never left their side for the rest of the journey... This pilgrim, like several others whom I met, interpreted the unanticipated relationship with a canine companion as part of the mystery of the Camino and suggested that the dogs were pilgrims in their own right. Some even suggested that they bore the souls of pilgrims who had never been able to reach Santiago.

— *Pilgrim Stories: On and Off the Road to Santiago.*
Nancy Frey.

A tiny, black ragamuffin of a terrier puppy turned up at our San Diego house one day in January 2001. As so often happens, after vainly trying to chase it away, or get the local animal shelter to answer the phone, Bonni and I ended up keeping her.

We cleaned her up in the kitchen sink, combing out her fleas and pulling off (we counted them, I'm not exaggerating) about three hundred ticks. There were also pencil-sized worms crawling around in her stools.

In spite of her problems, she was a feisty, fearless, friendly little thing, full of herself and full of fun. We had yard dogs, and we loved them and looked after them, but I wouldn't say I was close to them. But this new little puppy wormed her way into my heart. She was a born comedian. I only had to look at her to want to laugh and sweep her up in my arms.

We called her Penny. One day, gazing lovingly into her mischievous brown eyes, and feeling a mysterious rapport, I found myself saying, "Penny, I love you more than I love anything in the whole universe." And the terrible thing was, at that moment, I meant it. Thanks to that little terrier, day-by-day, in my eyes, every dog in the world grew in stature.

She also gave me a new appreciation for a little dog that my parents had years before I was born. I have a single black-and-white photograph of my mother holding it near London just before the Second World War. It wasn't the greatest photo, a little fuzzy, but it was one of the few my parents had from that period in their lives when they were too poor to own a camera or even have many pictures taken. But there it was with its little puppyish black nose poking from its black ragamuffin face—just like the little gal who'd come to us.

Many a time in my youth, growing up in a council flat on an "estate" west of London, I remember my mother pulling out that photo from her handbag, smiling, talking about her "Bonny," and how much she and dad enjoyed that dog, how much joy it brought to them in its short life—it must have been one of the few things making them laugh with the Great Depression still gripping the world and Hitler raising the specter of another war in Europe—and how upset they were when it died of "distemper."

I never asked but I'm sure my parents—who had met after coming to London from remote parts of Scotland and Ireland to look for work—had no money for shots or vet bills. Working by the hour and living week to precarious week, they probably had little enough money for their own health care. I never asked much in those days. I never listened much either. The television was constantly on in our house. As my mother reminisced, I'd try to sound interested but I'd always be looking past her rather than into her past, more interested in the nonsense on the telly than the recollections of a wonderful aging lady from County Clare.

We never had a dog; there was no room for one in our cramped little flat. So I'd never had a chance to develop a relationship with one myself. But my mother had tremendous compassion for animals. Her family had owned a donkey in Ireland and she spoke with as much love for that beast as she did for her Bonny, but sadly she never had a photo. To see her throwing breadcrumbs to the sparrows or feeding the ducks was like seeing St. Francis at work.

My father was as gentle, modest, and hardworking a soul as my mother. He had spent much of the Second World War in the British Eighth Army chasing Italians and Germans across North Africa, and up through Italy. I grew up barely knowing anything of his "Desert Rat" days, but in my later teens I realized my dad had been caught up in some amazing events, and I would delight in sharing a glass of whisky with him and listening to some of his tales.

I recall him telling in his beautiful soft Invernesian accent about the time his armored brigade had roared into Naples. The powers that be decided that there were too many stray dogs in the war-ravaged city and they were a serious health concern. His unit was ordered to take a break from chasing Germans and go on the offensive rounding up the dogs. It was an assignment my father had no enthusiasm for, but he graphically told how the strays would be wired to a generator, placed in a tub of water, and electrocuted. It was a disturbing image that I never forgot.

Chapter 3

Getting Involved

From their eyelids as they glanced dripped love.

— Hesiod c. 700 B.C.

Thanks to my growing fondness for Penny, the proposed San Pedro Mártir trip took the expected unexpected turn. Like most Baja travelers, I've seen the sad reality of a dog's life below the border and tried not to get involved, but sights that used to be just sad and depressing now started to seem heartbreaking.

One day in the spring of 2001, I pulled into a gas station two hundred miles down the main Baja highway, on the edge of the Central Desert, and there was a friendly young Mexican man asking for money to ride the bus north. As he seemed so pleasant I gave him a few pesos, a soda, and a packet of chips. A few minutes later, after I'd gassed up, I saw him and two other passers-by throwing stones at three or four inoffensive, hungry-looking dogs that had also come to the gas station to seek a handout. They were laughing as the bemused dogs were howling with the hits and fleeing down the road. Such was my disgust, I resolved to express my feelings on a grander scale than simply telling that person what I thought of him.

To help publicize the plight of Baja dogs, Penny and I could head up to the mountains together and I'd write about our travels...and what she was and what she would become. A summer with her would be full of fun.

But Bonni made two very important points: First, although we lived just a few miles from the border, Penny almost certainly wasn't a Baja dog. Second, with so many coyotes, bobcats, and mountain lions up there, taking Penny would be like "taking a chicken on a stick." Now, although I could have argued that Penny was anything but chicken—she would run unhesitatingly down the throat of a tyrannosaurus and start ripping out its tonsils—Bonni's points were well taken.

A stronger case could be made with a Baja street dog, one with longer legs and a better sense of self-preservation...and one, quite honestly, that I'd care a little less about.

I'd heard that there was a pound in Tijuana, just across the border, where as many as 60 to 80 homeless and abandoned street dogs were being barbarically killed every day with electricity—the Tijuana Hot Plate method they called it. Perhaps as an act of paternal atonement, I pictured saving a dog from there and calling it Sparky.

However, a friend informed me about a new animal sanctuary half an hour's drive below the border, near the Fox Studios where the movie Titanic was made. The staff, I was told, regularly go to the Tijuana pound to select as many dogs as they can bring to the sanctuary. I drove down to see the place and penned an article for the *Discover Baja Travel Club*:

BAJA ANIMAL SANCTUARY

This summer I'll be hiking around the Sierra San Pedro Mártir Mountains with a dog. During my six-month *Journey With A Baja Burro* I came to appreciate what great company an animal can be. Rather than take a pampered dog from the U.S., I decided to look for a Mexican "street dog" in need of a loving master...While looking for a suitable Baja mutt, a good friend directed me to the Baja Animal Sanctuary (BAS) in Rosarito Beach, and put me in touch with its president and founder Sunny Benedict...

As tourists we've all seen the dead dogs by the side of the road, and the parade of pathetic mutts wandering the streets of Baja towns—all skin and bones, and covered with ticks and mange.

Sometimes we stop and offer the unfortunate creatures a cracker or a bit of meat...and maybe a friendly, cautious hand. Sometimes we're so moved by their sad, pleading eyes that we end up taking the dogs home. But mostly we pass by, numbed, shaking our heads, trying not to get involved, saying inwardly "why doesn't somebody do something?"

Sunny Benedict is someone who did get involved. In 1990 she bought property in Rosarito Beach and built a home. Eventually she began working in a real estate office on the main boulevard, and there began to appreciate the scale of the problem as she watched abandoned and homeless dogs and cats going back and forth outside. "I just had to do something," she said.

From putting out water and a little food, she started bringing them home two or three at a time, cleaning them up and trying to place them with loving owners. She realized it wasn't enough. She couldn't work full time and give adequate attention to the needs of the animals.

So in January 1997 she placed an ad in the Baja Sun asking people interested in forming an animal sanctuary in Rosarito to attend a meeting in the real estate offices where she worked. Eighteen people showed up. Each donated $10. And so the Baja Animal Sanctuary was formed with assets of just $180.

The City of Rosarito promised to provide a piece a land, and while the energetic founders waited in vain for the "promised land," they ended up with almost 100 dogs and cats to look after in their own homes. Undeterred, a month later, they held another fund-raiser. This time 150 people showed up, and $1000 was added to the coffers.

The Baja Animal Sanctuary was then able to rent a few brick buildings and a piece of land about 4 miles east of the toll road, overlooking Rosarito Canyon. There was no electricity, and water had to be trucked in, but the Baja Animal Sanctuary (BAS) at last had a physical location. A generator, donated last summer, now supplies the power.

In the four and a half years since its founding, BAS has taken in well over 4,000 animals. They currently have about 400 dogs and 125 cats and kittens at the shelter. They have a no kill policy—except in cases where serious injury or sickness has robbed the animal of all hope of a reasonable quality of life.

Nearly all assistance and support comes from the U.S., though the Sanctuary has several dedicated Mexican workers (including two charming young part time vets.)

I met Sunny Benedict in Rosarito in May and followed her vehicle up the winding road to the Sanctuary. Around an impressive two-story building, scores of dogs were milling and loafing in fenced corrals, and pushing out curious noses from an assortment of kennels. Many "trustees" were roaming free and came up to greet us and settle down in the shade beneath our vehicles.

At first it was hard not to be overwhelmed by all the dogs and puppies. However, I was soon introduced to a few likely prospects. Many had sad stories. I was shown a white female

German shepherd that had been tied to a horse and dragged across a field till most of its fur and some of its skin had been scrapped off. When it managed to escape, it ran into the canyon. About three days later it appeared at the gate of the sanctuary and was taken in and cared for.

One unfortunate little fellow who had perhaps been too solicitous at a street taco stand had hot oil thrown all over him. The poor thing suffered terribly and still bore the scars, but is now recovering.

And there was Tyson—a big, friendly bullmastiff boxer which had been used for fighting—he was all scarred and "dented." When he had become too old for fighting he was just thrown out.

Sunny commented that when a Mexican dog develops a problem such as mange, all too often, rather than treat it, the impoverished owners simply abandon the dog and get another…

Inside the building I was shown the simple but well-stocked veterinary pharmacy and the surgery area where the animals were neutered and spayed. I was introduced to some of the cats and kittens. Two cats, Hobo and Peso, were found by the store near the highway toll booths where they had been scrounging food. They were brought to Sunny's house in bad shape with abscesses and fleas. Both have since been adopted by San Diego families.

Scattered around on the walls were scores of photographs of contented dogs and cats mailed and brought down to BAS by appreciative new owners. One was of a Dalmatian that had been left on the side of the road in Ensenada to die after being hit by a car. She was taken to the sanctuary where a leg was amputated in order to save her life. But she was eventually adopted by a family in California where she's living happily in the company of other Dalmatians. Also on the walls of the shelter were various newspaper stories about the work done by BAS, including some from the *San Diego Union-Tribune*.

The BAS brochure describes its mission as follows: "Our goal is to accept abandoned and abused animals, place them in a safe environment, attend their health needs, and to then find them loving homes." Sunny added that, "Educating the public regarding the proper care of animals is also one of our main concerns."

Recently, an opportunity came for BAS to take over a small veterinary clinic in town where they can now get to grips with the animal population problem by providing low cost neutering and spaying for anyone in town who can't afford to have it done.

As worthy as the diverse goals are, it was when Sunny talked about the "happy endings," the animals that had found loving homes in the U.S. or with families in Rosarito, that her eyes filled with tears. Finding good homes for the animals is clearly the greatest reward for all those working at BAS.

About 20% of the adoptions take place in the Rosarito area, almost exclusively with Americans and other tourists; nearly all the rest are placed in Southern California. (Though dogs have in fact returned with their new owners to Alaska, Utah, Montana, even Berlin.)

Last October the BAS adoption director, found an adoption outlet through PetsMart in the US. For a suggested $75 donation for each dog, BAS hosts a dog adoption every Saturday, 10 a.m.-3 p.m., at the Vista PetsMart.

Visitors and volunteers are welcome at the Baja Animal Sanctuary. If you don't want to drive down, or would feel more secure accompanying someone else, car pool visits can be arranged...

There is an orphanage down the road housing about 30 children aged between four and fifteen. Sunny added, "People have come here and have continued down the road to leave donations of food and clothes at the orphanage."

Further up the canyon, there is a Drug rehab' center. Required to do community service for a few weeks as part of their treatment, several of the residents have worked at BAS.

Sunny said enthusiastically, "The guys there who have been on drugs are called street dogs, that's their nickname, so we had "street dogs" working with street dogs. And it was really good to see the self-esteem that started to develop again with these young men who had lost everything because of their drug problem. They began to interact with the animals and they felt important, and I feel in a way the sanctuary helped boost them back into real life again."

There seemed to be just about every kind of dog available for adoption, and everything from the happiest, healthiest fellows down to the saddest most pathetic specimens that had just been brought in. But confronted with so many appealing eyes, I was too overwhelmed to make a decision at the sanctuary, so I went to the BAS adoption at the PetsMart store in Vista, near San Diego.

I felt like I had gone from Macy's to one of communist Moscow's department stores. There was just one dog left, which made my decision a little easier. It was described as a Rhodesian ridgeback mix, but I thought I could see more German shepherd and greyhound in him. Whatever he was, he was about 6 months old, small, slim, sweet, and a fairly uniform chestnut brown color. He had been up for adoption at the store for three or four Saturdays without success. The woman in charge of the adoption said she thought that the dog was waiting for me. It was an irresistible line; my sympathies were duly aroused. His name was Benny—that wouldn't do as it was too much like Penny; so I renamed him Pedro, in honor of our destination and, by extension, in honor of Peter of Verona, the Dominican saint who had lent his name to the mountains.

Chapter 4

Champion And
Ever Fervent Protector

I should count myself the coward if I left them my Lord Howard,
To these Inquisition dogs and the devildoms of Spain.
Let us bang these dogs of Seville, the children of the devil,
For I never turned my back on Don or Devil yet.
— Alfred Lord Tennyson—*The Revenge*

In the English-speaking world little is known about Saint Peter Martyr, perhaps because he had the dubious distinction of being the patron saint of the Inquisition. The very mention of that institution is enough to provoke the pugnacity of any true-blooded Englishman and have him spewing the most abhorrent associations.

But in Italy and Spain the patron saint of the Inquisition evokes other images. Many works of art have been commissioned about his martyrdom. Typically he is represented in Dominican attire, smiling serenely with a large knife or axe splitting his skull. In his left hand he holds a book where the first words of the Catholic Credo can be read, "I believe in God, Creator of heaven and earth."

According to Catholic commentaries, Saint Peter the Martyr was born in Verona, Italy, probably in 1206. His parents were adherents of the Manichean or Catharist heresy, which had become firmly rooted in northern Italy at that time.

His father, wanting to give him a sound education, sent him to a Catholic school. One day, his uncle asked him out of curiosity what he had learned at school. "The Creed," answered Peter, "I believe in God, Creator of heaven and earth."

His uncle was horrified. This was a denial of the fundamental tenet of the Manicheans which held that there were two first principles or creators—the one evil, from which came all material things; the other good, which was the origin of all things spiritual. In vain did his uncle try to persuade him that all material things were the work of the devil. In spite of the misgivings of the uncle, Peter's father decided to let him continue with the education he was receiving at the Catholic school, and eventually sent him to the University of Bologna.

There, he became even more confirmed in his "orthodoxy" by the teachings of St. Dominic, the founder of the Order of Friars Preachers, better known as the Dominicans. At the age of sixteen he asked St. Dominic to accept him into the order.

Peter aspired to preach to the heretics and bring them back to the fold. Seeing that he had a gift for touching hearts and "inspiring even the most stubborn with salutary fear," his superiors sent him throughout Lombardy and other parts of Italy.

He preached so vehemently against the Catharists that many forswore their heresy. The Church histories do not record whether Peter's parents or uncle were among the converted. He was developing a reputation as a "Second Paul" because he had turned from error and was assiduous in converting his former community.

Peter was fearless in entering the bastions of heresy. He thought it the greatest honor to make himself a sacrifice for the Church. Every day at the climax of the Mass he prayed, "Grant, Lord, that I may die for Thee, who for me didst die."

Because of his zeal he was appointed Inquisitor General for northern Italy. According to the Catholic historians, "It was always with reluctance that he acted with rigor against the obstinate. Never, in fact, did he resort to harsh measures until he had exhausted all mild means suggested by kindness and Christian charity."

In Milan, he had brought before him a Manichean whom those of that sect honored as their leading teacher. Peter of Verona decided to examine him publicly in an open square so that even the most obstinate defenders of this heresy would be forced to renounce their errors, when they saw them refuted before the people.

The examination was long, and the great heat of the sun was almost unbearable for the throng gathered to witness it. The exasperated Manichean suddenly exclaimed: "If you are as saintly as these deluded people think you are, why do you leave them to die of this awful heat? Why do you not ask your God to send us a cloud to protect us from the scorching rays of the sun that are burning us up?"

"I will do so," replied Peter without hesitation, "if you promise to relinquish your heresy, when you see my prayer granted."

The Manicheans called to their spiritual leader to accept the proposition; for, as the sky was perfectly clear, they felt he could run no hazard. Then Peter exclaimed: "That you may all know, and with one voice confess, that the omnipotent God, whom we adore, is not less the Creator of things visible and corporal than of things invisible and spiritual, I pray Him, in the name of His son Jesus Christ, to send a cloud to protect us from the burning rays of the sun." He then made the sign of the cross and cast his eyes to heaven. Within minutes both Catholic and heretic found themselves beneath a gathering of thick clouds, which formed a welcome canopy over their heads and did not disappear until the examination came to an end.

However, the black clouds of heresy did not disappear so easily. Dissatisfied with the progress being made, the Pope, on June 13, 1251 addressed a brief to Peter of Verona:

> We have resolved to strengthen the Inquisition here with all the more care, because the evil is nearer to Us. For this reason, We order you to...exert yourself heart and soul for the effectual extirpation of heresy. Against those whom you find tainted with heresy, or accused of it, you will proceed in accordance with the ecclesiastical laws, unless they submit themselves absolutely to the requirements of the Church. If necessary, you WILL invoke the assistance of the secular power. Should any wish to forswear their heresy, you will absolve them, after having consulted the diocesan bishop; but you must always take the necessary precautions to assure yourselves of the sincerity of their conversion.

> Above all things, We desire to see this business forwarded. You will therefore proclaim publicly and resolutely that, if any city or community, any nobles or other powerful persons, seek to obstruct Our efforts in the matter, We will avail Ourself of the sword of the Church against them. Nay, We will appeal to that of kings, princes, and crusaders, in order that heaven and earth may act together in punishing their atrocious rashness; for it is more essential to defend the faith near home than in distant lands.

The new climate of fear brought matters to a head. What Peter's miracles and preaching couldn't achieve, fear of the lash, the gallows, and the stake often did. Hundreds came forward to publicly abjure their heresy and to be admitted into communion with the faithful.

But it was not the same with the leaders of the Manicheans. They knew there could be no compromise or understanding with this zealous "defender of the faith," whose single aim seemed to be the destruction of their sect and the eradication of their cherished beliefs. Accordingly, they conspired to kill him.

In a sermon which he preached to some ten thousand people on Palm Sunday, March 24, 1252, in Milan, Peter exclaimed: "I know for certain that the Manicheans have plotted my death...Let them do what they will. I will accomplish more against them then than I have done during my lifetime."

The conspirators let the Easter festivals pass. On Saturday, April 6, 1252, Peter of Verona left Como to return to Milan on foot. The chief assassin, Carino by name, followed in eager pursuit. On the way, he was joined by his associate in crime. Peter and his companion were overtaken in a thick wood. Carino struck "the saint" on the head with a thick machete-like knife, which opened a terrible wound and caused Peter to sink to the ground. While the defenseless inquisitor was commending himself and his murderer to God and reciting the Creed, the assassins attacked the martyr's companion, and gave him several blows, from which he died a few days later. "Then, seeing that Peter of Verona, though no longer able to speak, was, through the sheer force of his will, using his finger to write the first words of the Creed in his own blood, Carino sank a dagger into his breast."

Thus, in the forty-sixth year of his life, Peter achieved the martyrdom he prayed for. The martyr's remains were carried to the Dominican Church of San Eustorgio in Milan for solemn interment. It was a somber occasion for the Catholics in Milan and the Order of Friars Preachers; many could think only of their lost champion and feared the worst.

However, it was as Peter prophesized. Immediately after his martyrdom the "atrocious rashness" of the Manicheans in Northern Italy was finally brought to an end. They became so despised that no one in those parts dared to admit that he was a Manichean. Some of the sect were driven from their homes and pursued by Catholics who had earlier trembled in their presence. Greater numbers than ever before publicly relinquished their heresy. Many of their leaders gave unequivocal signs of sincere conversion; for, not content to remain among the ordinary faithful, they joined the Friars Preachers, and led edifying lives. Several became fervent defenders of their new faith.

Naturally, veneration of Saint Peter Martyr is especially noteworthy in the Order of Friars Preachers, and many are the churches, chapels, and monuments dedicated to his name in the land of his birth. A church was built at the place of his death—the main altar erected over the spot where he fell and wrote the beginning of the Apostles' Creed in his own blood. His body is still preserved and venerated in the magnificent chapel of Saint Eustorgio, Milan.

John Paul II wrote from the Vatican, March 25, 2002:

> To my Venerable Brother Cardinal Carlo Maria Martini, Archbishop of Milan. I was delighted to learn that [you]...are preparing to celebrate the 750th anniversary of the martyrdom of St Peter Martyr, a Dominican religious who was killed for the faith on 6 April 1252...

> On this special, happy occasion, I rejoice with the Archdiocese of Milan that benefited from his zealous activity, promoted his canonization, preserves his mortal remains and the place of his martyrdom. I cordially unite with the Sons of Saint Dominic who in him honor their first martyr, an exceptional model for consecrated persons and for the Christians of our time...

> St Catherine of Siena notes that with his martyrdom, the heart of this outstanding defender of the faith, burning with divine love, continued to release "light in the darkness of the many heresies". His assassin, Carino da Balsamo, whom he forgave, was converted and later put on the Dominican habit. Remarkable was the widespread, intense feeling provoked by his brutal assassination. Not only did the echo spread through the Dominican Order and the Diocese of Milan but also throughout Italy and Christian Europe. The Milanese authorities, summing up the unanimous veneration of the martyr, asked Pope Innocent IV to canonize him. The canonization took place in Perugia in March 1253, a little less than a year after his death. In the Bull with which he was added to the list of martyrs, my venerable predecessor praised his "devotion, humility, obedience, goodness, piety, patience and charity", and presented him as a "fervent lover of the faith, its outstanding champion and ever fervent protector..."

San Pedro Mártir

Chapter 5

An Affirmation

Believe one who knows: you will find something greater in woods than in books.
Trees and stones will teach you that which you can never learn from masters.

— Saint Bernard

Pedro was a handsome, sleek dog with the thin, fast features of a greyhound, and the gait of a racehorse. He had a playful, friendly personality, but he seemed to have a timid streak too, as if he knew what was awaiting him. The first night in our house I couldn't leave him for ten minutes without him whimpering and whining. He only settled when I put him in a basket next to Penny, who was about the same age. They slept soundly together, but the seeds of doubt had been planted in my mind; perhaps Pedro wasn't quite ready to embrace martyrdom. But given my own inauspicious beginnings for an adventurer, I wanted to give the little fellow a chance and see if he was made of sterner stuff than what he had so far shown.

A week later, June 1, 2001…the day of departure came. Bonni was going to drive me up to the mountains and leave me there for exactly four months. I was checking my email for the last time before departure. There was an encouraging letter from the director of BAS supplying some background on Pedro:

Hi Graham…Pedro arrived at BAS with his mom. We "guess-timated" his age at the time to be about 5 weeks. He was in California about one month prior to you adopting him. His brother was adopted out three weeks ago, and we couldn't understand why Pedro wasn't lucky, as he is such a great little guy. I guess HE was waiting to make the final decision. Good luck on your ventures…I'm truly jealous, hope all goes well for you and Pedro. Hugs, Sunny.

But there was another email, which had been forwarded to me from a woman volunteer at BAS:

> I just want you both to know how very concerned I am for Graham and Benny. Graham may be an experienced camper and backpacker but I wonder if he realizes that a certain amount of training goes into getting a dog ready to take on such a venture. First of all he mentioned that Benny would be carrying a pack. Please let him know that Benny should be X-rayed to make sure his hips are sound before a pack is put on him…And does Graham have the following in order for the dog: proper ID, shot records, microchip, rolled collar, 6-foot lead, foot protection. Yes, foot protection!! Does he realize how hot the ground will be for Benny's feet? The dog needs some sort of foot protection. I'm all for giving a dog a career and a purpose but I feel more preparation and concern for the dog needed to go into this "adventure."

Given the awful circumstance of so many Mexican mutts, I was taken aback by the suggestion that Pedro should have boots, X-rays, and a microchip. I was looking forward to escaping as much as possible from the modern world and all its wonderful technologies, so the idea of taking a Baja dog implanted with a microchip seemed ludicrously sacrilegious. The writer was obviously coming from the world of pampered U.S. dogs rather than the world of a dog's chance south of the border. I was taking a few chances and preparing for a few discomforts myself; it seemed reasonable to expect the dog to do the same.

Nevertheless, I replied:

> Just to put minds at rest. Pedro won't be wearing a pack—that idea was really for a bigger dog…The ground won't be too hot; I'll be in a shady pine forest with lots of meadows. It will be cold at night. We just gave Pedro rabies and other shots, and while this is an adventure, I'll have weeks to assess his abilities and attempt to train him…if he can't handle it, I can send him home with my wife. Hope that helps.

It was about an eight-hour drive from San Diego to the park, allowing time for border lines and inspections. I was gung ho to go and arrive at a reasonable time, but before leaving I decided to do a few last minute errands including running over to a pet store and buying two or three vinyl-covered steel cable stakeout and run lines. I was willing to improvise with the chains and ropes I had but Bonni persuaded me otherwise. The lines would allow Pedro much more freedom in the early days before I'd trust him to run off line, and they would bolster my ability to quickly and safely secure him. It was about 2 p.m. by the time we left San Diego.

So on a fine Friday in June, we drove Pedro back into Mexico. We crossed the border at Tecate about 25 miles east of San Diego, then meandered south through the mountains on a relatively quiet two-lane road towards the port of Ensenada.

Fifty miles inside Mexico, a dozen miles from Ensenada, we pulled over to let Pedro out for a potty break at an isolated spot surrounded by parched chaparral-covered hills and valleys. And there we saw the heart rending reality of a dog's life in Mexico—beside a fence, sitting in a pile of trash was a classic Baja throwaway dog, a little puppy, a German Shepherd mix. Emaciated, mangy, forlorn, and pathetic, he had totally given up and was barely able to move.

It was as if he was put before me as an affirmation that I was doing the right thing. I was tempted to take him with me and attempt to clean him up, but concerned about him giving Pedro some disease, and as there was hardly any room in the truck, and wondering if the cold nights in the mountains might kill him, I reluctantly decided to leave the poor guy there. It was a real crisis of conscience. We left him enough dry dog food for two or three days and a large bowl of water, and decided that if he was still there when Bonni returned on Monday, she would pick him up and bring him home to San Diego.

As Bonni and I headed south in our Nissan pickup we saw the usual sad-looking strays and dead dogs by the side of the road—it's hard to drive ten miles along a Mexican highway and not see the bloated or mummified corpse of a dead dog.

About 170 miles below the border, we turned off the Transpeninsular Highway and after letting a little air out of the tires and a quick check of the vehicle, we headed east on a dirt road. I was glad to leave civilization behind. A sign proclaimed that the observatory was 60 miles ahead. In the evening light the mountains loomed majestic before us. I thought of that line from Genesis: "And the Lord God planted a garden eastward in Eden."

Sometimes we crawled slowly over bad patches of corrugated "washboard," and occasionally I'd get up enough speed to leave a cloud of choking dust behind us, but always I'd be looking ahead for any axle-ripping boulders or holes in the road. Pedro sat up front with us, mostly in Bonni's lap. In spite of the near constant juddering and banging, he didn't struggle, or strain to see, but just seemed to bask in all the attention. He closed his eyes and rocked his head when we scratched it, as if he was saying, "Umm…That's good. I like this adventuring. How about a little behind that ear?"

In the dry, sparsely covered foothills of the mountains, approaching the famed Meling Ranch, we stopped and I very carefully clipped Pedro on a leash, opened the truck door, stepped out, and invited him to jump down. While I looked around and admired the final lick of light on the tip of the peaks ahead, Pedro had a pee and a little roll on the ground. Almost immediately, I detected a strong smell of rank, well-rotted flesh. We jumped in the pickup and drove off. The stench came with us. Bonni and I were wondering if we'd trod in something—then we realized the smell was on Pedro's back. He must have picked it up when he rolled. Bonni tried to clean him with baby wipes, and sprinkled a little lavender perfume on him, but a vague odor of putrefaction lingered in the cab all the way up.

After the ranch, and crossing the dry riverbed of the San Jose Valley—in previous years there had been a sizeable stream there—the steepest part of the climb began. It was rapidly getting dark. More than once I lost traction on the dusty gravel road and was glad to feel the wheels bite again. We passed through several distinct vegetative zones as we went from coastal scrub through chaparral, oak and juniper woodlands, into the conifer forest. In a little over two-and-a-half hours drive time we had gone the geographical equivalent of from sun-baked Mexican desert to near tree line Canada—and had gone from needing maximum air conditioning to near full heat in the cab.

For the final dusty, rattling miles I looked beyond the moonlight reflecting off the white hood of the truck, strained to follow the sweeping beams of my headlights, and tried not to bounce from the washboard road down into one of the silvery, shadowy canyons.

As I had so much weight in the truck, I hadn't wanted to carry too much water, especially as I was sure we could fill some containers at a spring just outside the park entrance. It took us nearly an hour to fill them up; the flow through a pipe that had been wedged into the spring was much slower than it had been in previous years. The mountains were clearly dryer than normal, and it was perhaps the driest time of year—between snow melt and summer storm.

It was after 11 p.m. when we came to the park gate and a few wooden cabins. A sign welcomed us to the *Parque Nacional Sierra de San Pedro Mártir*. There was no one there, but luckily, the gate was open. After cracking a couple of celebratory cold beers, we drove several miles east beneath the towering dark pines. Inside the park, on the forested plateau, the road was in better shape.

At a viewpoint on a ridge in the "middle of nowhere" we passed a carved wooden sign, which said, in Spanish, *Chapel of Saint Peter*. I just managed to glimpse the chapel in the moonlight on a little rocky knoll. It was tiny and looked barely capable of holding two people and a dog. I might have stopped to investigate it if it wasn't so late.

"You know, Bon," I said, trying to keep us alert, "Pedro might be the reincarnation of Saint Peter the Martyr, sent back to earth as a punishment!"

"I think the road might have shaken your brain loose," she perceptively replied.

"No, seriously; I think he's been sent to me for punishment for being part of the Inquisition…I mean, he is the patron saint, no less."

"Well," Bonni added, "I'm sure he's come to the right person."

"And I intend to take my job very seriously."

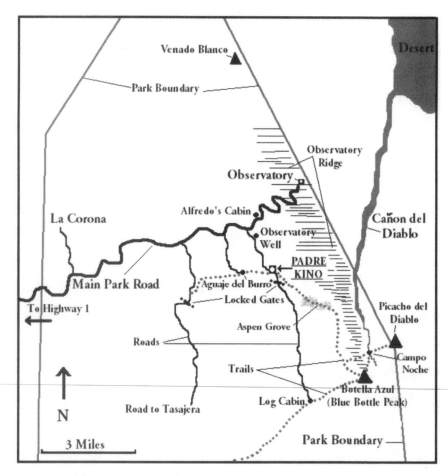

Map 2: Location of the Padre Kino camping area within
the *Parque Nacional*

Chapter 6

In the Forests of the Night

This other Eden, demi-paradise,
This fortress built by Nature for herself…
— Shakespeare

Mexico's National Observatory was at the end of the road. However, a mile or so before reaching the observatory gate, we turned right onto a little-traveled, single lane, dirt track and struggled not to lose it as we drove besides and occasionally across a dry riverbed dotted with aspens. Among the mix of dark pines and firs, and ghostly white aspen trunks our headlights picked out a rabbit, a coyote, and a swooping owl.

There was a steep forested slope on our immediate left. It was the western side of one of the most elevated ridges there in the mountains. On the other side, the whole San Pedro Mártir range dropped dizzyingly thousands of feet into the well-named *Cañon del Diablo*—the Devil's Canyon. A couple of miles behind us, out of sight, beneath a starry heaven of unmatched brilliance, the three great telescope domes of the observatory were dramatically perched on the crest of that ridge.

A mile or two across the other side of the canyon stood the highest point in Baja California—what most climbers, tourists, and guide books affectionately call *Picacho del Diablo*, the Devil's peak. (Although the Mexican government has bestowed on it the name of *Cerro de la Encantada*, and early Spanish explorers referred to it as *La Providencia*.) Actually, there are two white-walled, naked granite peaks a few hundred yards apart, and the Devil himself would be hard put to say which was higher. But most surveys give that honor to the north peak, which at 10,154 feet outdoes its neighbor by less than the length of a pitchfork.

As author John Robinson said "…whatever one wishes to call it— it is truly one of the finest mountains on the North American continent...*El Picacho del Diablo* is easily the most fitting name for this rugged peak, as any mountaineer who has scaled its precipitous crags would readily testify."

As I drove slowly the two or three miles south to what I hoped would be my campground for the summer, I had to concentrate on not losing the road as it occasionally meandered away from the valley bottom around the thick trunks of fallen pines. More than one trunk had been sawn in half after falling across the road. I could see just two hundred yards all around in the bright moonlight before the forest closed in and became a wooden wall.

Bonni and I were both so tired that our conversation now amounted to little more than slurs and grunts. Perhaps the deepest communication came when our hands touched while we were both stroking Pedro's head and neck. Our eyes met, we looked at each other's moonlit faces, and smiled. We had survived the journey up; we had made it.

It was almost midnight when we arrived at the apparent half-mile-wide head of a box canyon. It was bounded and protected on three sides by grandiose, rocky, pine-covered ridges that rose five hundred to a thousand feet above the valley floor. A rustic wooden sign informed us that we were in the Padre Kino Campground.

In the moonlight, I could see that a number of smaller valleys came down from the ridges towards the camping area. Their courses and the conjunction of the several valleys were blessed with a profusion of quaking aspens. Their whitish trunks were generally smaller and more densely packed than the conifers, which otherwise predominated on all the hills and slopes thereabouts.

Neither the valley nor the road ended there. The main valley turned sharply to our left and meandered a mile or two up to what I came to call "Observatory Ridge;" whereas the road, or rather the drivable track, continued four miles to the south to a dilapidated and abandoned log cabin, but a sign proclaimed, "No vehicles allowed—hikers only." Those who ignored the sign and attempted to drive up the steep slope would, within a third of a mile, be met with a heavy chain drooped across the road between sturdy steel posts flanked by car-sized granite boulders.

Enclosed in the rough right angle where the valley turned east, a "ring road" ran half a mile through the gently sloping forest marking an area of primitive camping; one could camp anywhere beside it. Down at the point of the turn, near the valley bottom, a few painted wooden signs and two large steel barrels serving as trashcans were the only concessions to civilization...and they had, courtesy of the *Parque Nacional*, been placed there just a year or two before.

After maneuvering around a fallen aspen, I turned on to the ring road and drove about fifty yards up from the valley bottom. Then, weaving around saplings and downed branches, I pulled onto a little rise in a small clearing, killed the engine and the lights, then lowered the windows. Bonni and I sat inside the truck for a few minutes, holding Pedro, whispering, listening, adjusting to the near total silence, sensing the forest. Very likely we were alone. We had camped ten days in the same spot the previous summer and hadn't seen anyone.

It was cold—probably close to freezing. The air smelled so clean it almost hurt. I was recovering from a sore throat and still felt the need to cough occasionally. It was comforting to see the waxing moon filling the forest with its silvery light and promising the security of several bright nights ahead. A broad band of moonlight illuminated a group of aspens down in the valley bottom...they stood soft, glowing, maternal, almost speaking in their goddess-like silence.

The more I sat there the more I was convinced that this clearing was the right place. It was about forty yards across; there were a few saplings growing there but the ground was mostly decomposed granite and dirt, and was remarkably clear of pine needles. All the big pines were some way back.

Although I was parked on a rise, it was not the highest point around. That was about 50 yards to the west, sandwiched between the road we came in on and the ring road. That hill would have provided the best all around view but I decided against setting up there for a number of reasons: I already had a good view of what was important—the road in from the north; I'd be better sheltered where I was, behind a screen of small aspens; I'd be less visible; I had the remains of last year's large fire pit which I only needed to shovel out; and most important, three big pine trees crowned that high point, presenting a danger from falling cones and branches, and from the many monsoon-like afternoon storms that visited the San Pedro Mártir range in the summer. One of the three lofty pines had been struck by lightning and almost its entire core has been burned out in a great spiral from half way up the tree to the ground. Those trees were three very big reasons for lightning to strike twice in the same place.

A ring of generally small aspens, most less than twenty feet tall, virtually surrounded the clearing. A yard or two back from those were two very prominent rotten pine stumps more than four feet thick and about 12 feet tall. The greater part of their trunks were stretched on the ground, almost forming a right angle, the reverse of the turn in the valley. Although soft, crumbling, and returning to the forest, they gave the site a sense of enclosure and protection south and east.

And above and beyond them, at what seemed to be a safe distance, stood a black palisade of pine trees, strong and paternal, many of their trunks as wide as my pickup and over 150 feet tall. "This is it," I croaked, "abandon ship."

Again I put Pedro on a leash, opened the door and stepped out. Pedro walked eagerly with ears flapping like gull wings. We crisscrossed the clearing and examined both the aspens and the pine trees. The ground was bone hard; the sound of dry pine needles crunched underfoot as Pedro sniffed the fallen cones and branches. It obviously hadn't rained for some time.

There was much to do. After temporarily tying Pedro to a pine sapling, I drove a metal stake into the ground in the middle of the clearing and attached one of the 15 foot vinyl-covered stakeout lines to it. Then I clipped Pedro on the other end. Now he could roam without me for a while so the master could enjoy another cold beer.

After examining the ground for sharp stones, sticks, and ants' nests, Bonni and I pegged out my 9 feet by 7 feet Coleman sleeping tent on the edge of the clearing beneath the shade and shelter of a spreading, very sound-looking, forty-foot-tall aspen. About six feet above the ground, the main trunk divided equally. It was as tall a tree as I dare camp beneath. We positioned the tent squarely on top of a folded tarp. The tarp would cushion and protect the tent floor from the ground and act as a moisture barrier, but I didn't want it sticking out to funnel rainwater or dew beneath the tent.

We threw our sleeping bags and blankets inside, shut Pedro in his home—a plastic kennel with some padding and blankets—closed up the car, and then gratefully retired for the night. It was close to 2 a.m.

I had a mild headache…it might have been due to the altitude, the long, eye-straining drive, my sense of responsibility for Pedro, or the dawning reality of what I'd be facing in the months to come. Thinking of the representation of Peter the Martyr with a machete cleaving his head, it seemed fitting to temporarily borrow him from the Inquisition and elevate him to the position of patron saint for headaches and seek his heavenly intercession.

Pedro slept through the whole freezing night. Apart from the occasional soft, contented snore we never heard so much as a whimper.

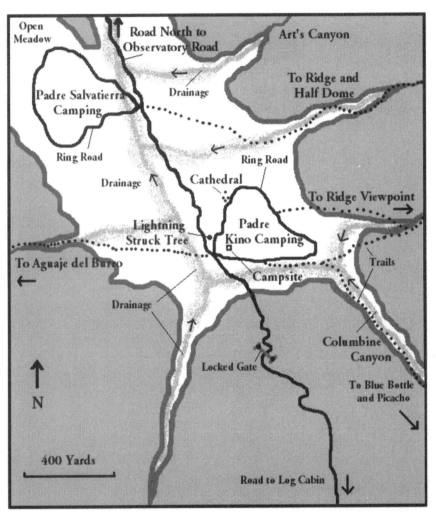

Map 3: The immediate surroundings of the campsite

Pedro's kennel   Sugar pines

Screen house and storage tent

Chapter 7

Playing House

Now air is hushed, save where the weak-eyed bat,
With short shrill shriek flits by on leathern wing…
— William Collins 1721-1759

It was a glorious first morning in the mountains. We all slept late and were able to emerge to feel the sun's warmth and bask in a rich and varied chorus of bird song. When I opened the door to Pedro's kennel he came out with a big yawn and a long arching stretch. I looked around at the open, uncluttered forest, and was tempted to let him run free, but decided to err on the side of caution so as not to prematurely lose the purpose of my trip.

With a mug of coffee in one hand and Pedro's leash in the other, I escorted a very curious puppy around the immediate environs of the campsite. We followed the warm shafts of light illuminating the flowers and fallen pinecones. There were so many different terrains within easy *walkies* distance: dry, grassy meadows bordered by lodgepole pines; aspen-lined arroyos filled with gravel and sand; rolling hills and slopes of Jeffrey and ponderosa pine; challengingly steep, bouldery rock faces studded with white firs and sugar pines.

I took Pedro over to see the lightning-struck Jeffrey pine atop the nearby rise. Standing maybe 140 feet tall it was a miracle of survival. Almost the whole core of the lower half of the tree had been burned out leaving little more than a foot thick spiral of bark and outer wood supporting the massive structure. Both Pedro and I could easily stand together inside the charcoaled trunk.

Then I led him over to another wounded Jeffrey pine less than 200 yards away—it had been struck near the top and the lightning had corkscrewed down the outside of the tree blasting off large chunks of wood and bark and flinging them forty yards all around.

Both trees served as dramatic reminders of the dangers of lightning. And there were scores of other trees, mostly scattered on the high points and ridges thereabouts, that had obviously been hit.

Following our stay in the Padre Kino Campsite the previous August, Bonni recalled an incident in an article she wrote for the Discover Baja Travel Club newsletter.

> I hiked out four miles to foray for fungus and…was somewhat alarmed to smell smoke, though I saw no indication of fire, near or far. The only ominous sign was that a lovely cumulus cloud was rapidly looming toward me, leading a bank of sonorous black thunderheads. Graham was relieved when I made it back to camp ahead of the rain and lightning…The next day we hiked back toward the [same spot]…Suddenly we…smelled the smoke. Graham sought out the burning source while I combed the woods and meadows for mushrooms. He found the smoldering base of a stump that must have been hit by lightning. Luckily it had been growing in a mound-shaped rocky outcrop that acted as a firebreak, but now it resembled a mini smoking volcano.

A pleasant warm breeze set the pine needles shimmering and moved through the quaking aspen branches creating a lovely rustling sound. It was hard to imagine a thunderstorm on such a cloudless day.

Dotted around the forest, we also saw several striking red snow plants, which range along the West Coast from the mountains of Mexico, through California, up to Oregon. Snow plants lack chlorophyll and cannot carry out photosynthesis—they live off decaying organic matter in the soil.

As John Muir wrote:

> The snow plant (*Sarcodes sanguinea*) is more admired by tourists than any other in California…Soon after the snow is off the ground it rises through the dead needles and humus in the pine and fir woods like a bright glowing pillar of fire. In a week or so it grows to a height of eight or twelve inches with a diameter of an inch and a half or two inches …The entire plant—flowers, bracts, stem, scales, and roots—is fiery red. Its color could appeal to one's blood. Nevertheless, it is a singularly cold and unsympathetic plant. Everybody admires it as a wonderful curiosity, but nobody loves it as lilies, violets, roses, daisies are loved. Without fragrance, it stands beneath the pines and firs lonely and silent, as if

unacquainted with any other plant in the world; never moving in the wildest storms; rigid as if lifeless...

There was so much to see and hear and smell. The air was full of the strident calling of pinyon jays. My eyes felt like pinballs bouncing between bluebirds, flickers, juncos, and hummingbirds...and at least one red-tailed hawk was patrolling just above the treetops. Bonni called me over to see a Williamson's sapsucker nest in a tall aspen overhanging the main arroyo—we watched the parents coming and going into the neat little hole drilled into the silvery white trunk.

Back in camp I clipped Pedro to his cable, which enabled him to run around and find sun or shade as he preferred. Letting him off-leash would be a big step, especially as he looked built for speed and showed great interest in chasing any little thing that moved.

Concerns about his timidity aside, Pedro came with a lot of positives. He was an even-tempered, good-natured, humble dog, who waited patiently for food or water. He had little inclination to lift his leg and spray on all the tents and gear; he simply stood and peed in a sensible place when he had to. While he amused himself playing with favorite toys, chewing on pine branches, tearing apart old cones, and digging for ground squirrels, I switched on my GPS and noted the camp position coordinates—115°27.04 W and a stone's throw short of 31° N—and the fact that we were at an elevation of 8,125 feet.

As Bonni and I started to unload the truck, I began to have mixed feelings about the abundance of equipment and supplies we had brought. It would be such a different experience from the "purity" of having my world in a backpack or on top of a burro. I hoped such "wealth" wouldn't detract too much from the joys of my saintly poverty.

After making a few adjustments to my sleeping tent, Bonni and I placed a couple of "kitchen tables" immediately beside it. I had a large, heavy-duty, silver tarp that I could pull over the tables and tent when it rained. It would completely cover everything a yard all around. I could then weigh it down with rocks and water containers. I was hoping it wouldn't be too big and heavy to be practical.

I needed to find a reasonably sheltered place for one of my 50th birthday presents—a Wentzel screen house, or gazebo. It would give me protection from sun and rain and flying insects, and offer a good view all round. If the summer thunderstorms weren't too threatening, it might be the best place to ride them out.

I ended up placing the screen house about ten or fifteen yards from my sleeping tent beside a line of small aspens and the trunk of one of the fallen trees. There was plenty of room inside to put a card-table, chair, and three large, lidded, plastic storage containers. Although it had two zip-up doors, the gazebo had no floor so I was going to have to coexist with the ants and bugs wandering over the ground.

I set up a second tent a little smaller than my sleeping tent. It would be the "store" for my food and excess gear. More concerned about ants finding their way into that, I took great care in its placing. I found a shady spot where there seemed to be no nest, then sprayed the ground with ant spray, placed a tarp down, and pegged the tent on top of the tarp. Politely ignoring Bonni's protests, I further sprayed around the bottom of the tent. It wasn't "politically correct," but it was practical and sensible. I also bagged and double bagged all the food that the ants might get into: nuts, bread, crackers, cookies, candy, dog crunchies. While I was at it, I made a mental note to spray under Pedro's kennel. As he would be locked inside at night for the foreseeable future, and given his tendency to roll in things putrid, I wanted to be sure the ants wouldn't devour him.

Bonni had brought a wire mesh, three-tier, fruit basket. She hung it from a branch of the large aspen above the tables, and filled it with potatoes, onions, apples, pears, plums, and oranges; then she draped a towel over it in such a way that it could be lowered and raised to keep off the dust and the sun. It worked great—no animals or bugs assaulted its contents.

I had three small solar battery chargers. I filled them with rechargeable AA batteries and placed them in the sun—then I filled a solar shower bag with water and left that out to warm up.

As the day got hotter, I was a little concerned about the number of small flies starting to land on everything. We hardly saw any the previous August. Although they weren't biting flies, I hoped they wouldn't be too much of a nuisance for Pedro.

I had to move Pedro a few times as he started whimpering if we got too far from him. To enable him to range even further, I ran a couple of forty-foot vinyl covered cables between trees and hooked him to one of them. That worked for a while. But when he started whimpering again, I tried shutting him in his kennel. I was reluctant to do so, thinking it was like jailing and punishing him, but he enthusiastically dashed inside, flopped down and enjoyed a long snooze. It was his secure den. To ensure the flies wouldn't bother him, I covered the kennel with a mosquito net.

With most of the chores done and Pedro sleeping, we found time to peruse some of our field guides. We had some difficulty identifying two of the common little flowers around the campsite—thanks to Bonni, I could at least say that one was a "little white phlox" the other "a pinkish half-flower phlox." Although abundant on the dry gravelly soil, they were not in our Western wildflower books. We suspected, correctly, that they were endemic to the San Pedro Mártir.

Near camp, a ground squirrel repeatedly emerged from its burrow and grabbed a mouthful of the "little white phloxes" then quickly backed into his hole.

In the summer of 2001, the San Pedro Mártir was as dry as I ever remembered. I had about a week's supply of water. Somehow I needed to find more. In previous years there had been a pool of water in a valley a little less than a mile to the east.

When Pedro awoke, we took him to it. He did a good job scrambling over the boulders and fallen trees in the valley bottom; I helped him once or twice. The pool was still there, but much reduced—it was little more than a stagnant 18-inch deep puddle in a natural rock basin. Pedro was happy to walk in and cool off a bit. It would be something in an emergency—even if it tasted of hot dog.

After finding the pool we strolled around to let Pedro see the lie of the land and leave his scent, increasing the chances that he could find his way back if he did wander off.

Shortly after returning to camp, we heard a vehicle coming. It was an older Dodge pickup, white with an official emblem on the door. It looked like a ranger making his rounds. That was a new development. In previous years you might or might not have to pay a couple of dollars "entrance fee" coming into the park, depending if anyone was at the gate.

The truck pulled into the clearing. A medium-sized, portly, kindly-looking man stepped out, wearing a khaki ranger outfit. He glanced at Pedro who was as silent and cowed as a Cathar before the Inquisition. I wondered what he was going to say about my plans.

I paid the new 70-peso park entrance fee (about $7.50 U.S.). He gave me the park brochure and map and said we were the only visitors in the entire 160,000-acre park that weekend. His name was Alfredo. He explained that the fee was for every vehicle entering the park; and after paying it we could stay as long as we wanted. I looked very deliberately at Pedro and asked, "Is it okay to stay a few weeks with my dog?" I thought it best not to mention "months" at this point.

"Si, no problema," Alfredo encouragingly replied. What a relief, and what a deal—maybe a whole summer for a few cents a day in a park in some ways as grand as Yosemite. I just hoped I hadn't misunderstood.

I explained that I wrote and lectured about Baja California, and showed him one of my books—it couldn't hurt my case when I finally found the courage to mention "months," all four of them.

At that point Bonni pulled out a letter of introduction that had been given me by Baja California's Secretary of Tourism—Juan Tintos Funcke. It was typed on white paper over a light blue printed Mexican eagle and looked impressively official with authoritative looking emblem, stamps, and signatures. It said, in essence:

> To all authorities civil and military, I present to you Sr. Graham Mackintosh author of the book Into a Desert Place. He will be making a journey in our state with the *"objetivo primordial"* of gathering information for another book about the attractions and beauties of our region. This Secretaría supports the project. To this end please look kindly on our petition and facilitate Mr. Mackintosh in order for him to achieve his objectives without hindrance.

Perhaps because of the paucity of people, or perhaps intrigued by my intentions, Alfredo seemed to want to sit with us and chat, but politely declined all offers of beer, coffee, or food. He was dignified, pleasant, and obviously keen to be helpful. I suspect he was being overmodest when he confessed he only spoke a few words of English.

We learned that he lived a few miles east of San Telmo, the village where the park road joined Highway 1. He was married with 3 children. His wife's name was Socorro. Several of his brothers and sisters were living in the United States, and many years ago he himself had lived and worked in Oceanside, California.

Alfredo had worked at the observatory before securing employment as a ranger. It was his third year in the job. He confirmed that for over ten years prior to his appointment, there had been no rangers in the park.

Obviously interested in nature, he spoke at length about the deer and the big horn sheep he'd seen, and eagerly related that when driving over he'd spotted a coyote with four puppies crossing the road. He lingered with us, talking about the park and learning about Bonni's interest in wildflowers and mushrooms.

Alfredo confirmed that it was very dry throughout the Sierra San Pedro Mártir. Usually there wasn't too much rain in June, he explained, but July, August, and September should be much wetter.

"Are the summer storms dangerous?" I inquired.

"No, you are in a good place here," he retorted.

I was working up to asking him about obtaining water when Bonni just asked him directly if he could help. He said he would be happy to bring me water from the observatory or from the observatory water truck when it was filling up from the well, two miles back down the road.

As a token of my gratitude, I gave him a copy of my latest book— *Journey With A Baja Burro*. He mentioned that the park director —Federico—would be arriving soon from Mexicali and staying in the park 3-5 days and would be sure to want to visit me. I wasn't quite out of the woods yet, but I was hoping it would be as pleasant with him as it had been with Alfredo.

Before Alfredo left, I asked him about rattlesnakes—"There are no rattlesnakes in this part of the forest, it's too cold at night," he said.

I asked if I had to be careful about rabid animals. He was adamant rabies was "not a problem in the park."

I went on, "Is it safe to leave things unattended? Is there a problem with…?" I was trying to recall the Spanish for "theft." Unable to do so, I asked, "Are there any banditos here?"

He smiled, and shook his head.

"What about mountain lions? Has anyone ever been attacked?"

He smiled at that one too.

It seemed to me that Alfredo embodied the Mexican attitude to not worry, and was politely telling me what I wished to hear, as if the most important thing in the universe wasn't truth and reality and confronting danger, but the need for me to be happy and relax.

As we shook hands, I thought Alfredo and I were going to get to know each other very well. I hoped he would return soon.

I dug out the ashes from our previous year's fire pit, and in minutes I had gathered sufficient firewood for the night. With all the pine needles, cones, and twigs on the ground serving as kindling, I soon had a blazing fire.

At dusk I brought Pedro and his kennel over and settled him inside by the warming flames. It didn't take much; he was as exhausted as his namesake after a hard day haranguing and hanging heretics. No doubt feeling the elevation, Pedro was dropping into his doggy dreams almost as soon as I latched the kennel door.

I was inside the sleeping tent putting on some warm clothes for the night. Bonni was sitting on her chair by the fire enjoying a beer. Suddenly, she screamed. I dashed from the tent expecting to see some huge, horrible creature dragging my poor wife into the bushes. Instead, I just caught sight of something small and black rising from her head and disappearing into the dark silhouette of the pine trees.

"It was a bat," Bonni explained. "Oh my God, it must have swooped down after a bug attracted to the fire."

"Did it scratch you or cut you?" I asked, concerned about rabies.

"No, it just fluttered around and brushed my watchcap. It didn't touch me."

"What a welcome to Mother Nature," I said as I closed up the tent and grabbed a beer.

Bonni and I sat feeding logs into the fire, staring at the flames. The aspens around the clearing leapt out in the firelight. They stood almost in a complete ring—half a dozen in each direction except to the west, where a solitary aspen stood as a close backdrop to our fire. The forest was now entirely still except the leaves of that aspen which jostled and danced with the rising smoke and heat. Every time a moth came close to my face, I was subconsciously pulling in my neck, expecting to see a squadron of bats dropping out of the moon.

Chapter 8

Bordering on Paranoia

He that's secure is not safe.

— Benjamin Franklin

Sometimes I envy the Mexicans their laid-back, happy-go-lucky approach to life. I am inclined to deal with danger head on, to perhaps exaggerate it, but always to be mindful and energized sufficiently by my anxiety to take preventative steps.

I had ankle-to-knee leather leggings for rattlers, a snakebite kit, a couple of sharp knives, a machete, and an assortment of other "weapons" handy for self-defense; and a first aid kit big enough to patch up an elephant hit by a jumbo jet.

Such focus and preparedness has served me well most of the time, but it comes at a cost. Focused fears can readily rise way out of proportion to any objective calculation of risk. And one can foolishly burden oneself with so much anxiety it's hardly worth the bother of living.

Having witnessed how violent thunderstorms could be in those mountains, I'd spent a good part of my time preparing for this trip reading about lightning and how best to deal with it.

The statistics are impressive. In the U.S. alone since 1960 there have been about 3,500 deaths and 10-12,000 injuries from lightning. The National Weather Service points out that lightning kills, on average, more people in the U.S. each year than tornadoes or hurricanes. There can be more than 200 million volts in a lightning flash, and typically between 10,000 and 100,000 amps. The speed of the lightning bolt can approach one-third the speed of light, and it can heat the air it passes through to temperatures as high as 50,000 degrees Fahrenheit.

Every year dozens of stories such as these appear in North American newspapers:

> Lightning struck one or more trees at the campground and traveled across and beneath the surface, striking people

holding onto aluminum tent poles or standing in pools of water. Twelve campers were taken to hospital, and ten others were treated at the scene.

Seven persons were hurt by lightning while attending a family reunion. Lightning apparently struck a tree and then "bounced" from it to the canopy tent under which they were standing.

Two women were killed by lightning while sheltering beneath a pavilion. The lightning split two of the pavilion's support posts. One woman received third degree burns over 35% of her body; two quarters fused in her pocket and the zipper to her jeans melted.

A 42-year-old man was injured when lightning struck the tent he was sheltering in. The lightning entered his right shoulder and exited through his right foot.

The "Lightning Safety Group" (LSG) of the American Meteorological Society recommends finding shelter in large enclosed structures (substantially constructed buildings), which tend to be much safer than smaller or open structures, or in fully enclosed metal vehicles such as cars, trucks, and buses. If caught in a forest, it advises, "waiting out the storm in a low area under a thick growth of small trees."

Once Bonni left with the vehicle, I would have to deal with lightning storms in nothing more substantial than one of my tents. Even so, I took at least partial comfort from the fact that I wasn't set up on the highest point, under tall trees, but rather the camp was nestled in a group of smaller trees, at what I deemed to be a sufficient distance from the big pines. Without camping in the bottom of the valley and running the risk of being washed away in a flash flood, I gauged that my little protected clearing would be as safe as anywhere thereabouts.

I had also read perhaps more than was good for me about mountain lions. I had seen one trotting across a meadow in the park a few years before. For much of the twentieth-century in the West, mountain lions were hunted and harassed, and thought to be a minimal danger to people. However, over the last twenty-five years, with greater protection afforded them, there has been a near exponential rise in attacks on humans, pets and livestock. And sadly for the sake of my peace of mind, I couldn't resist reading some of the graphic and horrifying accounts of what happens when fierce tooth and claw meets fragile human flesh. I entered the mountains feeling a bit like someone jumping into shark-infested waters after having seen the movie Jaws.

Although they typically weigh between 100 and 200 pounds—about the same as a human adult—they are capable of tackling animals many times their size with their powerful jaws, impressive teeth, and large sharp claws accommodated within oversize paws. Dr. Maurice Hornocker, a renowned mountain lion researcher, claims that "for sheer killing ability, [no cat in the world] surpasses the mountain lion."

A healthy mountain lion is able to kill an elk or a moose five times its own weight. In 1770, legendary frontiersman Daniel Boone saw one "seated upon the back of a large buffalo" that he estimated to weigh at least 1,500 pounds. The lion was hanging on with its claws while ripping a gaping wound into the neck of the buffalo with its teeth. Eventually, the mighty animal fell from loss of blood.

In 1851, "Indian fighter" Major John C. Cremony saw a lion attacking a grizzly bear in New Mexico. He graphically described how the cougar "tore open the back" of the bear and "ripped at its vital organs until it died."

A mountain lion usually ambushes its prey, stalking to within 20 or 30 feet, then leaping from behind and sinking its teeth into its neck. Its jaws are so powerful, it often prevails by severing the victim's spinal cord or by violently twisting and snapping its neck. The lion then drags the "carcass" to a secluded spot to feed. It usually eats the most nutritious internal organs first, leaving muscle tissue until later. After consuming its fill, the mountain lion will cover the kill with dirt, brush, and leaves, returning repeatedly to eat until the entire carcass has been consumed or until the meat spoils.

In recent years there have been a string of well-publicized attacks on people in California. In April 1994, Barbara Schoener, 40, was killed by a mountain lion while jogging alone on a path in Auburn State Recreation Area near Sacramento. Her body was found alongside several deer carcasses covered with leaves and dirt. California Department of Fish and Game (DFG) marksmen waited for the lion to return. A week later a female lion appeared at the carcasses and was shot.

In December 1994, Iris Kenna, 56, was killed by a mountain lion while walking alone on a road in the mountains of Cuyamaca State Park, east of San Diego. Those mountains are geologically and ecologically, in many respects, an extension of those south of the border. In the months before Iris Kenna was killed, a number of lions in Cuyamaca Park were shot for threatening or harassing humans.

In August 1994, two couples staying at a remote cabin in Mendocino County reported stabbing a lion to death after it attacked one of their dogs. Two of the people were injured in the struggle. The slain mountain lion was determined to be rabid.

California DFG reported 322 confirmed incidents of mountain lion attacks on pets and other animals in 1994. This compares with an average of just five to 10 confirmed incidents per year before 1975.

The Colorado Division of Wildlife has likewise reported a worrying rise in incidents of mountain lions confronting people with small dogs on hiking trails in that state. And Colorado has seen its share of fatal or near-fatal human-lion interactions.

The California DFG offered the following safety tips for people traveling in lion country:

- Do not hike alone. Go in groups, with adults supervising children.
- Do not approach a lion. Most mountain lions will try to avoid a confrontation. Give them a way to escape.
- Do not run from a lion. Running may stimulate a mountain lion's instinct to chase. Instead, stand and face the animal. Make eye contact. If you have small children with you, pick them up if possible so that they do not panic and run. Although it may be awkward, pick them up without bending over or turning away from the lion.
- Do not crouch or bend over. A person squatting or bending over looks a lot like a four-legged prey animal.
- Do all you can to appear larger. Raise your arms. Open your jacket if you are wearing one. Throw stones, branches or whatever you can reach without crouching or turning your back. Wave your arms slowly and speak firmly in a loud voice.
- Fight back if attacked. Some hikers have fought back successfully with sticks, caps, jackets, garden tools and their bare hands. Since a mountain lion usually tries to bite the head or neck, try to remain standing and face the attacking animal.
- Give that lion a healthy respect for humans.

All my reading had certainly given me a healthy respect for lions—some might argue an unhealthy debilitating respect, bordering on paranoia. One expert tried to put the risks in perspective by stating "your chances of getting struck by lightning are 10 times greater than your chances of attack by a mountain lion." Given my situation, I did not find that claim particularly comforting.

Others are quick to point out that such a claim is "a fiddled statistic" anyway. "It is true if you live where lions are rare. If you live or explore in the areas where lions and humans juxtapose, the odds begin to look a bit different." You could, of course, make the same point about the probability of being struck by lightning; if you spend a lot of time on high peaks standing under isolated trees during thunder storms, then you are just asking to get zapped.

One thing I could bet my life on, over the course of the following months, one or more lions would likely be aware of our presence. An encounter was a very real possibility. It would be prudent to remain watchful and prepared on all my solo wilderness hikes. In a face-to-face situation, with rock hammer or machete at hand, and stones and branches around, I felt reasonably confident that I could deter an attack or, if necessary, stand a good chance of prevailing. What concerned me most was being "ambushed," perhaps being taken by surprise walking around the camp at night and having my spinal cord severed, or being so severely mauled that I would be rendered defenseless, allowing the lion to drag me away and finish me at its leisure.

There were a couple of sources of comfort. One was if I could ever get Pedro to bark at anything, I would have his more refined senses to rely on. Another was at least there were no bears in the San Pedro Mártir.

Bonni has an eye for Nature

Graham feeling rejuvenated

Chapter 9

Fungal Filaments

Mushrooms can be every bit as beautiful as birds, butterflies, shells, and flowers, yet we never think to describe them in such flattering terms. When novelists or poets want to conjure up an emotion of fear, loathing, total revulsion, and imminent decay, they inevitably drag in the mushrooms and toadstools—malignant instruments of death and disease that appear only in the dankest and most abominable of situations.
— David Arora – *Mushrooms Demystified*

Sunday, June 3: It was another beautiful day, our anniversary. We had been married six years. In place of a present, I took to doing all the camp chores so Bonni could have fun in the forest. I threw down a stack of pinewood for our campfire. Many of the logs and branches shattered, throwing off bark and revealing mats of sulfur-yellow or white fungal filaments.

Bonni studied them with interest and explained, "Mushrooms are the fruiting bodies of fungi; they are the most dramatically visible part, but the great mass of nearly every fungus is hidden like these filaments, or hyphae, growing through the wood and the soil."

Bonni had a great love for nature. When we first met, her enthusiasm was for rocks and minerals. She was a member of the San Diego Mineral and Gem Society. But every aspect of nature caught her eye: birds, snakes, insects, wildflowers—all have occupied her attentions. Her latest fascination was for fungi. And there in the mountains of Baja California was where it all began. As Bonni wrote in her Discover Baja article:

Our interest in mushrooms was sparked camping in the Sierra San Pedro Mártir [in the summer of 1998] after the great El Niño winter. As a kid I'd observed plenty of fungi as I roamed the Wisconsin woods, but the appearance of many large red-capped, white-spotted "fairy tale" mushrooms in Baja was a first. This "fly agaric," or *Amanita muscaria*, got us noticing dozens of other varieties and we were hooked.

For our return, [in the summer of 2000] we armed ourselves with several fungus reference books and came to the park with great hopes for some serious mushrooming. Although we arrived at the park entrance after dusk, we could plainly see evidence of recent heavy rain along the roadside. The common summertime pattern of afternoon showers in the higher elevations makes for good 'shroom hunting.

Bonni, never one to be long mystified by a strange specimen, checked out books from the library, and then started her own impressive book collection. She even joined the San Diego Mycological Society. Before long she was well versed in matters mycological, and I wasn't immune to picking up a sporadic interest myself.

So there we were back in the San Pedro Mártir Mountains in early June 2001 with a fine collection of mushroom guidebooks. To the untrained eye, there was no sign of a mushroom, but Bonni now could home in on a 'shroom like a trained pig to a truffle.

On the forest floor there were a number of what looked like miniature moon landing craft, or more plausibly dried flower heads with extra thick petals. They were, in fact, the desiccated remains of earthstars—a type of puffball fungus. Conditions conducive for the release of spores result in the outer skin of this rounded mushroom splitting into star-like segments, which sometimes curve underneath revealing and lifting the delicate spore case within. In all probability, wind, rain, or perhaps some passing animal had long since dispersed the spores.

On the aspen trees she pointed out some brownish, velvety, bracket fungi that grew unobtrusively at old branch scars on the main trunk, like they belonged to the tree. This fungus—*Phellinus tremulae*—was about the size and shape of a horse's hoof, and can be found in nearly every aspen grove in the Western United States. Hidden hyphal filaments spread into and weaken the heartwood of the trees. Several aspens in the arroyo about our campsite had been flattened in rows by the wind, probably because of damage by this fungus.

Bonni also found the hard, foot-wide, dark brown, remains of another shelf-like fruiting body that had erupted from the roots of an ancient, decadent pine tree. Its hyphal filaments were likewise

growing inside the tree, actively rotting it. The tree was a
Before long, in tree terms, the mighty pine would come crashing down. But until that happened the fungus' fruiting bodies would continue to burst forth after rain. When fresh it is a massive, for a fungus, brilliant yellow polypore. For centuries it has been used for a yellow dye, giving the fungus, *Phaeolus schweinitzii*, the common name of the Dyer's polypore.

It was fascinating to think how much of the wood and general plant material in that forest was "infested" with fungi. Hidden all around, within the trees and underground, was a vast, network of fungal filaments, waiting for rain and the right conditions to produce fruiting bodies to spread their spores.

Indeed, the world's largest living organism is now thought by many to be not something as dramatically "solid" as a whale or a giant redwood but a fungus from eastern Oregon—a specimen of *Armillaria ostoyae*, popularly known as the honey mushroom. This pathogenic fungus began as a single microscopic spore an estimated 2,400 years ago, and now its filaments stretch 3.5 miles across, reach three feet into the ground, and cover an area equal to 1,665 football fields. You could be standing in the middle of the world's largest living organism and, apart from the unusual number of dead and dying trees about you, there would be little indication of its presence.

Surprisingly, the majority of trees in any forest, even the apparently healthy ones, are likewise "infested" with fungal filaments. Threads of these fungi spread throughout the soil and leaf duff, and reach within the tree's roots, sometimes penetrating between the root cells and even inside those cells. In most plant and tree species somewhere between 10-20% of all photosynthetic production is diverted to the benefit of these fungi. It would seem like a shocking case of fungal parasitism, another black mark for the fungi, for the vile decayers and rotters of the forest.

And I had brought my own rot with me. A red itchy patch had formed on my skin in the moist inner joint of my elbow. Bonni diagnosed it as ringworm, a fungal infection. I wondered could I have got it from Pedro or that little dog we'd seen beside the road. Fortunately, I had some antifungal cream. As I applied it to the affected skin I might have been forgiven for thinking that the best thing one could do for the forest and for every creature within it would be to spray the place with a particularly powerful fungicide.

However, the end product of such ill-informed do-gooding, like with facile fire suppression, would be the virtual destruction of the forest; we would end up killing most of the trees and plants, and stunting the growth of nearly all the rest. If we could reach beyond our prejudices against these seemingly destructive agents, and delve below surface appearances we'd see that the majority of the "host" trees and plants were by no means losing out with their fungal associations.

Take the snow plant. Its non-photosynthetic lifestyle is only possible because of the relationship its roots have with a fungus that enables them to better absorb essential nutrients from the soil. This "mycorrhizal" [fungus-root] association is mutually beneficial, and in the case of the snow plant "obligatory." It could not survive without its roots being penetrated by the hyphal filaments of the fungi.

And it is a similar story with the photosynthesizers. Only in recent decades have botanists and mycologists fully realized that as many as 95% of terrestrial plants live in a kind of intimate symbiosis with these root fungi. Plant scientists today consider these fungi to be the "biological cornerstone" of plant life on earth. The fungi might even have facilitated the plants successful colonization of the earth...and it seems likely that the two have been evolving together since.

As author, microbiologist and respected amateur mycologist Elio Schaechter puts it, "For the tree, the fungal filaments become enormously long and far flung drinking-straws." As well as serving as a secondary root system, reaching far out into the soil, extracting water, nitrogen, and vital minerals for their hosts, mycorrhizal fungi increase a plant's ability to tolerate stresses and adverse conditions. The fungal sheath serves the plant by absorbing and retaining toxic heavy metals such as arsenic and cadmium. They also help increase resistance to pathogen attack, especially from pathogenic root fungi. In return the plant or tree provides the fungus with the sugars, usually the products of photosynthesis, it needs.

Such is the importance of these associations that transplanted trees often fail to grow unless their mycorrhizal fungi are introduced with them. And orchid seedlings typically will not germinate without mycorrhizal inoculation.

Such crops as maize, wheat, and barley have shown growth rate increases of 2.3, 3 and 4 times respectively when inoculated with appropriate fungi. Onions so inoculated show growth rates six times greater. The beneficial yield effects of these fungal associations are usually far superior to those obtained with pesticides and fertilizers.

With eyes opened to the important ecological role of fungi in the forest, we realize that there may be more going on underground and under tree than we ever imagined.

In the April 2001 edition of *Nature*, John Klironomos and Miranda Hart, of the University of Guelph, Ontario, reported finding a "deadly partnership" between white pine trees and the *Laccaria bicolor* fungus, which grows into the tree's root.

According to them, the fungus preys on soil insects such as springtails to get animal-origin nitrogen and then "gives it" to the tree through their intimate root interconnectedness in exchange for the products of photosynthesis.

"We were originally trying to feed the fungi to the springtails," said Klironomos. "When we would introduce [springtails] to the soil...they would die immediately, and we wondered why. Upon closer examination, we discovered that the insects were really being attacked by the fungus. We think the fungus releases a toxin that paralyzes the insects, infects them, grows inside them, and then eats them alive." Using radioactively labeled nitrogen, Klironomos and Hart tracked the animal nutrients as they passed first into the fungus and then into the tree.

The tree and the fungus have developed a mutually beneficial relationship, a vast and hidden "swap-meat" whereby the fungus preys on insects to get animal-origin nitrogen and then gives much of it to the tree in return for carbon the fungus needs for its growth and metabolic activities.

"When we think of the fertility of a soil, we do not think of living animals," says Klironomos. "This study suggests that...plants may tap into this 'living' nutrient pool."

Root fungi similar to *Laccaria* are near ubiquitous among trees. So maybe fungi are more important than we realize. Without fungi the soil may become overrun with springtails—which typically inhabit a square meter by the hundreds of thousands—and other insects or animal pests.

Another fungus, *Arthrobotrys dactyloides*, is a very important element in controlling eelworm populations in soil samples. Its hyphal filaments are adept at capturing and "throttling" passing eelworms with nooses that inflate at the slightest touch. The fungus then penetrates and sucks out the victim's innards.

Such findings should make us more hesitant in our desire to shake up and improve ecosystems.

In the Aspen Grove

Jeffrey pine or ponderosa?

Chapter 10

Barking Up the Wrong Tree

*It is during cloudless windstorms that these colossal pines
[ponderosas] are most impressively beautiful. Then they bow like
willows, their leaves streaming forward all in one direction, and,
when the sun shines at the required angle, entire groves glow as if
every leaf were burnished silver...This species also gives forth the
finest music to the wind.*

— John Muir

Monday, June 4: Although the previous day's maximum
temperature was over 80°F, it dropped to well below freezing in the
night—my thermometer was showing 24°F at dawn. It promised to
be another fine morning; there was no wind and not a cloud in the
sky. By eight o'clock the sun felt hot on the back of my neck.

Knowing Bonni would soon be gone, I started picking her brains
about identifying some of the trees and flowers.

As for the pines, the lodgepole pines with their tiny cones, and the
sugar pines with their long cones and spreading canopies, were easy
to identify...but I had trouble accepting—what most popular writers
seemed to repeat each other in suggesting—that the majority of the
pine trees on the San Pedro Mártir plateau were Jeffrey pines, with
ponderosa pines not meriting a mention.

> The forests of the San Pedro Mártir are generally more open
> than those of the Sierra Juarez. Jeffrey pines are dominant in
> most areas, interspersed with Incense Cedar and White Fir.
> Sugar pines largest of all the pines occur on the higher ridges.
> There are also Quaking Aspens and Lodgepole pines...
>
> *Baja California Plant Field Guide — Norman C. Roberts.*

Above 1,500 meters, thickly forested glens leave the Baja
desert mythos behind. Here you will find piñon and Jeffrey

pine, incense cedar, white fir, sugar pine, and at least three species not found elsewhere in Baja—quaking aspen, lodgepole pines and the endemic San Pedro Mártir cypress.

Moon Publications — BAJA.

To my arboreally untutored mind, the supposed Jeffrey pines were made up of two very different kinds of tree. One had darker, more furrowed, brownish bark, smaller downward-pointing Christmas tree-like branches covering most of the trunk, and comparatively large cones. The other had lighter, orange-red, platy bark, massive straight branches that emerged higher up the trunk, and smaller cones. The difference between the two tree types was so obvious that I was frankly mystified. Bonni concurred. How could they be the same tree? The differences couldn't be accounted for in terms of age; even fully grown trees obviously hundreds of years old were patently distinct.

I was naturally reluctant to go out on a limb and question the considered opinions of so many fine authors, but a little perusing of tree books left me with the strong conviction that the darker, less ponderous trees were Jeffrey pines while the more orange, platy barked specimens were in fact ponderosas. And delving deeper into the literature reveals that the problem of identification between these two trees has a long and thorny history. Indeed, the problem ultimately leads into some profound philosophical questions as to what is and what is not a separate species.

Lewis and Clark encountered and described ponderosa pines in 1804, but it was Scottish explorer and plant collector David Douglas who, after coming across specimens near Spokane, Washington, named the tree in 1826. The name "ponderosa" was inspired by its ponderous appearance. "Since that time," as one writer states, "the taxonomy of the ponderosa complex has been the subject of continuing dispute."

When Jeffrey pine was "discovered" in 1852 in the Shasta Valley of California by John Jeffrey, another Scottish botanical explorer, he classified it as a variety of ponderosa pine.

Even John Muir referred to Jeffrey pine as a variety of ponderosa:

"The Jeffrey variety…forms magnificent forests scarcely invaded by any other tree. It differs from the ordinary form in size, being only about half as tall, and in its…more closely furrowed bark…and larger cones; but intermediate forms come in which make a clear separation impossible, although some botanists regard it as a distinct species..."

— The Mountains of California

A number of attributes have been suggested for distinguishing between the two trees including cone prickliness, cone size, and the smell of the bark.

Jeffrey pine cones are described as having prickles that are curved in, so they don't hurt one's hand when grasping, whereas ponderosa cones have prickles that stick out. Hence the phrase, "Gentle Jeffrey, prickly ponderosa." Admittedly most of the cones from the trees around my campsite seemed to be of the "gentle" type, but some were prickly, and others prickly in places. I had to wonder if too much credence had been given to cone prickliness in identifying the trees of the San Pedro Mártir and subsequent denial of the painfully obvious.

I went to collect cones from two huge but strikingly different trees growing fifty yards apart. The cones of the slightly smaller, more Jeffrey-like, tree were nearly twice the size of those from the larger more ponderosa-like tree. That alone strongly suggested to me that the orange-pink plated trees were ponderosas, or at least they weren't typical Jeffreys.

The scent of the bark and the crushed twigs of Jeffrey pines has been likened to lemons, vanilla, and pineapples, also violets and apples. Whereas that of ponderosas is described as having a pleasing, "pitchy" smell, similar to turpentine. However, after pushing my nose into the bark crevices of scores of trees and detecting everything from glass cleaner to mother's gooseberry pie, I thought that aromatic variation was simply too subjective to be a reliable tool of tree identification.

Even botanists and other scientists admit that it has been notoriously difficult to tell Jeffrey from ponderosa pines in the field because they are similar in so many ways, and yet display considerable variety.

With respect to ponderosa pines, there is a remarkable level of uncertainty as to how many subspecies, varieties, and races there are. William W. Oliver and Russell A. Ryker in their summary of the literature write:

Ponderosa pine (*Pinus ponderosa*)...is one of the most widely distributed pines in western North America...Within its extensive range, two varieties of the species currently are recognized: *Pinus ponderosa* var. *ponderosa* (Pacific ponderosa pine) (typical) and var. *scopulorum* (Rocky Mountain ponderosa pine)... Arizona pine (*P. arizonica*), sometimes classified as a variety of ponderosa pine is presently recognized as a separate species.

Ponderosa pine shows distinct geographic variations over its widespread range...var. ponderosa consists of three major geographic races and var. scopulorum of two major geographic races.

Natural crosses of ponderosa pine with Jeffrey pine have been observed in California where their ranges overlap, but they are rare...Ponderosa pine crosses with...P. arizonica...

Another writer claims, "Forestry studies indicate the existence of four distinct 'races' or 'ecotypes.' These...are morphologically distinct and would normally be treated as subspecies, but most have not been formally described at this rank."

In her comparison of the forests of the San Pedro Mártir with those in Southern California, Melissa Savage stated: "An undetermined number of pine trees...at Barton Flats [In the San Bernardino Mountains] may have been ponderosa pine or hybrids of Jeffrey with ponderosa pine."

In *Nature Notes* for Crater Lake National Park, Volume XXVI – 1995, Ron and Joy Mastrogiuseppe wrote:

In the late 1970s it was reported that Jeffrey pine, *Pinus jeffreyi*, occurs in the forested panhandle of Crater Lake National Park...The biologists...based their determination primarily on seed cones which did not appear like cones of typical ponderosa pine, *P. ponderosa*. Apparently those biologists were unaware of another contender, *P. washoensis*, a rare pine similar to ponderosa but with smaller cones. As it turned out, the ponderosa variants in the panhandle are actually closer to Washoe pine than to Jeffrey pine based on cone length and diameter. There still is the need, however, for additional study of local populations as one part toward understanding variation on a larger geographic scale because the widely-distributed variants of ponderosa pine are so difficult to interpret.

Some scientists have taken their attempt to distinguish these two tree "species" down to the level of chromosomal attributes. Researchers at the National Forest Genetic Electrophoresis Laboratory (NFGEL), part of the US Forest Service, reported:

> It can be difficult to correctly distinguish ponderosa pine from Jeffrey pine in the field. ...we developed isozyme markers that may be diagnostic at distinguishing ponderosa from Jeffrey pine.
>
> Isozymes were processed at 23 loci for 9 known Jeffrey samples, 14 known ponderosa, and 9 unknown, morphologically intermediate individuals...Eighteen of the loci were found to be informative and six principal components explained 85% of the variance. Two of the ponderosa were mis-identified and are really Jeffrey pine. Of the 9 unknowns, three appear to be Jeffrey, five are ponderosa, and one fits neither profile well and may be a hybrid.

Clearly, even that basis for distinction isn't entirely satisfying. Such attempts to separate these trees makes one wonder if any features are truly "diagnostic," and provides considerable insight into the difficulty of applying static concepts to what is essentially a fluid process of evolution.

Correctly identifying Jeffrey and ponderosa pines has, on occasion, been more than just an academic issue—getting it wrong has sometimes proved fatal.

Pine resin has been an important shipbuilding commodity since at least the time of Noah who was divinely instructed to "pitch the ark within and without." During colonial times, pines in the South Carolina and Georgia colonies produced copious resins of excellent quality for the construction and repair of British and colonial ships, and for the manufacture of turpentine.

During the Civil War, when Union forces were cut off from these sources of pitch and turpentine, production was shifted to the pine forests of California. When the resin was taken from ponderosa pines, there was no problem, but the resin of Jeffery pine is unique in that it is supposedly the only pine that contains aldehydes and a hydrocarbon, n-heptane (a constituent of gasoline), rather than terpenes to protect the tree from insect and fungal attack. The fragrance of Jeffrey pine bark is caused by these aromatic aldehydes in the resin. Misidentifying the trees and firing up a turpentine still inadvertently filled with sap from Jeffrey pines was like building a fire under a gas tank.

Bonni was packed and ready to go. Before leaving she helped me dip Pedro with a combination flea, tick, and mange solution, which thanks to one of its main ingredients, an "aromatic petroleum distillate," left him reeking of gasoline.

Then we sat together in the shade, by the cooling embers of yesterday's campfire while she read me the *Daily Word*:

> My heart soars with appreciation for you so that I am in touch with the sacredness of all life. My mind expands to take in wonderful possibilities that are mine to experience. As I commune with you in prayer and as I observe your presence everywhere, my spirit is renewed.

I kept pulling Pedro away from the still-smoking fire pit in case a spark sent his heart soaring and scattered his presence everywhere.

After a long, lingering hug and kiss, Bonni drove out saying she would try to return by July Fourth. Pedro started whimpering as soon as he saw the pickup disappearing in the distance. Without a vehicle, a couple of hundred miles from home, I felt like doing the same. Pedro and I were alone together, looking at each other very doubtfully.

I busied myself getting organized and putting the final touches to my campsite. From now on the experience would be very different. There would be more tension…more silence…and I would spend more time looking around, scanning the forest for coyotes or lions or people.

Pedro was the unknown factor. What difference would he make? Would he prove to be a good watchdog? Would he alleviate my loneliness? Would he light up my life?

Or would he be more trouble than he was worth?

Chapter 11

Pockets of Pus

A better insight into your dog...should heighten the sense of responsibility we as humans have, not just for our fellow creatures but for each other and for all creation.

— The Monks of New Skete

It was time to explore. We could hike north or south from my campsite on the small dirt road, or east and west on trails. Those were the four directions of my compass. We explored three of them in quick succession.

First I took Pedro back up the road we drove in on, heading north. That was relatively flat, easy, and relaxing as we were following the only way a vehicle could approach my campsite. I studied the painted wooden signs by the road...messages in Spanish invited visitors to respect nature and help preserve the park for future generations.

A solitary female deer appeared on the road ahead. We stared at each other for half a minute before she calmly stepped out of sight. Pedro didn't seem to see it but he was intrigued by the scent left where the deer had stood. As we walked on, he found other things interesting too—I caught him sampling sun-baked cow cookies and deer droppings.

After returning to camp to give him some water and let him rest awhile, I took Pedro on a longer hike out of the valley, over a pine and manzanita-covered granite ridge, a mile to the west, down to the corrals of an old cattle camp called *Aguaje del Burro*—the Burro's Water Hole. It seemed odd leaving so many of my possessions unlocked and unguarded. I would have to get used to that.

My floppy, wide-rimmed hat lent my shadow an Aussie look, inducing me to sing *Waltzing Matilda*. I sang it loudly, over and over, not just because it was such a great "marching" song, but also because if Pedro became lost its familiar strains might be another means for him to find his way back to me.

At one point, Pedro tiring of the march and perhaps my singing, sat down on what seemed to be a nice cozy patch of leaf litter. Moments later he jumped up like a very unjolly jumbuck, frantically shaking and sucking his paw. I looked at it and noticed a number of two-tone, red-and-black ants, which I brushed off. The ants were different from those at my campsite—they were larger, and obviously biting or stinging. A few yards away, a foot-tall nest of pine needles and twigs was surrounded by a shimmering horde of the ants. A little beyond I saw another smaller, swarming mound where the ants were busily dismantling a dead bird, possibly a youngster that had fallen or been harried from its nest. I led Pedro away fast.

We reached the roofed, rock-lined, spring-fed water hole at Aguaje. I was surprised to see how low the water level was, and how stagnant and green it had become since the previous summer. I was even more surprised to see Pedro happily lapping it up. I discouraged him from doing that by stamping my feet and saying, "No, no, no, no." I then poured him a bowl of clean water from my canteen.

Mindful of rattlesnakes, I also discouraged Pedro from poking his nose under fallen trees or in rocky crevices. And such thoughts brought up a serious question. What if Pedro was bitten? What if he were mauled by a cougar…or attacked by a ferocious pack of coyotes…or zapped by lightning? What if he were suffering terribly?

How exasperated I get when I see a book or article discussing, for example, how to deal with a rattlesnake bite, that offers just a few first aid suggestions and then ends with the facile, cop out suggestion, "Get the victim medical help." What happens when there is no medical help? Or when first aid isn't enough? How about facing up to some "last aid" possibilities.

The previous summer Bonni and I had seen an emaciated and mangy coyote walk across the road a few yards in front of us and then scramble up a gravelly slope. It stopped to look at us. One side of his head was so infected it bulged like a volleyball; and the eye on that side was an open oozing yellow mass of pus. We threw it a slice of bread but it was too far-gone to care about eating. He turned and stumbled into the forest to die. Never had I wished for a rifle so much in my life.

I forced myself to address the question of what to do if Pedro was in an equally hopeless state? Do nothing and let him suffer? Or did I owe it to him to put him out of his misery? If so…how? The machete seemed too crude and ineffective. Crushing his skull with a rock seemed too brutal…and I didn't want Pedro's last sight to be me bringing a machete or rock down on his head. Cutting his throat, although horribly messy, seemed the best option. I pictured myself, weeks into the trip, sitting on the forest floor holding his head in my arms, cutting his throat with tears in my eyes while I sang Waltzing Matilda.

Such were the necessary thoughts going through my mind. I had to think the unthinkable, imagine doing the unbearable…to have a plan, to be ready. Yes, sometimes I longed for a more relaxed Mexican outlook.

However, there was an upside to such wild imaginings. And it was a part of why I have so often felt compelled to wander into the Baja wilderness alone. I would find myself believing things untaught, and being assailed by visions and notions that surprised, delighted, and disturbed me. Baja was my crystal ball, my Holy Land, my temple, the place where I communed with my God.

I recall while camped beneath a cactus one cold and clear desert night coming to the conviction that it was every man's duty to escape deadening failing tradition, to throw open his mind, and to be gently led to the divine—not to be scared, constrained and whipped into a sad conformity.

It seemed as clear as the heavens above, that no child should be permitted to follow the religion of his parents; he should be forced to be free to worship at another altar. We should all aspire to be like Jesus, Buddha, Mohammed—born into a spiritual tradition to transcend, if not fundamentally reject, it. Jesus was the first Christian heretic. With all due respect to the patron saint of the Inquisition, who was himself a heretic to the faith of his fathers, perhaps it is incumbent on all Christians, on all men to aspire to heresy. How few have the courage.

I approached the camp tired from the thin air and perhaps a little exhausted from my imaginings. It was hot—it felt about 90°F—but mercifully it was a western dry heat. The distant shining silver gray roof of the gazebo looked like a space ship had landed in the forest. Pedro was tired and eager to sleep. I encouraged him into his kennel in the shade, and covered it with the mosquito netting.

In the cooling late afternoon we found the energy for another hike, a mile up the road to the southern ridge, past the locked gate. It was steep, but looking back through an opening between the trees I was rewarded with an excellent view of the undulating high plateau of the San Pedro Mártir—its craggy mainly north-south ridges enclosing scooped-out valleys and occasional park-like meado And down below was the valley in which we were camped. Beca of the trees I couldn't see my campsite...or anything manmade except a two-mile distant "road" zigzagging up the steep "Observatory Ridge" to the east.

Closer to me along that ridge were two obvious saddles. Passing through them brings you to the eastern edge of the plateau and the spectacular sight of Baja's highest peak immediately across the great gorge of Cañon del Diablo. If I had climbed much higher I would have begun seeing Picacho del Diablo's naked white walls of granite rising slowly, massively, beyond that ridge.

Hiking up to Observatory Ridge was a challenge that I was looking forward to undertaking when I was sure Pedro and I were both ready. For now, I was content to explore a little of the mesa over which the road ran to the south.

With fat trees and stumps, dense clumps of manzanita, and tall house-sized rocky outcrops, I was increasingly aware of being in lion land, in perfect country to be "ambushed." I appreciated more than ever Pedro's nose, eyes and ears—and hoped they were all wide open.

A 35-foot-tall pine tree caught my eye. The main trunk looped through 360 degrees as it grew up, down and back up again. A heavy snowfall when the tree was a sapling probably accounted for the eccentricity.

I picked a couple of red tubular flowers and headed back to camp to try to identify them with my plant field guides. Their color and long thin tubes suggested they were pollinated by hummingbirds. Having had so much trouble identifying other San Pedro Mártir flowers I was pleased to conclude that it was almost certainly *Monardella macrantha*, or the scarlet monardella.

Washing up that evening I half noticed a couple of wasps flying around but didn't give them much thought till mindlessly wiping my wet hands on my shorts. There was a sudden sharp painful burning in my left palm. A wasp flew away.

Perhaps because of my loud curse, Pedro woke and began whimpering inside his kennel. I let him out and secured him to one of the long lines stretched between two trees. Instead of running or playing he began maniacally eating grass.

Unable to discourage him, I left him to it while I prepared a ham, tomato, and broccoli sandwich. The number of little nuisance flies hovering around the food took the edge off my appetite—it was hard not to take a bite of the sandwich without taking in a fly or two. While I was trying to nibble it between vigorous hand waves, Pedro started retching and upchucked a foamy whitish green mess. I put the sandwich in a bag for later, got my shovel and buried the vomit.

A little while later Pedro seemed fine, so I fed him his standard fare of mixed dry and canned food. There was certainly nothing wrong with his appetite. He finished a bowl of it and was looking around for more. With darkness descending, I built a nice fire, put Pedro back in his net-covered kennel, his line attached to a stake in the ground, and the door open. Apart from the noise of the fire, an almost audible silence hung over the moonlit forest.

Pedro had been sleeping for an hour; the flies seemed to have disappeared, so I tried to eat once more. I had hardly begun when Pedro pushed his way out from under the mosquito net, took a few steps, and then started throwing up the barely digested remains of his dinner. By the time I'd buried that and washed my hands, I ate out of duty rather than interest.

Bundled up in my warmest clothes against the freezing night and still coughing occasionally, I peered into Pedro's kennel. In the dancing firelight a single inscrutable eye looked up at me from a head sunk deep on the soft padding. I began to question again if Pedro had the constitution or the temperament for this trip.

About eleven o'clock, I gently pulled him from his kennel, so he could go potty before being locked in for the night. While he was attending to that, I moved his kennel away from the fire and put it next to my tent—almost door to door.

Suddenly he started barking. He was staring at some brush beside one of the fallen trees. I grabbed my flashlight and the nearest weapon—a hammer—and carefully approached. There was a rustling noise from inside. Pedro was still barking, and making little light-footed leaps side to side like he was primed to pounce or spring for his life. Following his pointing nose deep into the bush…and down into the leaf litter, I was amazed and somewhat relieved to see a pair of toads. Knowing there wouldn't be much sleep with them rummaging around so close to my tent, I picked up the cold clammy creatures and put them beneath another clump of bush much further away. With Pedro settled in his kennel, and my hands washed yet again, I retired for the night.

The thin nylon walls of my tent brought a ridiculous sense of security. There could be mountain lions, rattlesnakes, and ten-ton toads outside, but safely ensconced within, I felt relatively relaxed. It would have been nice to have put on my earphones and listened to the radio, but needing to be sure I could hear Pedro if he had a problem I put the radio away and settled down to sleep fully-dressed inside my sleeping bag.

Sure enough, at 1:30 Pedro started whining. Before I could unzip the tent and get out he began throwing up inside the kennel. While I was cleaning up that pile of yellow vomit, Pedro was energetically running around eating all the grass he could.

What on earth was making him ill? There were plenty of candidates: the flea and tick dip, eating the cow and deer poop, drinking stagnant water, chewing on pinecones and pine branches…maybe eating a toad?

I had barely warmed up inside my sleeping bag and gotten back to sleep when I was woken by more retching noises. It was 2:30. As I suspected, this time Pedro was throwing up little more than greenish puke. I tried to distract him from eating more grass as I dashed about cleaning up the mess from his kennel with paper towels and soapy water. After so many washings in near freezing water my hands were painfully cold.

Shivering beneath the stars, in the silence of the forest, I had a moment of severe self-doubt and started to really, really appreciate the responsibility of having a young dog with me. Compared to the freedom of being on my own, the situation began to seem onerous. Needing to be so focused on Pedro, I wouldn't be able to lose myself in a radio program, read a book or concentrate on anything.

Tired, troubled, and sleepless in my tent, I wondered if Bonni had made it home safely and if she had picked up the dog we had seen on the way down. If he was still there, we had decided to call him Sparky.

As it turned out, when Bonni returned to the trash-blown, roadside pull over, the plastic water bowl was empty, the food had gone, but there was no dog. She whistled and called while filling up the bowl. Suddenly he emerged desperate for water, but looking a little more lively than before. After he drank, Bonni gave him a dog cookie, and perhaps the first loving words and touches he'd ever known. Then she opened the back of the truck—which was almost empty after dropping off my supplies—and began preparing a space to take him home. Turning around, she was amazed to see another little puppy, this one a light tan color, possibly a golden lab or a pit bull mix. Although wearing an old leather collar, the poor thing was emaciated, dehydrated, and both eyes were pockets of pus. Bonni couldn't leave him—so now she had two puppies!

Driving home, she had to pass through a couple of military checkpoints; the soldiers just glanced in the camper shell window and motioned her on.

She stopped at a veterinary store in Mexico to buy worming pills and antibiotics. If the puppies were going to live, her nursing talents would have to suffice.

At the border, the inspector just asked her citizenship and waved her across. It was late by the time she got home. One of the puppies had been sick in the back of the pickup. She fed them a little and gave them water before placing them in kennel cages for the night. Sparky was left outside in the garden because he was very mangy; "Tanner" was brought in and his kennel was placed on the floor heater in the bathroom.

Next morning, Bonni did her best to attend to their needs. Tanner's eyes were so filled with pus she had to check to see that he even had eyeballs. One eye seemed okay; the other was cloudy, shriveled, and obviously useless. She applied veterinary ophthalmic ointment. She then bathed and dipped both dogs with flea, tick and mange dip, started them on antibiotics, and examined their sores. While she was bathing Tanner the water turned red—there was such a stream of blood from his chest she thought his throat had been cut. But he was so infested with fleas they were literally sucking the lifeblood from him. Sparky's paws and lower legs, especially the joints, were clumps of abscesses, full of pus where foxtails had become embedded. She tried to squeeze and clean them out as gently as she could. He was perfectly calm as if he knew she was trying to help.

Dog training expression

Chapter 12

Howlers

I am the Alpha and Omega, the beginning and the end…
— Revelation 22:13

It was 29°F at sunup. I had to pour Pedro out of his kennel to go potty. Having managed that, and vainly trying to upchuck again, he was eagerly scrambling to get back inside. I anxiously consulted my dog books—do I give him antibiotics, worm him, let him rest? I was like a new mother with a colicky kid.

The vomiting continued for two more days and nights. My hands started to crack from being washed 25 times a day. I gave Pedro less food and fed it to him earlier. I discouraged him from eating more grass; and kept from it, he seemed less desiring. Gradually, Pedro's energy and enthusiasm returned. I could have shed tears the first time he got through the night without being sick.

As Pedro seemed more up to it, I did a little leash training with bits of dog biscuits, a few hugs, and lots of kind words. Three or four times a day for about ten minutes we marched together around camp while I firmly called, "heel," and tried to keep him beside me. We also practiced a few simple commands: *sit, stay,* and *come.* The last was the most important. Pedro needed to come to me when other people or animals appeared or when danger threatened.

A neighbor had lent me a book called *How To Be Your Dog's Best Friend* by the Monks of New Skete. The monks were members of the Orthodox Church in America; their monastery located "high on Two Top Mountain" in upstate New York. The New Skete monks have been breeding, raising, and training dogs, mainly German shepherds, for decades. They have an international reputation and many well-qualified and influential supporters.

In the book's foreword, Michael W. Fox, author, veterinarian an' Director for the Study of Animal Problems, writes "this special book. In fact, it is a unique and major breakthrough i of animal training. It rises above the usual 'cookbook' texts of how to train a dog, by providing a wealth of insights that will help the trainer/owner understand, appreciate, and respect his or her canine companion."

Thomas Wolski, with a higher degree from the Cornell Graduate School of Veterinary Medicine, has been taking care of the New Skete dogs since 1983. He said in an interview that the New Skete approach is "wonderful. I recommend the monks' work all the time and have for quite a while. They based all their advice on very, very sound behavioral principles. Some of the other training books out there unfortunately rely on very complicated and elaborate training techniques. The New Skete approach is basically common sense; if it doesn't seem right, it probably isn't."

In spite of such accolades, the monks themselves display a disarming humility. They caution that "dog training is an evolving field, and no one author has all the answers." And they suggest that if you must train your dog solely with a book, read at least three different books. It was advice I failed to follow, for the very practical reason that their book was the only dog-training manual I had…and the fact that I liked what I read of their philosophy.

In the introduction to *How To Be Your Dog's Best Friend*, they say, "Honest and effective communication serves as the foundation for more advanced and constructive interaction…. Your efforts to key into another being…to read its reactions and to register nuances of its behavior can heighten your ability to empathize with all God's creatures."

As it was going to be the first time that I had ever consciously trained a dog, I decided to basically adopt the Monks' approach and see if it worked for Pedro and me. Like all good theories and models, it would be a guide and a tool to frame my thoughts, and would always be subject to common sense and revision. Would it help me understand and train Pedro? I wanted Pedro to be, within reason, attentive to my commands. I didn't want to crush his spirit; as far as I could see he was on the eager-to-please side anyway.

The central assumption of this training method is that dogs are, deep down, wolves and no matter how much they have been naturally and selectively bred into something different, the wolf propensities and instincts still underlie their behaviors, and training methods should address these innate traits.

As the monks put it:

...every dog claims the wolf as an ancestor. Understanding wolf behavior will help you to understand your dog...Both are innately pack-oriented and prefer not to be isolated for long periods of time. Both are hunters who chase down their prey instead of ambushing it...Both are responsive to leadership from an 'Alpha-figure' to whom they look for order and directives. Both use a wide array of body language to communicate within the pack and with outsiders...To learn about dogs, learn about wolves.

The monks add:

At first, pack leadership (the figure of the Alpha) is exclusively revealed in the mother. However, early on in the development of the litter a pecking order among the pups develops, and each littermate fits into a particular role in the pack... When a pup goes to its new home, it becomes a member of a new pack, and will begin to act like a pack member, testing its limits, trying to determine where it fits in. It is absolutely essential for the owner(s) to assume the role of Alpha in their pup's life...they have to understand that dogs require a leader and that this must be their role.

Within that framework, I fixed the following clear and compelling ideas in my mind.

It would be so much easier if we could explain to our dog what we wanted them to do. Needless to say, that approach doesn't work...Dogs learn by trial and error, by making mistakes...By applying simple behavioral principals to our training sessions, we can make rapid progress with a minimum of stress. In this connection, remember that dogs tend to seek what they find pleasant and avoid what they find unpleasant.

...praise is absolutely necessary. It is the cornerstone of any successful dog-owner relationship...praising a dog is a physical and verbal involvement with the animal...it is more than treats, more than an occasional physical pat, and more than a reward for good actions. Praise is an attitude, a stance.

Thus, in training, you'll want to use only that amount of force (negative reinforcement) necessary to get the dog to change its behavior to what you're asking; the force of your leash corrections, for example, will depend on what the dog requires to correct itself. As each dog is an individual, what might be too heavy for one dog will be insufficient for another. To find the proper level for your own dog, you'll have to experiment, starting from a lighter correction, to one that is sharper. Your dog's response will speak for itself. However, after the correction is made and the dog adjusts itself, praise your dog immediately, so as to associate in its mind the praise with the specific behavior it is doing. That way, it will begin to prefer following your command.

"Make sure the dog knows what you want. Be sure your message is clear and you are not sending out mixed signals." Don't confuse the puppy. Stick to simple, repetitive commands.

"Discipline...we have developed several methods that depend less on violent physical force than on timing, a flair for drama, and the element of surprise." And in disciplinary interactions, they stress holding the dog's attention by maintaining eye contact and pointing frequently towards your eyes, then releasing your gaze.

When discipline was urgent and necessary, the book advocates a technique [which I have found useful in my marriage] called the Alpha-wolf roll-over (or "Alpha roll" for short) whereby, after sitting your dog, you vigorously shove it onto its back:

At this point, most dogs will go into the classic submissive posture of all canids. The dog will bend its front paws to its chest, spread its legs wide open, push back its ears, possibly tuck its tail between its legs, and look up fearfully. This is the moment to make eye contact, and continue scolding the dog. Keep the dog pinned on its back by applying steady pressure with your hand on its neck area. Your verbal discipline may now be quieter, but no less firm and direct than it was...You are acting as the Alpha-wolf. In a wolf pack the leader will often pin subordinates for misbehavior in this same position.

The monks emphasize that it is a technique only to be used for the most serious infractions, and they stress that the idea with this technique is not to physically hurt the dog but to be "dramatic." It is "more play-acting than anything else, although the dog must not know it." It is, they claim, "better to administer discipline effectively and meaningfully once, rather than dozens of times in an ineffective way."

Other discipline "do's and don'ts" I took to heart were:

If you must discipline your dog, do it immediately after the bad action or forget it; after a certain point the dog will not associate the correction with the misbehavior.

"Never call a dog to you and then discipline it." The dog will associate coming to you with something negative. Go and get the dog. "Even if a chase is involved, go and get the dog."

Remain passive and distant from the dog for one-half hour after disciplining for a serious infraction. Then do something fun together.

I was conscious that not everyone agreed with the New Skete approach. Thus in their 2001 book *Dogs*, Raymond and Lorna Coppinger state:

Today the popular dog press seems to feel that if dogs descended from wolves, they would have wolf qualities...we are advised to act like the pack leader, the alpha-male, and treat our dogs as subordinates...We are a much different animal than the apes in spite of our common genetic ancestry. The same is true of the dog and its ancestor...the dog is first and foremost a biological being, and no mere subspecies of the wolf...our dog lying out there under the car on a hot day is not an evolved wolf in its simulated cave. It is a highly evolved specialized new animal with behaviors that adapt it to its niche... [scavenging from and interacting with people.] Asserting dominance over one of my favorite working dogs by pressing it onto the ground and snarling at it is prepos- terous. I don't want my sled dogs rolling on their backs and urinating in the air like some subordinate wolf every time I show up...Dogs do not understand such behaviors because the [hypothetical original] village dogs didn't have a pack structure; they were semisolitary animals...The biological reality of all this is that the wolf is now the distant cousin of the dog. That canid family tree split, and wolves and dogs went along their separate branches.

I didn't have time to enter into a debate about how far dogs were or were not wolves. The bottom line was I had never trained a dog; I needed a little guidance; the New Skete method made sense theoretically; it had obviously worked for the monks; and it had clearly impressed many others who work with dogs...I had the book, the approach applied in the sensitive way advocated by the monks seemed humane and flexible; so I chose it as my initial guide. I just wanted to do what worked.

Even the Coppingers admit that Alpha rolling may work with a dog: "A trainer who pretends to be the alpha leader of a wolf pack—say, by turning a dog over on his back and getting down and growling at its throat is intimidating the dog no doubt."

If Pedro was wired to accept that I was the Alpha...great, and if snarling and Alpha rolling worked, even as just an extreme example of negative reinforcement—and there was plenty of evidence that it did—then I'd be content. Pedro could think of me as the alpha, the omega, or whatever he wanted.

I would try to be a leader to Pedro...and if my acting like a wolf and throwing him on his back a few times helped to train him I was willing to commit a few howlers. I hoped it wouldn't come to that, but nevertheless I studied the Alpha action and filed it away in readiness.

Again, the bottom line was the result. If Pedro turned into a vicious monster or a cringing coward or ignored my every command, then at least I'd know that the New Skete method wasn't going to work for him and me. And hopefully long before that ever happened I'd have the insight and common sense to discern what was going wrong and how to correct it.

Anyway, until in possession of some empirical feedback, I had a borrowed theory, and an ability to test it against the reality of Pedro's development. I kind of suspected he was both pack wolf and solitary, slinking dump dog. But for testing purposes he was a wolf—a very sweet one to be sure.

Chapter 13

Return of the Condor

Give me a condor's quill! Give me Vesuvius' crater for an inkstand!
— Herman Melville

Federico, the park director, paid me the expected visit. He stepped from his late-model, dark green Dodge pickup, looking pleasant, proper, and dignified. He was of medium height and build and was smartly dressed in an ironed, light beige park uniform. I was hoping to make a good impression. Pedro, wanting to make an impression of his own, surprised me by barking loudly, almost menacingly. My pointed stare and firm "NO" restored calm.

Federico welcomed me to the park, and I welcomed him to my campsite. I was fetching a couple of cold sodas from my cooler when Pedro now decided to offer his wolfy welcome by jumping up and planting his dusty paws on Federico's clean pants. After shouting a very firm "NO. NO. NO," I apologized to the director who was indignantly brushing himself down, handed him the soda and motioned for him to take a chair.

As we sat down in the shade, Federico looked over at Pedro and lamented, "Your first ticket will be for the dog." I gulped, and pictured myself alpha rolling Pedro all the way down to the bottom of Cañon del Diablo. Then, seeing Federico smile, I realized he was just kidding.

Talking in a mixture of Spanish and English, he asked me about my Baja trips and I asked him about the park. He said that the park gate was open from 7 a.m. to 8 p.m., May through November. A maximum of 10 vehicles were allowed in the Padre Salvatierra, Padre Kino, and Cucapa campgrounds; and 20 in the Kiliwa, Pai Pai, and Padre Linck campgrounds. Camping was restricted to the area 20 meters from the ring road around each campsite. None had ever come close to being full. Much more likely was the chance that the entire park would be devoid of visitors.

Federico explained that he was a rancher from Sonora, and he had a long-standing commitment to conservation. He had taken on the directorship of the park at the State Governor's request. He said that it was his intention to keep 97% of the land in the park pristine and safe from all tourist and commercial development.

Federico confirmed that there was indeed a plan to release four to six young California condors in the park in the summer of 2002. That would be fitting, as it was almost exactly four hundred years before, in 1603, that the crew on one of Vizcaíno's three ships exploring the Pacific coast of the Californias noted several giant vulture-like birds feasting on a large carcass along the shoreline. They were possibly the first Europeans to see the California condor, the largest and the heaviest flying bird in North America. Certainly, Father Antonio de la Ascensio, one of the friars ministering to the expedition, was the first European to document the existence of these incredible scavengers with their near ten-foot wingspans.

It thrilled Federico to think that North America's largest flying bird would be reintroduced to the mountains and canyons of Baja that it first called home forty thousand years before.

Federico wasn't quite so quick as Alfredo to put my mind at rest about the hazards of summer thunderstorms; rather he emphasized that they could be very dangerous for anyone outside. He advised me to avoid tall trees, stay off peaks and ridges…and lie flat on the ground when lightning was crashing all around.

The latter opinion has been long held. The 1972 Funk and Wagnall Encyclopedia, for example, claims the safest place for a person outside in a thunderstorm is "lying flat on the ground in the open." Microsoft's 1996 Encarta Encyclopedia expresses the same opinion.

However, most authorities now recommend squatting or crouching rather than lying flat. For example the U.S. Federal Emergency Management Authority (FEMA) advises "get to an open space and squat low to the ground as quickly as possible…if you feel your hair stand on end (which indicates that lightning is about to strike), bend forward, putting your hands on your knees. A position with feet together and crouching while removing all metal objects is recommended. [This incidentally places you perfectly to kiss your ass goodbye] Do not lie flat on the ground."

The Lightning Safety Group (LSG) of the American Meteorological Society recommends, "If there is no shelter, avoid being the tallest object in the area. If only isolated trees are nearby, crouch on the balls of your feet in the open."

Federico explained that the park was working on banning cattle—an important but controversial move. He said he felt like the sheriff in

High Noon when trying to explain that necessity to the cattle ranchers, including the powerful Meling family, whose livestock had been enjoying the fine summer grazing in the park for generations. Indeed, because of the rugged terrain and the long absence of any decent entry road, cattle ranching has traditionally been about the only economic activity in the sierra.

A new and potentially devastating logging venture recently started on the western edge of the park was an activity that Federico looked upon with great suspicion. A U.S. based company had acquired the timber rights from the local ejido (or cooperative) headed by one of the Melings. Federico made clear that the park would be monitoring the logging company's activities to assess the extent of the damage to the forest, and scrutinizing the nature of the permits under which they operated.

Upon his appointment, Federico had chosen the names for the six camping areas—three for local Indian tribes (Cucapa, Kiliwa, and Pai Pai) and three for Jesuit missionaries (Salvatierra, Kino, and Linck). He offered a little background on the three missionaries.

Salvatierra was the indomitable Italian Jesuit who founded the first permanent European settlement in Baja California at Loreto in 1697, two-thirds of the way down the peninsula on the Gulf of California.

Padre Wenceslao Linck, a Bohemian Jesuit, led the first expeditions into the Sierra San Pedro Mártir in 1765 and 1766, where he encountered deep snow and bitter cold. The missionary and his accompanying Spanish soldiers were the first Europeans to get a "bird's eye" view of what would be involved in establishing a land route between the missions of Lower California and those of mainland Mexico.

Linck's explorations did not lead to the naming of this highest mountain range on the peninsula. In 1767, the Jesuits were suddenly expelled from all Spanish territories. Padre Junipero Serra and his Franciscans were invited to take their place in California. The Franciscans held sway for just five years before moving their enterprise north from the peninsula to what became the U.S. State of California. The Dominicans were invited to take over missionary activity in Baja California. They established Misión San Pedro Mártir de Verona in 1794 on the western fringe of the mountains. Although the mission was always marginal and was abandoned in 1806, the forested mountain range was destined to take the name of the Dominican Saint Peter.

Clearly, Federico's tribute to Linck and Salvatierra was sincere and perfectly justified; however, when Federico spoke of Padre Kino, he did so with undisguised respect and admiration, confessing that Kino had long been his "hero."

Padre Eusebio Kino, a contemporary, countryman, and close friend of Salvatierra, was born in a small village in the Italian Tyrol in 1645. Kino's parents, recognizing his abilities, sent him to the Jesuit college in nearby Trent (Austria) where he studied mathematics, cartography, and astronomy. While at the college he fell seriously ill and vowed that if his patron, Saint Frances Xavier, the founder of the Jesuit Order, would intercede for his recovery, he would devote his life to the Church. He regained his health and joined the Society of Jesus in 1665. Father Kino fervently hoped to serve as a missionary in China but his superiors, placing all in the able hands of God, cast lots to decide his fate. Father Kino was destined for Mexico. His contribution there was well summed up by his biographer:

> Eusebio Francisco Kino was the most picturesque missionary pioneer of all North America—explorer, astronomer, cartographer, mission builder, ranchman, cattle king, and defender of the frontier... For a quarter of a century Kino was the outstanding figure on the Sonora-Arizona-California frontier. A score of present day towns and cities began their history as mission pueblos founded by him or directly under his influence. Over a vast area in the Southwest and adjacent Mexico, cattle ranching and the introduction of European cereals and fruits owe to him their beginnings... Kino's maps of Western North America made him famous in Europe even in his own day... Because of his personal influence over the natives, in the defense of the Spanish settlements he was declared to be more potent than a whole garrison of Spanish soldiers...
>
> — Herbert E. Bolton *Rim of Christendom*

Soon after his arrival in Mexico, he was sent as missionary and royal cartographer on an expedition to Baja California commanded by Admiral Isidro Atondo y Antillon. After many setbacks, the admiral's three ships reached the Bay of La Paz on April 4, 1683. There, Kino divided his time between learning the Indian language, preaching as best he could, and drawing maps.

Following a serious incident whereby the Admiral fired on the natives, killing several, the expedition was forced to abandon La Paz and establish a new site at San Bruno, just north of present day Loreto, in October 1683.

In December 1684, Atondo and Kino led the first European expedition to cross Baja California from the Gulf of California to the Pacific. Kino kept a meticulous account and made detailed maps of the exploration. Largely because of drought and supply failures, San Bruno had to be abandoned in May 1685.

Kino's plea to be allowed to remain in Baja California was rejected. He wrote of the Indians they were leaving behind:

> Everybody was very much grieved to see such gentle, affable, peaceful, extremely friendly, loving and lovable natives left deserted. Already many of them were begging for holy baptism...it was not easy to find another heathendom so free as these people from the ugliest vices, such as drunkenness and homicide.

Regardless of the apparent failures of the Atondo expedition, Kino began to make a name for himself for zeal, industry, wise counsel, hardiness in the saddle, and the excellent notes and maps that he had made.

In 1686, he was given permission to establish three missions in Sonora, in the lands of the Pima Indians. On March 13, 1687, he founded his first mission, Nuestra Señora de los Dolores, which became his home and base camp for the remainder of his life.

Although indefatigable in his missionary work and explorations in the Northwest corner of New Spain, the needs of California were always on his mind. After Padre Salvatierra had established himself at Loreto in 1697, Kino was quick to send all the aid that he could. As transport by sea was at that time a costly and hazardous affair, Kino dedicated much of his exploratory activities to seeking out a land route to Baja California. He had become increasingly convinced that the widespread belief that California was a long narrow island was incorrect. Through his explorations, Kino proved to the satisfaction of many that the Sea of California was a gulf and California itself was not an island but a peninsula.

A good deal of Kino's activities took place in what is now the State of Arizona. In February 1965, Father Kino's statue, representing the State, was unveiled in the Capitol Rotunda in Washington, D.C. Federico was not alone in his admiration. Kino is held in the highest regard by two nations.

And I held Federico in the highest regard. He was a modest, gracious, informative, intelligent man with a great sense of humor— and a crusading conservation vision that was almost radical. He had quickly put me at my ease and made me feel at home. If I had a problem, he assured me that Alfredo or any member of the Park staff would get a message out on their radios or provide whatever assistance they could.

Pedro was much better behaved with his goodbyes. By the time Federico stood up to leave, Pedro had clearly accepted him as one of the pack. He just sat there quietly as Federico rewarded him with a pat on the head.

Chapter 14

Nergal Unleashed

Alone in the night
On a dark hill
With pines around me
Spicy and still,

And a heaven full of stars
Over my head,
White and topaz
And misty red…
— Sara Teasdale

I had been up in the mountains exactly a week. It was just about dark. I was well wrapped in thermal underwear, sweat pants, and sweaters, reading by lamp light in the screen house with Pedro in his kennel beside me.

Pedro started barking. I looked up to see vehicle lights approaching from the north. Being so isolated I was naturally a little concerned about who was arriving at such a late hour. Could it be Alfredo again? As the vehicle pulled up by the trash bins, a quick glance with my binoculars revealed that it was a pickup with California plates. Two people got out and started talking. I couldn't quite hear what they were saying above the noise of my propane lantern. As I listened to them unloading and setting up, I was itching to walk down and introduce myself, but first I decided to let them settle in a bit. It was hard to concentrate knowing I was up on my little rise, lit up like someone inside a lighthouse. I was almost relieved when one of the guys walked up, beer in hand, and called out a friendly hello.

Pedro only managed a couple of halfhearted barks before I shushed him. The stranger looked pleasant enough, he apologized for disturbing me, introduced himself as Mark and said that he and his companion were from San Diego. He explained that they were attempting to climb Picacho del Diablo; they would be leaving the following morning and hoped to return after three nights camping out. He invited me over for a beer.

I left Pedro in his kennel and went down a few minutes later, Mark introduced me to Pete, a jolly, heavy set, powerful-looking man who was sharpening one end of a six-foot-long spear-like aspen branch. He impaled a large hunk of meat the size of my head on the end and held it over the fire. They were both flipping tortillas on the coals with their fingers. These were real campers.

Pete said he was a fireman; and he had run the San Diego Marathon a few days before. His first two tortillas did not turn out well. One emerged as black as a moonless night. The other was burning like the sun. Pete skillfully shook out the flames and then continued to shake his smoking fingers.

Mark asked if I was "an Aussie," and I owned that I was a Brit. Pete wondered if I knew another Brit who had walked around the coast of Baja. "That crazy dude is my hero," he said as he pulled another flaming tortilla from the coals. "Took him two years, and he wrote a fantastic book."

"Into a Desert Place?" I enquired.

"That's the one. Do you know the guy?"

"That's me!" I replied as modestly as I could.

His jolliness now knew no bounds, "Oh man, you are my hero. You're not as tall as I thought. Let me shake your hand."

To help keep my feet on the ground I confessed that my wife thought I was more of a wimp than a hero. "She calls Pedro and me Wimpy and Whiney." He laughed and offered me some meat. After I'd sampled a few hunks, I accepted a nice fatty piece for Pedro, bade them good night, and retired to my campsite to check on my buddy.

I gave Pedro his treat and walked him around for ten minutes, then I stayed up awhile emboldened by the presence of my friendly neighbors and the light from their fire. Two men by a fire in the forest, laughing and talking freely, about to face a daunting challenge together—it was an evocative, timeless image.

The night was still moonless. I sat mesmerized by the subtle dancing of the firelight on my tents and the nearby trees. Then out of the corner of my eye, I saw what I thought was the fire reflecting off an aspen above me. Instead it was the "solid," silvery brilliance of the billions of stars in the Milky Way.

The dry air above the deserts of Baja often affords the most breathtaking views of the night sky—and it's even more incredible in the mountains. Someone who had never ventured far from a sea level city would be amazed by how many stars there are, and how milky is the light from the Milky Way. I stepped into the middle of my clearing. And even as I threw my head back to drain a can of beer, there in that chance moment a shooting star flashed across the heavens like a far off, silent bolt of lightning. It led my eyes to Mars. In all the twinkling blue-white wonder of the heavens, the red planet leapt out, dramatic, like a ruby in the celestial crown.

Astronomers had much to say about Mars in the summer of 2001. There was excitement about a special *Mars opposition*, where Mars and the sun would be on opposite sides of the Earth. Mars would be visible throughout much of the night, rising in the east at sunset, tracking across the night sky, and setting at sunrise.

> While Martian opposition occurs every other year, the minimum distance between the two planets is not always the same because of the elliptical orbits of the two bodies, particularly Mars. *Jet Propulsion Laboratory*

All summer long and into October, Mars would be larger and brighter than usual. The planet would be at its closest distance from Earth since 1988—just 42 million miles.

Students of myth have long pointed out ancient man's obsession with the red planet. In both the New and the Old World, Mars has been almost universally proclaimed the harbinger of war, pestilence, and apocalyptic disaster.

In the "cradle of civilization," the Babylonian empire centered on modern day Iraq, astronomical texts identified Mars with the war-god Nergal—the great hero, the king of conflicts, the champion of the gods, king of eternal darkness.

Mars to the ancient Greeks was Ares, the god of war, the son of Zeus and Hera. He was portrayed as fiery, bloodstained, and murderous. The contemporary astronomical sign for Mars, a symbolized spear and shield, dates to the Greek conception of Ares.

In Roman mythology, Mars was both the god of war and the father of the Roman people. According to legend, King Numitor was deposed by his younger brother Amulius, who forced Numitor's daughter Rhea Silvia, to take a vow of chastity. Subsequently, when she bore twins, Amulius commanded that the two boys be drowned in the flooded river Tiber. However, Mars was the father of the twins. He influenced the soldiers not to drown them but to place them in a basket and let them float away with the churning current.

The basket drifted to the bank beneath the Palatine Hill where the infants were found and nursed by a she-wolf, an animal sacred to Mars. Eventually, they were taken in and raised by a herdsman and his wife. When grown to manhood, these sons of Mars—Romulus and Remus—killed the usurper king, restored Numitor to the throne, and founded Rome on the Palatine Hill above where their basket had come ashore.

With Mars so dramatically there in the night sky, I wondered what catastrophes astrologers were prophesizing for the summer of 2001. And in case prognostications for carnage and bloodshed were not favorably enough written in the heavens for 2001, the next Mars opposition will occur in August 2003, when the two planets will be the closest they have been in at least 60,000 years—approximately 34.6 million miles.

What might the Babylonians make of that? And what foreshadowing might there be in the month of Mars in such a year? No doubt, their wise men would see their land engulfed by bloody war, with Nergal, the king of conflicts, finding rich employment.

Before retiring I walked Pedro around the trees a final time then closed him in for the night. Taking advantage of the freezing nights, I emptied most of my cooler onto a table to allow all the bottles, cans and produce to chill down. In the morning I would place it all back in the cooler. It was a great system. Even without ice, I had cold drinks and food throughout the warm day.

Pedro had a good night; I guess he didn't want to throw up his unexpected treat. I got up early, took him for a warm-up walk and then went down to chat with Mark and Pete while they were having breakfast. Pedro now displayed his burgeoning guard dog talents by barking loudly at one of their backpacks leaning against a tree.

I decided to take Pedro and go with them a mile and a half up the trail in "Columbine Canyon." I christened it thus because although there were orange-yellow columbines scattered throughout the valleys and gorges of the range, that deep, steep sided valley leading southeast from the Padre Kino campsite was full of them. And for some reason, most of the firs and pines clinging to its rocky slopes were draped with masses of lichens.

While Mark and Pete labored with their heavy packs, Pedro actually went in front on the leash sniffing out the trail and following it perfectly. I used my machete as a walking stick, and occasionally dragged the point along the ground to help mark my way back. I had the camp coordinates entered into my GPS, but having on a previous excursion into the San Pedro Mártir had my malfunctioning GPS inform me, "Do not rely on this product as your only source of navigation," I was firmly wedded to the notion of redundancy.

The trail took us into a broad sunny valley where we said our good-byes. I watched with mixed feelings of envy and pity as Mark and Pete carried their burdens further along the trail towards a steep craggy gully. If all went well, that night they would be in the bottom of Cañon del Diablo, the next day they would attempt to hike straight up to the peak and back down to Campo Noche in the canyon bottom. It was something I would love to have attempted, but with Pedro with me that was out of the question.

After twenty minutes rest, Pedro and I headed "home." Looking up at all the rocky crags and pine-covered slopes, I was once more mindful of lions. I took comfort from my sheath knife and even more from my long machete, which I continued to use as a walking stick. Pedro was feeling the heat. All the way back he was dashing from one shady spot to another. If I declined to stop, he would look at me with pleading eyes. He did the same when I stood up after resting and stepped back into the sun. I had to drive him a little bit to get him back to camp in a reasonable time.

It was the toughest hike we'd taken so far. Back in camp, I inspected Pedro's paws—they were no cuts but two had blobs of pinesap with gravel and bits of wood attached. Suspecting they might be causing him discomfort I did my best to cut, scrape and dissolve them off.

My own "paws" were getting worse every day...or more accurately, every night. The cold dry air, the constant washings in freezing water, and holding them before the fire were producing deep and painful bleeding cracks.

While the climbers were away, Alfredo came over with a big, old, friendly dog called Baltasar. It sounded like he didn't really belong to anyone in particular, but Alfredo had borrowed him from the observatory to accompany him on his rounds. He looked like a German shepherd/Labrador mix. He offered his paw for shaking as if he were welcoming me to the park and to my adventure promoting dog welfare in Mexico. Baltasar had a few scabby, bald areas over his head and ears. And Pedro, like Saint Francis kissing the sores of a leper, wanted to lick Baltasar's face almost continuously. I had to work on my qualms as he and Pedro romped together—was he bringing fleas, mange, worms, or worse to my buddy?

Alfredo said he had to leave the park for a few days to visit a sick family member. He said that Federico would also be gone, so he declared, "You are now in charge. You are the sheriff." This was a most unexpected promotion. And he gave me a handful of entry permits and maps to issue to new arrivals. He asked if there was anything I needed. I gave him $10 to buy me some milk, tortillas, bread and fruit.

Alfredo hadn't left but a few hours when I saw what I thought was the first real cloud of my trip. But as it grew and turned a very uncloudy reddish brown, I realized it was smoke. Bits of ash came raining down. There was a major fire a few miles to the west.

I could think of nothing more rangerly to do than take a shower, clean my teeth, and put on clean clothes. If I was about to be burned to a crisp, it seemed important to look and smell my best.

Confronted with a devastating conflagration, the sensible course of action seemed to be to grab Pedro and the other stuff I couldn't do without and head into one of the large meadow-like clearings. Luckily before I stuffed Pedro into a backpack or took down any tents the smoke cloud began drifting in another direction and then grew less massive. The fire looked like it was burning itself out—a validation of what researchers such as Richard Minnich have claimed, that fires in such unmanaged old-growth forests tend to be frequent and nondevastating.

The following afternoon, the exhausted but ecstatic Picacho climbers returned looking severely mauled not so much by their successful ascent of Picacho as by their getting lost on the plateau coming back. Pedro was glad to see them; he sat at their feet and licked the blood still flowing from the many scratches on their legs. Mark's boots had practically disintegrated, making his ascent and return particularly challenging. Pete kept repeating, "Never again."

To cheer them up I slapped cold drinks in their hands, told them I had been appointed park ranger, gave them their park literature, and charged them $7 for their pains. Even so, they were still gracious enough to leave me some butter, tortillas, and other much appreciated items before heading back to San Diego.

It had taken 12 days but I finally found the courage to let Pedro off line and leash, at least around the camp. My heart was pounding as I released the clip. Would he run off, or go crashing into my tents and tables?

Once he knew he was free, he sprinted away effortlessly, gracefully, like a natural athlete. In seconds he was a brown speck in the distance.

Chapter 15

Sense of the Sacred

There used to be a charming myth that the Gothic cathedrals with their high pinnacles and their tall columns had been constructed in direct imitation of those forests in which the Teutonic invaders of Europe had spent so many years of their lives...the histories of art of a few generations ago had the people of the early middle ages construct churches with high vaulted windows to surround themselves with the atmosphere of their ancestral forests.

— Heindrik Van Loon

When Pedro was about 150 yards away I yelled, "Come," and was relieved to see him immediately sprint back towards me like a greyhound chasing a hare. He nearly bowled me over in his enthusiasm to return. I was sure he could outrun any coyote in the forest.

He ran around with his big feet sounding like a horse; then he dug and chased, and chewed sticks, cones, and bones to his little heart's content. He was in his element. I reveled in his freedom and shared his exhilaration.

If I walked away from camp he would dutifully follow, sometimes at my side, sometimes cavorting around after the birds and squirrels, but always staying in sight. When I called he came straight to me for a well-deserved pat and a hug. I also made a practice of blowing a whistle to call him in for treats so he would associate the sound with "come" if my voice wasn't adequate.

One crisp, cold morning, I emerged from my tent to see three deer backlit where the morning sun was shafting through the trees. I watched them silently for a minute, but when I unzipped the screen house to get my camera, they slowly melted into the forest. Because of the deer, I walked Pedro on a leash, in the opposite direction, along a broad band of warm sunlight. As we walked briskly, I watched his ears flapping like he was flying. "Hermes—messenger of the Gods," I chuckled.

I lifted him over a couple of fat fallen trees and then we scrambled to the top of a granite outcrop. Seeing a fine clump of paintbrush, I picked one of the beautiful orange-red flowers intending to identify the species. Two hundreds yards from camp, convinced the deer were far enough away, I released Pedro from the leash. As soon as he was free, he grabbed the flower from my hand and ran off with it, clearly delighted by this new game. I entered the camp to find him stretched out on his favorite towel in the sun, chewing on a pinecone looking very pleased with himself, the sorry remains of the flower beside him.

After breakfast we went for another walk. I recorded:

Pedro was following me around the Padre Kino ring road. I was singing *Nearer my God to Thee*. It was like a mantra. I just kept singing it, walking up the road, feeling really happy with my buddy here, who was kind of half walking and half playing. I looked over at four big ponderosas among all the Jeffries and thought, they looked like wonderful red plated columns holding up the blue sky…It's like they form a cross, three of them at one end and one at the other. And it suddenly occurred to me that the space between those trees will be my church, my cathedral in the mountains. I walked "inside" with Pedro. He scraped aside the pine needles right in the middle, right where if you drew two lines across from these four trees it would be the exact center. He lay down and I crouched down with him. He then rolled on his back with his little paws up looking like a praying mantis. I was petting him and rubbing his belly and he just looked so blissfully happy. It was a real special moment, and almost without any conscious intent, there I was on my knees, inside my cathedral, singing, "*Nearer my God to Thee.*"

The "cathedral" stood on the edge of a football field-sized clearing, about three hundred yards from my tent. And I guessed those mighty ponderosas were at least four hundred years old. Perhaps they were mere saplings when Vizcaíno's ships were exploring the coast of California in 1602-3.

I looked maybe two-thirds the way up the massive naked platy trunks to where the branches began. The westernmost tree was the grandest; and most of its main branches ran opposite each other in a north-south direction as if spread to welcome the morning sun or give thanks at sunset. The largest pair of branches was so stout and ponderous it was hard to believe that the limbs wouldn't at any moment come crashing down under their own weight. They were themselves as big as many of the fine Jeffrey pines thereabouts. The whole arrangement of branches in the upper third of the tree suggested by turns a mighty mast or a series of massive crosses, one on top of the other. In the right light, on your knees, thirty feet from its base, looking up into the blue, that single tree seemed just about as awesome and impressive as anything, anywhere, created by man. And in the sky above, I saw my first swallows of the summer.

My cathedral was perhaps more beautiful than many an "authentic" cathedral because it was devoid of the compulsions and cruelties of man. In its giddy heights, only bluebirds and sure-footed squirrels held sway, there were no pressed "jolly tars" or shunned and hunted hunchbacks. In the grand plaza or courtyard beneath, there were no stocks or gallows or stakes. My cathedral was not mindlessly inherited but freely chosen—as freely as I had chosen Pedro, or he had chosen me! My cathedral was not integrally wrapped in a dubious package of self-serving dogma but there, so solid, simple, and natural that even Pedro seemed to feel the need to be at its very core. The simple sense of the sacred intrigued and comforted me; it was a sense that came sharpest when alone and perhaps a little overawed in the wilderness.

Although it would not be a good place in a lightning storm, I knew that that space would be my personal spot, my spiritual refuge, a place to go when I needed a little courage, inspiration, or attitude adjustment.

The fallen wood littering the ground within the cathedral seemed sacrilegious. I began to carry and drag it back along the road to stack by my campfire. There was abundant wood for burning closer to camp, but it seemed right and noble laboring to improve my temple.

Every time I returned to the cathedral for more wood, Pedro would desist from play and sit down where he'd cleared away the needles, right in the center, and look up at me balancing another branch on my shoulder, singing my mantra of praise. Looking at Pedro's loving eyes it was easy for "Nearer my God to Thee" to morph into "Nearer my dog to Thee."

> It is so beautiful at this time of day. I guess it's five o'clock. The long shadows on the pine needles, the warm sun, the lovely sound of the breeze, my wonderful companion here, boisterous and playful…I feel like it has been a special day for me and a big step on this journey.

The breeze dropped to a perfect calm. I got a blazing fire going with the cathedral wood. Although Pedro could have stayed free he chose to snuggle into his kennel. I stared in at him, and felt a great sympathy. What an exhausting day he'd had—having accompanied me on five walks and several firewood runs to the cathedral—yet he looked so content and comfortable. Did a dog ever have a happier, freer life?

Alone and away from the prejudices of the world, I reveled in my own freedom and felt my heart and imagination were likewise being unleashed.

That night, just before retiring, I experienced the downside of such liberation. After gently encouraging Pedro from his kennel for a final potty walk, I was warming my hands on his ribs as he stretched and looked around, when suddenly he tensed up, stared into the night, and emitted a barely audible growl.

I shone my flashlight all about but could see nothing moving. Eventually I got Pedro to do his business, and settled him in his kennel. After driving the point of my machete into the ground outside the door, I was glad to get inside the tent and slide into my sleeping bag.

For the first time, I didn't sleep well. I was accosted by a brooding loneliness that further stirred my imagination. It was as if the sacredness that I had sensed was double edged, and I had grave doubts about my ability and readiness to deal with it.

I woke to the first very windy morning. The violet-green swallows were in their element, flying like little short winged jets among the trees. While Pedro amused himself, I fetched a dozen heavy stones from the arroyo, then tied and weighed down everything in camp as best I could.

Another uniformed ranger came over and introduced himself as Ruben Góngora. He was slightly taller than Alfredo, well spoken and clearly well educated. He explained that he was currently making observations and compiling statistics about the wildlife, questioned me about the deer and birds I'd seen, then told me that Alfredo was still out of the park visiting his family, and reiterated all Alfredo's offers of assistance.

The first real clouds came floating in from the southwest like little bursts of antiaircraft fire. Suspecting a possibly dramatic change in the weather, I didn't wander more than a kilometer from the campsite. By midmorning the blue sky was rapidly disappearing and fast moving battalions of shadow infiltrated the sun-drenched forest.

I hurried back mindful of the need to prepare my defenses, brought up more rocks from the arroyo, then partially unfolded the tarps and laid them on the ground ready.

However, the sky brightened by late afternoon, and was almost entirely clear at dusk. I had been spared, but wondered what tomorrow would bring.

Two views from Observatory Ridge

Looking down Cañon del Diablo

Chapter 16

Mother of all Exit Wounds

No mountain or mountain range, however divinely clothed with light, has a more enduring charm than those fleeting mountains of the sky.

— John Muir

June 18 began sunny and warm—not long after breakfast I was wearing shorts. The violet green swallows continued to flit masterfully among the trees. The little daredevils seemed to enjoy retracting their wings and dropping like stones to see who could come closest to the ground.

I decided the time had come to risk taking Pedro to see the view from the Observatory Ridge. We followed the steep, generally well-marked trail up the valley to the east, taking many rests in the shade.

Perhaps it was the thinness of the air or the difficulty of the struggle or the increased tension and exhilaration of wandering deeper into the wilds, but for whatever reason I felt my senses accentuated. "The air was just reeking of sage" and the flowers seemed more colorful as we climbed—blue lupines, red and orange paintbrush, yellow lotus, red penstemmons, rose sage, purple locoweed. What a splendid bouquet I could have brought down.

On some high points, looking to the west I could see the Pacific Ocean, or perhaps it was the sunlight reflecting off the silvery "marine layer" of low clouds marking its position.

Approaching the ridge, we emerged from the partial shade of the forest into an increasingly blue sky. There were more white firs and sugar pines among the Jeffreys and ponderosas. Many of them had been burned or shattered by lightning. The rocky outcrops were reddish, striated, and daubed with silver-gray lichen; they looked more like fossil wood than the metamorphic rocks they were.

After so many limited forest vistas, we crested the final rise and were suddenly confronted by the awesome, intimidating, naked gray slopes of Picacho del Diablo. And beyond Picacho, we could plainly see the blue Gulf of California to the north of San Felipe and even the low-lying mainland coast of Sonora.

I made myself comfortable on a protruding flat rock, and couldn't have wished for a more dramatic viewpoint. Such was the drop before me, I felt like I was flying out in the canyon. It was exciting to think that the gently whispering air might soon be filled with the whoosh of the condor. I was sure that I had found another sacred spot, another place of pilgrimage. Pedro was more concerned about catching up on his zzzz's—he excavated a little shady place for himself beneath a manzanita bush, then laid his head on a fold of his cheek and neck like he had brought his own built-in pillow.

It was hard to take my eyes off the peak. My mind, newly liberated from the more intimate vistas of the forest, hadn't adjusted to the change of scale. One moment I felt I could reach out and touch it; the next it seemed a hundred miles away.

I studied it with my binoculars, trying to imagine how one could approach the summit, and wondering where Pete and Mark had struggled up. So many ridges and canyons apparently dead-ended in spectacular, dizzying, sheer walls of rock.

The great veins in the side of the mountain revealed what a contact zone there must have been between the original rock and the invading magma; and how deep in the earth the vast chamber of liquid rock must have pushed against, penetrated, and defiled the older sedimentary rocks, baking them, changing them. The veins, some as wide as trucks and houses, told it all.

Thousands of feet below, boulder-strewn Cañon del Diablo snaked its way down from those precipitous rock walls, through V-shaped, tree-studded slopes to the sparse, blistering desert.

If the journey up from the west or the south had been relatively gentle, and that's a very big relative, the drop from the plateau to the desert was daunting. A brave man with mountain goat in his genes might safely make it down, but it would have been almost impossible to get riding mules and pack animals to follow. I recorded:

> Looking at the desert one appreciates what the padres and the explorers must have thought when they first looked down from this ridge. It looks so brown and burned and empty down there; it must have looked like the formidable barrier that it is.

As Federico had informed me, the first European to espy this sobering vista was Padre Linck. When he gazed down at what beckoned, he wisely decided to venture no further. Yet, how tantalizingly close it must have seemed.

Thanks to the dry, clear air I fancied I could see every scraggly mesquite and ocotillo for fifty miles. Yet at the same time the scale of the scene was continental; the mind breaks the picture up into mountains, deserts, and sea. While all was unsullied blue over the San Pedro Mártir, looking over at the mountains of Sonora, perhaps 100 miles away, a line of giant thunderheads ran up to the U.S. and way south along the west coast of Mexico.

I was looking across at the region that Kino explored, mapped, and missionized—that part of northwest New Spain, now divided between two countries proudly calling him founder and Father. I was also looking down at the answer to a question that vexed geographers for generations. Was California an island?

It was one of the most resilient myths in the history of exploration. Even as Kino explored higher and higher along the mainland shores of the Gulf; even as he saw the mountains of mainland New Spain and those of California coming closer and closer, he found it hard to doubt what so many had confidently asserted since that great epic of Spanish literature—*The Adventures of Esplandian*—spoke of the mythical Island of California, largest in the world, at the extreme edge of the Indies.

Kino admits that in spite of what his eyes saw: "I persuaded myself that farther on and more to the west the Sea of California must extend to a higher latitude and…must leave or make California an island."

However, on another exploration, Indians near the Colorado River gave Kino a gift of some large blue abalone shells, which, he was convinced, could only have come from the Pacific coast of California. And when those Indians informed him that the Pacific coast was ten or twelve days journey overland to the west, the implications were immediately obvious. The missionaries could enter California from the north and drive much needed livestock to the infant and precarious Jesuit outpost at Loreto.

His friend Salvatierra was hanging on desperately. The Californian Indians were hungry—the very people that he had taught, befriended, and written about so enthusiastically at the time of Atondo. The uncertainty and prohibitive expense of shipping livestock and provisions by sea made an overland drive so attractive.

When Kino communicated his peninsula opinion to his colleagues, there was much excitement. Salvatierra wrote eagerly from Loreto: "we are desirous of knowing whether from that new coast which your Reverence traversed, California may be seen and what sign there is on that side whether this narrow sea is landlocked."

Another Jesuit missionary declared: "What great news...that it is possible to pass overland to California...news truly the greatest if it is verified, but which although it is desired so long it has never been possible to confirm."

In 1700 Kino strove to learn more about the route by which the blue abalone shells came to Sonora and the lands of the Pima Indians. To that end, he dispatched messengers to the surrounding Indian chiefs summoning representatives to his mission near Tucson.

Delegates from the western Indians came. Kino wrote, "We talked with them a great part of the night...in regard to the eternal salvation of all those nations of the west and the northwest, at the same time continuing various inquiries in regard to the blue shells...They admitted that they came from the opposite coast of California and from the sea which is ten or twelve days journey farther than this other Sea of California, on which there are pearl and white shells but none of those blue ones..."

Again, his fellow missionaries shared Kino's excitement: "May our Lord grant that there be a road as royal as we think and desire, for thereby the labor as well as the care of California will be lessened," wrote Father Kappus.

"I greatly desire that your Reverence may finally make this most desired expedition by land into the Californias...if you accomplish this we must erect to you a costly and famous statue," added Father Manuel González.

With the new yeast of adventure in his soul, Kino once more took the long trail. He would find the land passage to California if one there was. Then all the old geographers would see the error of their ways. And he would indeed "lend a hand" to Salvatierra. His vaqueros would drive cattle around the head of the Gulf to Salvatierra's very dooryard at Loreto!

Rim of Christendom

On September 24, 1700 Father Eusebio Kino left Dolores with ten servants and sixty horses and mules. The journey lasted five weeks and covered a thousand miles. On October 6, he arrived at an Indian village that he had named San Pedro—the place where, the year before, he had been given the abalone shells that had been the catalyst for his new thinking. He wrote: "They welcomed us now very affectionately, even giving the dog which was with us water and 'porridge' in a little basket, with all kindness, as if he were a person, wondering that he was so tame and faithful, a thing never before seen by them."

On October 7, Kino wrote: "I ascended a hill to the westward, where we thought we should be able to descry the Sea of California. But, looking and sighting towards the south, the west, and the southwest, both with and without a long range telescope, we saw more than thirty leagues of level country, without any sea…" They were above the head of the Gulf. He was sure the old maps were wrong. A celebration was in order

"Returning to our stopping place, we ate lunch, adding some sweetmeats for joy that now, thank the Lord, we had seen the lands pertaining to California, without any sea between and separating those lands from it!" All he had to do was decide on the best route, and send what was needed around the head of the Gulf so that the California mission need not be abandoned again.

Salvatierra was as optimistic as Kino. Late in December 1700, he crossed the Gulf "with firm and well-founded hopes of returning by land in latitude thirty-one or thirty-two degrees" to his mission of Loreto.

His joy knew no bounds when he saw Kino again after a five-year separation. They set off from mainland Mexico in March 1701 with twenty mule loads of provisions and 150 saddle and pack animals.

It was an arduous, dangerous expedition. Some Indians, fearful they would die of thirst, deserted the party rather than cross the vast area of sand hills approaching the shore.

"Do not judge them too harshly till you yourself have faced those sand dunes," said Bolton in *Rim of Christendom*.

The expedition made camp by some springs near the shore. "Since there was still some light," wrote Salvatierra, "without dismounting, I went towards the sea as far as half a league from this place, where before sunset we distinctly and with great clarity saw California and its mountain chain, and still more clearly after sunset, when it appeared to us that the sierra must be distant from us about ten or twelve leagues, and that the land before the sierra must be even closer than that."

Kino noted that, "In the north, the mountains of the two sides of the Gulf curved towards each other, seeming to meet."

Hoping for a better view, they headed back east and climbed another mountain in what they estimated to be 31°degrees with their banner of the Lady of Loreto fluttering bravely in the breeze. They were delighted to see that the mountains of California and New Spain came together. "With this view of the straight we sang the litany of Loreto as a sign of Thanksgiving."

Although they wisely decided not to attempt an expedition to Loreto at that moment, Salvatierra declared, "I felt sufficiently satisfied with what I had seen with my own eyes and with the reports from the Indians…that we would be able…to succeed in opening communication by land between New Spain and California." Kino drew a map dated 1701 indicating California was a peninsula. It became the standard map of the region for decades.

Another round of congratulations poured in. Jesuit Visitor Leal said: "I have rejoiced greatly that your Reverence has now returned from your journey, which has been made with hopes so well founded as to constitute certainty of the continuity by land."

From Loreto, Father Piccolo wrote Kino: "I give your reverence a thousand congratulations for your discovery. May our Lord grant us the boon of seeing California carry on trade with New Spain by land for the relief of these missions and the salvation of so many souls."

To make absolutely certain about this "certainty" Kino and Salvatierra agreed to head up their respective sides of the Gulf in October 1701 and meet at its head. But lack of a ship prevented passage from the mainland of horses for Salvatierra's expedition. Kino was deeply disappointed when he heard the news.

Kino decided to go it alone on perhaps his most ambitious journey. "At present I am equipping myself to enter, with divine favor…very far into California, until I get sight of or until I reach the very South Sea [Pacific]…and in order to go as far as possible…towards the mission of Loreto Conchó, where lives the Reverend Father Salvatierra."

Kino set off November 3 with only one Spanish companion and his Indian servants. As he traveled down the Colorado River from Yuma his entourage had swollen to 300 Indians. When the party approached a new Indian village, Kino's only European companion lost his nerve and fled. Kino was concerned he might falsely proclaim that some disaster had befallen his expedition.

Kino was floated across the river in a large basket. He now entered a thickly populated region that "was full of small but very continuous villages, with very many people, very affable, very well featured, and somewhat whiter than the rest of the Indians." He passed "most beautiful corn fields very well cultivated with abundant crops of maize, beans and pumpkins..."

At a village he was met by a delegation of Indians from the north. They brought gifts, "in particular many blue shells from the [Pacific] or South Sea...saying that they were not more than eight or ten days journey to the westward, and that the Sea of California ended a day's journey farther south...this very large volumed Rio Colorado and two other rivers emptying at its head."

> Kino had crossed the Colorado. He had reached California by a land route. The head of the Gulf was south of him. To the west, hardly a stone's throw, lay Cócopah range, and just beyond it the Sierra Madre of California. Still beyond was the South Sea, source of the Blue Shells. The map had unfolded.
>
> *Rim of Christendom*

Kino decided to turn around, increasingly uneasy about the mischief that might be set afoot by the timid Spaniard who had fled...and because "already this much disputed but now very certain land route to California had been discovered, for the sea did not ascend to this latitude of thirty-two degrees..."

> Kino recrossed the river on the raft used the day before, swimming chiefs and tribesmen towing it over...Few men of his day were held in higher honor or warmer affection among the natives of the western hemisphere.
>
> *Rim of Christendom*

When he at last arrived at his home mission of Dolores, he reported his journey to his superiors and colleagues and made amendments to the map he had drawn earlier. California was certainly a peninsula.

Kino saw the full implications of his discovery: Not only was the land route to Loreto a reality, but he visualized a port on the Pacific coast, perhaps at San Diego Bay, from where a supply route could run directly to Sonora and all of northwest New Spain.

> At the same time through this port...the lives of so many of these sailors [manning the Manila galleons which came across

the Pacific to Acapulco] who every year are prone to fall sick and die from the painful disease of scurvy can be saved, since with fresh food they are easily cured and freed from this evil...

Kino reported to Rome:

In a short time, with the favor of heaven, we shall send cattle by land, and shall have ranches in California itself near the land passage...The father visitor...and I, and others, are of the opinion that this California near the new land passage recently discovered might be called California Alta, just as the preceding region...as far as 30 degrees of north latitude, might be called California Baja.

It was a distinction that eventually took hold. Again the acclaim was general. Many missionaries were thrilled by the idea of participating in an expedition "even to where the California fathers were in Loreto..."

In February 1702, hoping to reach the shores of the Pacific, Kino and Father Manuel Gonzalez set out to the west in "another Kino cavalcade." At a watering hole on the way Kino observed a comet in the constellation of Aquarius. And this comet would indeed carry a dire portent, both for one of the missionaries and for the whole enterprise. They then headed down the Colorado with their usual entourage hoping to reach the very place where the river pours out into the sea. Kino's fame was such that at one point hundreds of curious and friendly Indians swam across the river to see him.

The missionaries crossed the river near its mouth and traveled far enough west to see the sun rising over the Gulf, "proof most evident that we were now in California." However, Father Manuel Gonzalez had become dangerously ill. It was impossible to go on.

As Bolton proclaimed, "Kino had been cheated out of complete triumph by circumstances—the illness of a friend." How different might have been the history of California if Kino had been able to push on to the Pacific and foster the development of his grand scheme.

After a return that was described as one of the hardest marches imaginable, Father Manuel Gonzalez worsened; Kino administered the last rites, and shortly thereafter he died.

That tragedy aside, Kino could now state:

Hence it is plainly to be inferred that...many...modern cosmographers, in their various printed maps, with notable discredit to cosmography, deceive themselves as well as others, by extending this sea, or arm, or straight of the Sea of California from thirty-two to forty-six degrees, making it thereby an island, and the largest island in the world, whereas it is not an island but a peninsula.

And yet there was still skepticism by those who had not seen and those averse to such revolutionary ideas. As Salvatierra lamented, "They are not going to be silenced until they are completely done for." There was talk of another expedition. But Kino was prevented from further explorations by the urgent requirements of his mission lands.

Although Kino was right about the existence of a land route between California and Sonora, he had a sense of only the beginnings of the difficulties involved. The route was through such forbidding deserts and over such daunting mountains that in fact not one horse or pack animal made the journey during the entirety of the seventy-year Jesuit occupation of the California missions.

With tired legs, we made our way down from the ridge. "What a hike, what a view, and what great aerobic exercise," I said. Back in camp, an exhausted Pedro was ready to crash inside his kennel. I pulled the mosquito netting down over it and looked inside to see a contented brotherly eye looking back at me.

While Pedro slept, pearly masses of billowing cumulonimbus clouds moved rapidly against the tops of the pines, spreading in all directions like they were alive and growing. Then came the sound of angry rumbling as the clouds turned gray and blocked the sun. A cold, gusting breeze stirred the trees and scattered the bugs.

With thunder echoing around the valley and the occasional heavy raindrop descending, I put on my rubberized army-surplus jacket and pants over my T-shirt and shorts, and began securing my campsite against the threatening deluge.

I covered the two tents and my kitchen table with large tarps, which I weighed down with rocks and heavy water bottles. I pulled my green army galoshes over my tennis shoes; they comprised two right feet of different sizes, but as I'd bought them from a swap meet for fifty cents the pair I wasn't complaining.

Thinking it was time for Pedro to go potty while he could, I encouraged him out from his kennel, then clipped him on a line.

Brilliant flashes were followed ever more rapidly by dramatically loud bangs. Outside in the forest the noise was unbelievable—I was concerned about damage to Pedro's hearing. My wildly blowing hair felt like it was half way to the clouds; and the fur was rising on Pedro's back—I hoped a sign of fear rather than of an imminent lightning strike.

Helpless before such power, one prays and beseeches Jesus and Mary, and apologizes for all one's sins, and appeals to everything one deems holy. It seems important to remove all reason to be struck.

Just in case my appeals were falling on deaf ears—the cracks could deafen the angels—I thought about the metal I could discard. I pulled my penknife from a pocket, took off my wedding ring, made sure I had no zips. I kept on my metal framed glasses even at the risk of terrible facial burns and blindness—the scene was too awesome to miss, and I might have to deal with some emergency any moment.

Like much that is familiar, the phenomenon of lightning is not clearly understood. One theory pictures the "negatively" charged base of a thundercloud sending invisible downward "leaders" like the snakes on medusa's head pulsing towards earth "seeking out active electrical ground targets." And along the ground, beneath the cloud, a pool of "positively" charged "particles" gathers and shadows the storm. These particles are drawn to the highest points in the area—trees, fences, poles, peaks, buildings, people, animals, lightning rods, etc.—investing them with varying degrees of electric charge so that "upward streamers" are launched from these objects, reaching up like a mess of charmed cobras. Mostly around tree height, "collection zones" of these upward streamers become established. When leaders connect with these collection zones or individual streamers, it's like the closing of a switch. Snakes alive! Flash/Kaboom. We see cloud to ground lightning.

I decided to try riding out the storm in the "comfort" of the screen house. I brought Pedro's kennel inside with me and locked him in. As I expected, the rain came pouring through the mesh of the sidewalls. I needed to cover the kennel and the table in the center with a plastic sheet.

The heavy beating of the rain on the nylon above was strangely reassuring. The rain turned to hail. The ground became wetter and whiter. And it was cold. The temperature felt like it had dropped from 80 to 40 degrees. Next time, I vowed I'd put on a sweater and long pants before climbing into the rain gear.

At first, I felt somewhat protected by the low clump of trees about me, and my rubber boots, but with seemingly never-ending flashes and cracks, and more and more water pooling on the ground, I didn't feel quite so secure. I could envisage, and even sense, those leaders and streamers snaking all about. I kept looking at all the metal objects around me every time the lightning lit up the forest—the aluminum chair inside the gazebo, the metal legs of the table, and the tent poles locking over my head.

With the noise of the storm rising to a heart-thumping crescendo, streams and sheets of water began to run between the trees and the tents. I mulled over all the expert's suggestions in my mind, and even contemplated exiting the screen house and throwing myself face down in the mud. The high ground and bushes turned white; it looked like it had snowed. The silver tarp covering the tent and tables outside stood like a little glacier with all the unmelted hail on it.

Statistics for U.S. lightning-associated deaths and injuries were not comforting. Most occurred in the afternoon; over 80% of the victims were male; 75% were struck during the months of June, July, and August; and 90% of the incidents involved just one person. I decided to have a beer.

The fact that in the U.S. lightning consistently kills more men than women might suggest that God is inherently prejudiced against men, but more likely reflects the fact that men are more prone to be hanging out in screen houses in the mountains during thunderstorms.

Having drunk the beer, I had to go outside to pee in the midst of the storm. With every step I was sloshing in puddles or crunching hail underfoot. I looked at the "streamer" of steaming pee hitting the pine needles and wondered if there might be another explanation for the disproportionate propensity for men to be zapped. Not only are we more likely to be outside in such weather, but we're more likely to be drinking beer, therefore peeing more, and as is our nature standing taller for the act...so alas are we not at such times perfect lightning rods? I imagined that if lightning struck nearby, the current might run through the water on the ground, up the stream of pee and deliver a very nasty shock, or if hit from above I might end up with the mother of all exit wounds. I decided to pulse pee like the water jets used for cleaning power lines.

The storm abated a little. I let Pedro out so he could try his luck peeing on a bush. That done, he had a blast jumping in puddles, and poking his nose in the hail.

Well it was certainly exhilarating and spectacularly beautiful to be out in a wild and violent thunder storm, but I have to confess that any relief attendant on the passing of the storm was tempered by surging anxiety at the thought of dealing with it all again. I felt like a soldier who had just come through a terrific bombardment, wondering if his nerves could stand another one.

Pedro looked up in such a way that I followed his gaze. I was amazed to see a small car parked just across the arroyo, two hundred yards away, on the road to the old log cabin and Blue Bottle Peak. Because of the noise of the rain and the storm, I never heard it arrive. It seemed like a strange apparition, this mysterious little vehicle suddenly, silently, just there in the drizzly, dripping forest. Curious, I wandered over with Pedro.

It was a black Suzuki Samurai with Oregon plates. There was a single occupant—a bearded male. He probably thought the green hooded, misty-spectacled, figure walking towards him was a Mexican soldier. So I dropped the hood to reveal my red hair and Van Gogh bearded face. The man started his engine and drove slowly toward me...then just as slowly lowered the window.

The driver introduced himself as Matt. I guessed he was in his late forties. He was gaunt and had sunken, sad, sensitive eyes, like those of an abused puppy. He struck me as being an old, slightly burned-out hippie. He said he was on his way to Southern Mexico to look for mushrooms but seeing the great thunderheads above the San Pedro Mártir he, on impulse, decided to drive up and check out what the mushrooming was like.

In heading to the mountains of Southern Mexico he was following a route that had become almost a pilgrimage for his countrymen after the appearance of a 1957 *Life Magazine* article entitled, "Seeking the Magic Mushroom." The author R. Gordon Wasson, was a former investment banker turned ethnomycologist. Since its publication a constant procession of American "tourists" have journeyed to Mexico to find enlightenment, including Timothy Leary, the 1960's drug counterculture guru. Wasson wrote:

> ...on the night of 29–30 June, 1955 I participated...in a midnight agape conducted by a shaman of extraordinary quality. This was the first time on record that anyone of the alien race had shared in such a communion. It was a soul-shattering experience...And all the time...the priestess in Mexico sings...The singing is good, but under the influence of the mushroom you think it is infinitely tender and sweet. It is as though you were hearing it with your mind's ear, purged of all dross. You are lying on a petate or mat...It is dark, for all

lights have been extinguished save a few embers among the stones on the floor and the incense in a sherd. It is still, for the thatched hut is apt to be some distance away from the village. In the darkness and stillness, that voice hovers through the hut, coming now from beyond your feet, now at your very ear, now distant, now actually underneath you, with strange ventriloquistic effect… All your senses are similarly affected: the cigarette with which you occasionally break the tension of the night smells as no cigarette before had ever smelled; the glass of simple water is infinitely better than champagne. Elsewhere I once wrote that the bemushroomed person is poised in space, a disembodied eye, invisible, incorporeal, seeing but not seen. In truth, he is the five senses disembodied, all of them keyed to the height of sensitivity and awareness, all of them blending into one another most strangely, until the person, utterly passive, becomes a pure receptor, infinitely delicate, of sensations. As your body lies there in its sleeping bag, your soul is free, loses all sense of time, alert as it never was before, living an eternity in a night, seeing infinity in a grain of sand… At last you know what the ineffable is, and what ecstasy means. Ecstasy! The mind harks back to the origin of that word. For the Greeks ekstasis meant the flight of the soul from the body… Can you find a better word than that to describe the bemushroomed state? In common parlance, among the many who have not experienced ecstasy, ecstasy is fun, and I am frequently asked why I do not reach for mushrooms every night. But ecstasy is not fun. Your very soul is seized and shaken until it tingles. After all, who will choose to feel undiluted awe, or to float through that door yonder into the Divine Presence…

Matt looked like he'd been a little too long in the Divine Presence himself, but he assured me that he was only interested in edible mushrooms such as matsutakes and morels. He was indeed from Oregon, and had long made a living picking wild mushrooms mostly, in the Pacific Northwest. He asked lots of questions about what I'd found and where to camp. Although he was obviously a fascinating person, I couldn't help feeling slightly uneasy about the sudden presence of this stranger who arrived with the storm— especially after he confessed that for fourteen years he had been heavily into hallucinogenic mushrooms and other drugs. I was relieved when he drove away looking for a place to camp. I guessed he had made camp in the Padre Salvatierra campground about a mile back along the road.

The silver tarp was heavy with water and hail. Pedro was still cavorting and splashing. All around in the forest, suddenly sodden cones and branches were thudding and crashing to the ground. It was clearly hazardous walking beneath the tall trees after so much rain.

Pedro is a funny old thing. I went for a walk after Matt had gone and he was just running and playing, enjoying himself, tearing through puddles, just having a blast. He's a happy fellow. He is really, really enjoying being up here in the woods. It's going to be a shame in a way when he has to go home.

A little warming sunshine shafted through the trees before dark. With everything so damp, it took considerable effort to get a huge smoky fire going. Pedro was secure in his kennel by the fire. The sinking sun was reddish brown through the smoke that was drifting and hanging throughout the valley like wispy fog or like chimney smoke on a cold, still morning.

Chapter 17

Astral Projections

The Sierra de San Pedro Mártir became a national park in 1947, and work is now underway for it to be designated as part of the International Biosphere Preserve, a most worthy distinction for this unique place.

— Dick Schwenkmeyer

It had been a mild night—the temperature never dropped below 40 degrees—but nevertheless patches of hail lingered around the tents. I decided that I needed an easy, domestic, drying out day, so Pedro would have to limit himself to wandering around camp.

The pine trunks were soon steaming in the sun, and mist was rising from the forest floor. The clouds were gathering early as if all the misty vapor from the damp forest was being slowly drawn up like a guillotine before its thunderous crashing down.

I was sitting in the screen house, coffee in hand, reading, when I noticed a deer—a doe—grazing just fifty yards away. It hadn't seen me. I stepped outside slowly and watched it for several minutes before it took off. Pedro was so rapt chewing on a large cow bone that he'd dragged back to camp, he had no idea it was there.

The rain seemed to bring out a rush of life. Jays and juncos were noisily flitting in every direction; a flycatcher was perched just a few feet from my head; ground squirrels were scampering far from their borrows; two hummingbirds were boldly checking out all the reds and oranges around camp—I was worried that Pedro might leap up and grab one as they flew by his nose. I squashed my first mosquito.

About midmorning, with the gods molding and kneading some rather dramatic clouds overhead, Matt returned in his sandals. He had indeed made camp near the Salvatierra campground. For someone about to venture to the southernmost parts of Mexico, I was impressed by how under prepared he was. Although he had a small tent, he had no stove, pots, or pans, little food or water...and he almost proudly related that he had no Mexican auto insurance.

"Have an accident in Mexico without insurance—your fault or not—and you'll be lucky to escape jail time," I warned.

He replied that he didn't believe in U.S. auto insurance either. "It's all a rip off," he declared. As vehement as if he were refusing to do drugs so as not to support the murderous drug lords, he insisted that there was no way he was going to put his money into propagating the heinous criminal conspiracy insurance companies were foisting on the public. Clearly he was a serious man of principle. I offered him a beer—which he declined. Our values didn't quite match—and, for a while, neither did our conversations.

It seemed that he needed to talk. And the way he talked about people getting attacked and murdered below the border would make even a native paranoid. I tried to reassure him by tactfully telling him that I'd been traveling through Baja California for over twenty years without any serious problems—but I emphasized that I didn't hang around big cities, tourist dives, drug dealers, drunks...or do risky things like camp alone beside highways after dark.

We chatted for over an hour, and I made him several cups of tea. You could characterize a conversation with Matt in many ways—being dull was not one of them. He was certainly fascinating and informative on the subject of wild edible mushrooms.

Harvesting wild mushrooms such as matsutakes, morels, chanterelles, and boletes in the Northern Hemisphere is a major industry, with annual sales estimated to exceed $1 billion. However, most Britons and Americans don't care to indulge, and limit themselves to eating white button mushrooms grown commercially.

Matt talked up matsutakes like a fevered forty-niner ranting about nuggets. He spoke at length about their various sizes, grades, and prices, and the big bonanza days that he had known. I had only the mistiest notion as to what a matsutake was. Matt explained that they were delicious white, cinnamon-smelling mushrooms usually harvested in the autumn. In a good year matsutakes are abundant in the pine forests of the Pacific Northwest, including Oregon, Washington and British Columbia.

The crop had been lightly exploited till rising demand from Japan and other Asian countries sent prices skyrocketing. Demand had increased as many Asian forests had shrunk or disappeared, taking with them the wild mushrooms that grew in association with the trees. Matsutakes are a "no expense spared" status symbol in Japan, prized at weddings and other special events; they were at times selling for over $400 a pound.

For a while there had been easy pickings and big profits supplying that market. Matt joined hordes of other hopefuls raking away pine needles to reveal the elusive "buttons." Many lived in temporary camps set up in the forest. Buyers attended the camps, offering immediate cash. Seasoned pickers at the time of the best prices could make more than $500 a day.

At first, the majority of pickers in the Pacific Northwest were from Mexico and Southeast Asia (especially Cambodia.) But more and more people got in on the act. Matt spoke of virtual range wars with people defending their woodland patches with almost the same ferocity as drug growers. Ugly hostile confrontations, assaults, and even murders had occurred.

In places, local Indians resented the intrusion of outsiders on their ancestral mushroom grounds. And many unemployed timber workers in the region turned to mushroom picking to supplement their incomes. Matt told me of his run-ins with them. Some who were already violently resentful of longhaired hippies "screwing up their livelihood for the sake of an owl," no doubt found Matt an easy target. In spite of the hazards, the rewards brought Matt and other pickers back, year after year.

Notwithstanding his former drug addictions and current radical notions, Matt was a genuinely searching soul. The more we talked the more I put aside my reservations and came to sympathize with him. I lent him a spare gas stove and a large saucepan, and gave him some water, tea, and a few snacky foods. He said he had found a small spring of water to supply his needs, so I gave him some iodine tablets to purify the water.

Not long after Matt left, Alfredo came over to the camping area to pick up my empty water containers and paint the wooden signs by the road. While he worked, the sky became black and threatening, and the sharp cracks began resounding through the forest. I looked nervously at Pedro digging under one of the bigger pines and called him to me. Some of the bolts lit up the trees with a brilliant blue light. One awesome discharge went on and on and on…a prolonged, pulsing magnesium flash that seemed brighter than sunlight.

Alfredo was still painting his sign, calmly studying each brush stroke. I felt like a rookie soldier watching a grizzled veteran nonchalantly playing cards while bombs and shells were falling all about.

Perhaps seeking a little reassurance, I wandered down to ask: "How often do these storms come?"

"They could come every afternoon now through July and August."
He said.

Over two months of this! The thought depressed me.

Only when the rain picked up did Alfredo step back, look satisfied, get into his truck, and drive off.

Almost immediately, the storm moved overhead. I pulled the tarps down over the tents and stacked sufficient dry wood and kindling under them to help get the evening fire going. Before slipping into my rain gear, I put on sweat pants and a sweater and other warm clothes. I was learning.

As the rain started and the mighty bangs rent the air, I hurried Pedro into his kennel and re-questioned the wisdom of staying inside the screen house during the storm. And again I reasoned that it was probably as safe as anywhere because if lightning did strike the screen house, the aluminum poles running overhead would presumably act like lightning conductors and take the current down into the ground. Standing in my rubber boots on dry soil I felt I wouldn't be a good path to ground…and I imagined that a dry Pedro in his plastic kennel would be relatively safe too.

The storm brought just half an inch of rain, but the thunder seemed louder and more menacing than the day before. When I was confident that it was over, I let Pedro out to run around, play with his toys, and chase a few birds. Although vivacious, he was wonderfully mindful; he never bothered my tents, tarps, solar battery chargers, camera, or anything I left out. I felt like I'd made a good choice for a camp companion.

Next day, Alfredo returned with my filled water containers and finished painting the signs. When he left around noon, I walked Pedro over to the Salvatierra campground to look for Matt and invite him over to my camp to have lunch. I found him in his tent, unwell with a stomachache. He said he was nearly struck by the previous day's lightning—"a bolt hit the ground just yards away."

Nevertheless, he recovered quickly and drove over to my camp a few minutes after I'd walked back. Another storm was threatening—the wind stirred the trees; the aspens leaves were quaking like crazy; and a rainbow seemed to be arching over a massive rising thunderhead. It turned cool, gray, and dark. Thunder was booming all around, but it never rained. Matt and I chatted for another two hours glad, I think, of each others reassuring presence.

After he drove back to his campsite, I found my first obviously living fungus—a lemony yellow sponge-like mass enveloping some pinecones and twigs at the base of an old failing Jeffrey pine. It was the fresh fruiting body of the Dyer's polypore. The rain had likely brought it out.

At sundown the air became filled with big, bumbling ten-lined June beetles (*Polyphylla decimlineata*). Perhaps the rain brought them out too. They were about an inch long, light brown on top with one short and four long white stripes on each wing cover. They had fuzzy dark brown hair under their thorax; and their antennal "clubs" consisted of long broad plates.

Viewed through a hand lens from on top, one looked a bit like a striped squash with legs, and a pair of "horns" that would have graced a big horn sheep. From beneath they looked like monstrous hairy aliens, hideous enough to make Sigourney Weaver hurriedly abandon ship.

They flew enticingly about at head height and landed clumsily, hissing and waggling their antennae. Pedro enjoyed chasing and eating them. He especially liked to leap up and grab them from mid air. And boy could he leap. I tried to save a few from his mouth, but it was pretty hopeless.

Ten-lined June beetles belong to a group of scarabs known as chafers. The adult emerges from the pupa stage usually in June or July. They normally feed on the foliage of conifers. The C-shaped white larvae are subterranean and feed on roots, and take a heavy toll of the seedlings of various conifers. Out of the forests, they can become serious pests of such crops as potatoes, corn, sugar beets, and various fruit trees.

Pedro snagged and broke his dewclaw chasing one of the beetles. He let me inspect his foot without flinching. His whole paw seemed to swell. Then that evening he exploited my concern by cheekily jumping onto my chair by the campfire; he stretched out and starting licking his injured paw as if he knew I wouldn't have the heart to throw him off.

I had a glass of malt whisky and quipped, "It's a good life up here, especially if you're on my chair." I had a second camp chair so I let him keep that one. And that became his favorite fireside spot for the rest of his time in the mountains.

Next day, his paw seemed much better; certainly he was running and chasing with all his old enthusiasm. Matt drove over and returned everything I'd lent him and took off back down to the highway heading for Southern Mexico. He hadn't found any mushrooms but he was confident they would soon be appearing. I wished him luck in his quest for 'shrooms—sacred or otherwise.

A party of five Americans arrived and made camp down in the valley bottom. I was glad when they said they'd be staying three or four days. One of them, Dick Schwenkmeyer, was a respected lecturer and joint author of a book on the *Natural History of Southern California*. I had a copy in my little camp library. He also brought a message from Bonni confirming that she was planning to come up in a few days. Another one of the party was an affable, energetic sixty-year-old woman called Jane; she had brought her large black and brown dog with her—a hound-rottweiler mix. He was well named, Bear.

Pedro was at first too excited and puppyish for this older dog, who was probably a little tired after his long drive up. When Pedro sprinted towards him and accidentally collided, he growled his displeasure.

That misunderstanding aside, Pedro acted like he'd found his long lost buddy and totally forgot about me...and virtually all his training. He had no interest in eating even; all he wanted to do was visit and romp with the other dog. So much for the supposed bond we'd forged.

Wanting to give Jane a break, I fetched him back to my camp and clipped him to a line. He whined. I tried putting him in his kennel, hoping he'd sleep. He just whimpered some more. I clipped him back on his line, and eventually he took a nap.

I joined the group on a number of hikes. First we went to the viewpoint on the ridge. Pedro and Bear were in their element hiking together. I hardly had to think about him the whole time. Dick was a most informative guide. He knew all the flowers, including the ubiquitous little white flowers, which he identified as *Linanthus melingii*, a San Pedro Mártir endemic. No wonder I couldn't identify it from any of my California wildflower guides. He put a name to many of the nondescript bushes and shrubs that constituted the underbrush and were scattered in the arroyos. Perhaps the most widespread was the snowberry; Dick said that later in the summer the bushes would be covered with pea-sized white berries.

The white fir trees were heavy with cones, especially around the crowns. Dick explained that the female cones were on top and the male cones much lower down to diminish the chances for the tree self-fertilizing. On the ridge, a line of grumbling thunderheads stretched above us, sandwiched between blue skies east and west. The rain held off till we got down.

Pedro had a great time with Bear and wanted to stay with him in camp. But as raindrops fell, I led him to his kennel to give the others a rest from his boisterous playfulness.

Another day we hiked several miles to the south and we were all so focused on the flowers and the wildlife that we lost the trail and got turned around and disoriented. The sun was right overhead and not much help. What we swore was east was in fact north. We had to consult compass and GPS to be sure of the direction back to camp. Even so, we found ourselves traversing a seemingly endless forested plateau of rocky outcrops and little valleys, essentially devoid of reference points. We had to scramble around some impossibly steep high points and down a deeply set, boulder-filled valley before we spotted some marker "ducks"—little cairns of rocks—and regained the trail and our sense of security.

On another hike, we headed to the broad, sunny meadows west of Aguaje, and standing among the pink and white showy evening primroses, we could see the red A-frame roofs and white domes of the observatory complex along the ridge to the east.

At one point Pedro started running towards some cattle in the meadow, but luckily a young bull stared him down and he came smartly back. I promptly put him on his leash. In just an hour, the sky went from mostly blue to mostly full of thunderheads. As they loomed menacingly above us, great booms were echoing off the ridges. A few sprinkles fell, but we just beat the main downpour back to camp. I settled with Pedro in the gazebo to weather the storm.

Later that afternoon, with the sun shining again, Federico came over with his son to hike around. Thankfully, Pedro was a model of courtesy, and this time treated the park director with due consideration. We chatted a bit about hiking trails and discussed a proposal by various environmental groups and academics such as Richard Minnich to give the park International Biosphere Reserve status. Federico wasn't totally wedded to the idea. He argued that Mexico ought to keep national control of the park's priorities, including phasing out the summer cattle grazing and returning it to the most pristine state possible.

Federico mentioned that there was a scientific team from the University of California in the park taking blood samples from coyotes and vultures to ascertain if they had dangerous levels of lead or other toxins in their blood. It was an important last step before committing to the release of the California condors.

Emboldened by the presence of my neighbors, I took Pedro for an early evening photo session to the ridge. He was on the leash to begin with as I had no doubt he would happily divert to see Bear. When we were far enough away from camp I released him. I was a little tense because we were alone, it was late in the day, and it would be a bad time to lose him.

But Pedro seemed to be back to his old normal, mindful self. He stuck reasonably close to me even though we encountered a deer coming over the final ridge. I allowed myself half an hour to admire the rich evening light on Picacho and enjoy the unusual warm stillness there on the overlook.

Heading down, about a third of the way back, in one of the most craggy, intimidating areas along the trail, I lost sight of Pedro. I looked up and there he was standing on a twelve-foot-high boulder. Silhouetted against the fading blue sky, he looked like a coyote or a mountain lion. Even though I knew it was Pedro, I still did a double take and my heart speeded a little.

My heartbeat hardly had time to return to normal when Pedro could contain himself no longer—he just blatantly took off down the trail leaving me calling in vain. He was gone! It was rapidly becoming dark and I was alone.

What made him run away? I was almost hoping it was because he couldn't bear to be separated from Bear. Otherwise, I speculated, something might have spooked him. I gazed anxiously around and gripped my machete. Then I raced down the trail picturing all kinds of scenarios from throwing Pedro on his back and yelling, "You disloyal son of a bitch," to using him as a Frisbee and throwing him half way to Picacho.

As the silence of the night dropped heavy about me, accentuating my heavy breathing and the sound of my boots grinding on the granite, I realized it was really my fault for not training him better; and it wouldn't achieve much coming down on him like a falling ponderosa as by then, recalling the Monks of New Skete, he probably wouldn't know why I was so furious.

Sure enough, he was in camp having the time of his life with Bear. He even had the audacity to greet me by running up and licking my hand. I just jabbed a finger towards him softly growling, "You bad boy. You bad boy, Pedro."

Soon all was forgotten as Pedro and Bear entertained us with their antics chasing the hovering June beetles, and we humans settled by the communal fire and bonded with wine, beer, and good conversation. The wet weather usually meant pleasant mild nights.

As well as his glue-like attachment to Bear, Pedro had also big time bonded with Jane. She was a remarkable lady who had climbed Picacho several years before, and she clearly had a fantastic rapport with and knowledge about dogs. By the campfire, if there was one thing Pedro preferred to settling on my chair, it was stretching on her lap.

Next morning, once again, Pedro wasn't interested in eating; he just wanted to get down to run with his buddy. Before indulging him, I took him on a ten-minute training walk; but he couldn't focus for ten seconds—all he could think about was Jane and Bear, Jane and Bear. I had to get tough with him and give him what I hoped was a passable attempt at an alpha roll. After that, he was a little more attentive when I said sit or come…but not much. There was still work to be done.

Dick had been a wonderful, informative, patient, enthusiastic teacher, and his enthusiasm brushed off on me. By the time he left I felt I knew virtually every common plant and bush in the San Pedro Mártir. Admittedly, he had given me a list of all the plants he had identified there, but without a teacher to help put name to plant it wouldn't have been much help.

And then suddenly, one frosty morning, our newfound friends were just a memory. Pedro and I were alone together, standing over the cold ashes of their fire, listening to the racket of the pinyon jays—mostly squabbling, unruly fledglings mercilessly harassing their parents.

With Bear gone, Pedro seemed at first to be depressed and then sullen and withdrawn. I let him mourn his loss, and gradually his moodiness passed and he was back to playing with his toys and chasing June bugs.

I was back to being more on edge, alert, and intimidated by the blackness. Pedro was a worthy match for my timidity. Every night I had to almost pour him out of his kennel to take a pee, and having managed that he usually scrambled with unseemly haste to get back inside.

Stormy weather past, the nights were again bitterly cold, and I delighted in huddling by a blazing fire. Yet, the sight of the new moon goaded me to enjoy the night sky while I could—it would soon be washed out by bright moonlight. As the closing parenthesis of a moon disappeared, I let the fire burn down, then stepped into the clearing to study the stars.

I turned my binoculars to the familiar summer constellation Sagittarius. Early astronomers tracing imaginary lines between stars had seen Sagittarius as a centaur—half man and half horse. Some have speculated the figure might have originated from the amazement ancient peoples felt when they first saw warriors on horseback, and thought they were seeing a human head and torso rising from the body of a horse. Indeed, the natives of Mexico believed that is what they beheld the first time they saw Spanish cavalry.

Today's stargazers are more likely to see Sagittarius as a teapot with handle, lid, and spout. And those fortunate enough to observe the "teapot" in a location such as the San Pedro Mártir on a clear moonless night will plainly see a great cloud of "steam" about the spout. And one can readily understand how those who saw centaurs in the sky might have seen the Milky Way as the dust from their galloping hoofs.

Sagittarius may not be a centaur, but near the spout, 30,000 or so light-years away is what many astronomers believe to be center of our galaxy and the location of an enormous black hole. Training binoculars on this area reveals perhaps the finest concentration of star clusters and nebulae in the heavens.

Before retiring, I stared long and hard at the overarching splash of the Milky Way, and realized that it wasn't a uniform, undifferentiated mass of starry liquid light. I could see shapes and structure. I confessed to my tape recorder—"Definitely has two components to it…it's almost like two forms copulating or indulging in some strange sexual practices; the more I look up, the more I can see different practices going on up there."

I was brought down to earth when Pedro suddenly raised his head from his chair and growled. I shone my flashlight all around and subconsciously moved closer to my shovel, which was resting on a log beside the fire. The shovel would probably be my weapon of choice if confronted by a mountain lion—I could use it as a shield, and swing, stab, and throw dirt and stones with it.

And as my beam swept through the trees, and crazed galloping centaurs raced through my mind, I was shocked to see in the direction of my cathedral several glowing orange eyes silently looking back at me.

It was such a surreal image in the coal-like blackness, I couldn't be sure if they were two yards, 200 yards, or an eternity away. Needing to know what they were, I left Pedro hooked on his line and slowly walked away from the fire with flashlight in my left hand, shovel in my right, and my heart in my mouth. As I walked, the eyes seemed to be moving up and down and around in hypnotic circles. Fifty yards out, I quickly shone my light back towards camp and saw what I hoped were Pedro's eyes, equally orange and floating.

The mysterious eyes beckoned me on. They must be coyotes, I thought. But as the animals turned and noisily crashed away, I realized with considerable relief that they were just cows and calves grazing in some bushes.

Next morning, there was ice in the kettle and frost on the ground. Pedro wouldn't leave his kennel...it was too cozy in there. Without Bear's inducement I had to drag him out to go for a walk.

I hiked back up to the ridge. It was the clearest day yet—I could see mountains way over in Sonora that I hadn't seen before. Coming down, we ran into two families of quail. Pedro took off after one of them. A dozen chicks were running all over. Pedro ignored those and went after one of the adult females. She cleverly ran ahead using patches of brush for cover—clearly leading Pedro on. Suddenly, my dog was hundreds of yards away, across the valley; and then he was gone. I sat and waited, whistled and called, for 20 minutes...before he nonchalantly ambled up to me. Not wanting to send the wrong message and discourage his return, I greeted him effusively, glad he was back; but he was a dog under sentence. I thought his backsliding had gone too far. Next time he refuses to "come," I'll go fetch him and then he'll get the treatment.

Back in camp I occupied him with a few focused training sessions. If there was one word of English he was going to learn, it was, "Come."

After dark, I kept looking up at the Milky Way and north along the road wondering if and when Bonni would come.

A mysterious rapport

Chapter 18

Superdog

It is not good that man should be alone.

— Genesis 2:18

June 27: The sun had gone down. It would soon be dark. There was no sign of Bonni. I had pretty much given up that she would come that day, when Pedro sat up so sharply he spilled from his chair. A few moments later I heard a horn. It was our Nissan pickup hurrying down the road.

When Bonni pulled into the campsite, I was surprised and delighted to see Penny's little black nose and stubby paws pressed to the side window, her brown eyes full of eagerness as she barked to get out. Bonni had brought her up to give her a few days break in the mountains.

Bonni recounted that Penny had been sitting on the front seat on a blanket and she had been carsick three times near the border, but had perked up since. I made a big fuss of her and then clipped her on a line; she walked around, sniffed the air, listened to the sounds, and then played enthusiastically with Pedro. Pedro was ecstatic to have another, and this time familiar and equally boisterous, friend. Bonni said she was being a nuisance at home, chewing things and digging holes all over the garden. Here she could chew and dig all she wanted.

It is quite a challenge to describe Penny. She's certainly a brown-eyed, dirty-nosed, coarse-haired ragamuffin. She looks like a chunkier, cuter, darker, floppy-eared version of Toto—Dorothy's dog in the Wizard of Oz—or like a black Benji, or Scuppers, or a little bow-legged hippo with the face of a gentle orangutan or friendly sea otter. She had a silver-streaked goatee hanging down from her cute black nose giving her the air of a Mandarin sage. Her head in profile looked somewhat like a cartoon bearded Viking—like Hagar the Horrible.

She had a great way of lying down—she would stretch out both her little front and rear legs till she just dropped onto her belly, and she was very fond of just sitting like that. One hardly knew which end was which. She was good with her paws; a skill she used to full effect to roll and raise things so she could grab them with her mouth.

When we got the fire going, Pedro pulled himself back up on his chair and Penny settled into her cozy soft basket, which Bonni had brought up. She also brought up another closeable plastic kennel, similar to the one Pedro had. Just to be on the safe side, even by the campfire, I clipped a line to Penny's collar; she's an impulsive little thing and she'd think little of chasing off into the night if she heard something.

Pedro, asleep on the chair, looked so handsome and noble, whereas Penny in her basket looked unbearably cute. I called them Little Penny and Old Pedro.

Bonni and I sat up late into the freezing night sharing our news and drinking beer. She told me about her rescuing Sparky and the other dog, which they had named Tanner, and how well they were doing now. When it was time to retire, I put Pedro and Penny's kennels together next to our tent, and all but covered them with towels and tarps to help keep them snug. In spite of the fire, Bonni and I were both so chilled it was hard to warm up even in our sleeping bags inside the tent.

It was a cold morning too. We kept Penny clipped on one of the run lines as we unloaded all the supplies. By turns she chewed on pine cones, played with Pedro, and stared about in apparent wonder as the sun sent its warmth and brilliant light shafting through the forest clearings.

To give Penny a better sense of where she was, we took a few short walks with her on a leash. Then as the sun rose higher, Bonni and I enjoyed a hot shower, put the dogs in their kennels, and retired to a now wonderfully warm tent to talk about what I had seen in the Milky Way. We had a stellar time.

And somewhat later we took Penny and Pedro for a long walk up a deeply set little flower-filled canyon with beautiful intimate pools and an on-again, off-again trickling stream. I had come to call it "Art's Canyon" after Dick had mentioned that an old Baja explorer named Art liked to camp there.

Next day, we let Penny off the leash. As she ran free with Pedro, her little elephant-like floppy ears flapped around her face. Her black raggedy tail stood erect like a little fir tree or a snow plant. In spite of the altitude she only had two speeds—a happy romp, and flat out fearless like a charging wild boar or a little, four-legged cannon ball careering along the ground. She was always eager to go from one entertainment or delight to another.

On Penny's first encounter with a cow she uncharacteristically just stood and stared, shooting a couple of enquiring glances at me—she had no idea what to make of it. However she knew exactly what to do with dried cow pies; she'd pick them up and run, getting Pedro dashing after her. She was such a tease.

The forest or the mountains certainly didn't intimidate her. On her first off-leash "hike," she disappeared for several minutes. I called anxiously. I was about to go looking for her, when she came charging down a rocky slope, jumping over branches and boulders, I winced as she launched herself into the air like an obese, short-legged gazelle and landed at my feet; then it was all tail wagging and greetings, and licking. She probably had got lost in the boulders and manzanita, and was trying to get down.

A little while later, Penny jumped off a fallen trunk on a steep slope. There was a big drop on the other side. She somersaulted on the pine needles, landing with a hard body slam, then stood apparently dazed. It looked like she might have hurt herself. Bonni was so concerned, she ran forward and scooped her up intending to reassure the poor thing, but as Bonni stood up she was under a low hung pine tree and both she and Penny crashed into a canopy of branches. Somehow, in spite of our good intentions, Penny had a knack for getting into—and mercifully usually getting smartly out of—sticky situations.

Before we even had a chance to convince ourselves she was okay, she ran off and came barreling down a slippery, pine needle-covered slope, lost control and looked certain to crash full speed into a boulder at my feet; but somehow she twisted aside—her rounded dumpy shape concealing her incredible agility.

Given the fact that her belly is only about three inches off the ground, she was amazingly good at jumping over fallen trees. She seemed to glide over them like Superdog, pink tongue hanging out, cute little paws stretched to the front and back. All she lacked was a little cape. She was having so much fun, and her antics were so ridiculous, I only had to look at her to laugh.

Miss-hap would have been a good name for her. It was going to be a challenge to keep her safe, but I thought we could probably manage it for a few days. And even Pedro was doing his bit. He seemed to be shepherding her and teaching her the ropes. When I called him, he'd look around for Penny before dashing over, and she would follow flat out.

While Bonni was preparing dinner that evening Pedro was tearing around camp in a big circle. Penny, not quite able to match his speed, was cutting corners and launching herself at him growling. I wondered if they were really fighting, but minutes later they were curled up together—a cute black and tan bundle catching the final rays of the sun. Pedro seemed to be sheltering her; she was snuggled up inside his legs, her back to his belly, a perfect cozy fit.

Every evening, Penny and Pedro delighted in chasing bugs together—especially the ten-lined June beetles. Occasionally they would run around too vigorously, kicking up dust and Penny would go crashing into tables and tents. She was hopeless, untrained and undisciplined, but she was generally desirous to stay with Pedro. My only sure means to call her back when she ran off was through Pedro who had reverted to being the dependable responsive one.

Penny had a body about the size of a chubby two-year-old human child. She was so tactile; it was almost instinctive to pick her up, cuddle her and rub her belly. That's something she played on—at the slightest issue between us, when she heard an angry voice, she'd rely on cuteness by rolling and presenting her less hairy underside. It was her doggy-wolfy way of submitting when she had been bad, but it was as if she were saying, "Look. Be nice. I'm almost human." She had me perfectly trained; it worked every time.

When, during a training session, I had Pedro walking on the leash, Penny grabbed his leash in her mouth and then started running, dragging me on one side and Pedro on the other. It was very comical. To keep her in line I put her on her own leash. She seized that in her teeth and was soon leading me through the lupines. You can't keep a good dog down.

Unlike Pedro, who would practically inhale whatever food I put down, she was amazingly halfhearted about eating; she needed to be coaxed, except when something was particularly to her liking. Anything flavored with ginger or garlic was well received. And she loved bits of apple—she would eagerly chew as many as I gave her. Whereas Pedro, like a wise and horrified Adam tasting future woe, would let them drop from his mouth.

Chapter 19

Observatory

Nation will make war on nation, kingdom upon kingdom; there will be great earthquakes, and famines and plagues in many places; in the sky terrors and great portents.

— Luke 21:10

I was catching up on the news, reading the June 27, 2001 copy of the *San Diego Union-Tribune* that Bonni brought up. A story caught my eye about the problems of light pollution in the mountains north of the border.

In response to the City of San Diego's plans to install brighter street lighting, Paul Etzel—Director of Mount Laguna Observatory in the mountains of San Diego County—pleaded:

> The remote mountains of San Diego County represent a National Treasure. We have the best overall mix of dark skies, clear weather, and smooth dry airflow of any location in the Continental United States. The City and County should embrace the opportunity to protect this resource of global importance...Increasingly light pollution will limit various forms of research that are done with the telescopes of SDSU's Mount Laguna and Caltech's Mount Palomar Observatories...We San Diegans are trustees for two very significant observatories that contribute to the global study of the universe. We must not blind them with foolish, extravagant street lights.

Fortunately, the San Pedro Mártir Mountains had no such problems. An observatory brochure claimed:

> The Sierra de San Pedro Mártir is one of the most favored sites in the world for astronomical investigation because of its

meteorological characteristics—clear skies, freedom from city light pollution, and calm dry air. Only the mountains of Mauna Kea, over 4,000 meters high, in the Hawaiian Islands offer comparable conditions for astronomy in the Northern Hemisphere. So it is important to conserve and develop this location as a sanctuary for astronomical observation.

While I had the truck, I drove Bonni and the dogs up to the observatory for a photo shoot. It was a little over four miles from my camp to the maintenance and administration buildings by the observatory gate, then a further steep mile or so up to the telescope area. We passed two smaller domes and parked beneath the huge white dome housing the main 2.1-meter telescope. The dome rose majestically on a promontory, the manmade equivalent of nature's commanding peak looming across Cañon del Diablo.

Although we could hear whirrings and soft bangings from deep inside the building, there was no one in sight. We just walked the dogs on leads around the dome, read the dedicatory plaques, and peered over some pretty awesome cliffs.

The San Pedro Mártir National Astronomical Observatory is the most important astronomical observatory in Mexico, and can be seen as the culmination of a long and proud tradition of studying the night sky that extends back to the Aztecs, the Mayas and beyond.

Pre-Columbian civilizations—especially the Mayan—made notable astronomical and calendric advances, but their knowledge was largely suppressed and wiped out by the Spanish conquerors.

The first colonial teachings about astronomy were conducted at the *Universidad de México*, which was established in 1553. The course content was heavily influenced by religious presupposition, and more akin to astrology than astronomy. The books used were typical medieval texts promulgating an earth-centered universe—eternal, immutable, and divinely perfected.

However, the vast reach of the Spanish Empire gave a powerful boost to practical astronomy. In 1584, the Spanish monarch sent instructions to his colonial officials to accurately observe and record all eclipse phenomena, and also outlined a simple method for building an instrument that could determine the different phases of eclipses in order to use the data to determine the geographical positions of the observing sites. Knowing, for example, the exact duration of an eclipse in relation to those recorded further east and west would give a good estimate of longitude.

The clash between practical astronomy and the dictates of Catholic dogma rumbled on for over a century. Copernicus, in the early 1500's, had presented the theory that the sun is the center of the universe, not the Earth. Other scientists began to offer evidence supporting his belief. In 1616, the Roman Catholic Church declared the idea heretical and in opposition to the official teachings of the Church.

Galileo publicly defended the Copernican theory because his telescope observations provided strong evidence for its validity. In 1633, the Inquisition tried Galileo for heresy. Fortunate to escape the stake, he lived the remaining years of his life under house arrest, and died in 1642.

Although the Inquisition had been established in Mexico in 1571, it was a relatively mild institution compared to that in Spain and Italy, and had markedly little influence on colonial culture. Thus, in 1638 the *Universidad de México* opened its School of Astrology and Mathematics. Despite its name, the school dared to discuss and critique the latest European developments in astronomical science. And at the same time the first telescopes designed specifically for astronomical work arrived in Mexico.

Gradually, the intellectual and empirical approach to studying the heavens won out over the dictates of the theologians, and the ideas of the more liberal, progressive sky watchers slowly pervaded colonial society.

After the 1680's there was even a relaxation in the severity and zeal of the Spanish Inquisition. And so there arose in Spain a new movement, that of the *Novatores*, which began to introduce many of the ideas of modern science into that country.

But elements of superstition and Church influence in the field lingered throughout the seventeenth-century. A particular controversy arose over the great comet—now known as Halley's comet—that appeared in 1680 and was visible for many months. Without a true understanding of the nature of comets, there was a great deal of fear about its portent.

In November and December of 1680, while waiting for a passage across the Atlantic, Padre Kino had the opportunity to carefully describe the motion of Halley's comet in Seville. And after January 1681, Kino continued to make observations on the comet aboard a small mail ship, part of an armada that arrived in Vera Cruz, Mexico, May 3, 1681. Kino quickly left the unhealthy tropical coast for the more agreeable climate of Mexico City, where he studied the comet from his new vantage point.

He had scarcely arrived in the capital when he was introduced to Carlos de Sigüenza y Góngora, perhaps the *Novatore* movement's most important representative in New Spain. He was born in Mexico and was a professor of astrology and mathematics at the Royal University of Mexico. He had also made extensive observations on the comet, and being contemptuous of what he regarded as ignorant superstitions, wrote a book entitled— *Philosophical Manifest against Comets stripped of their dominion over the Timid*—which was intended to calm public fears by asserting that the comet was entirely a natural phenomenon.

Kino became a welcome guest at Sigüenza's home, who in turn took him to visit his long time friend Sor Juana, one of the greatest poets in the Spanish language, a nun whose "convent cell became the intellectual center of Mexico City." She owned a telescope, and had the largest library in the city.

Kino couldn't totally divorce his astronomical observations from his theological assumptions, and insisted that the comet foretold great and terrible events. Thus he took a very different position from Sigüenza when he wrote his own book called *Expósicion Astronómica de el Cometa* published in 1682. The dire portents of comets were patent to everybody, he wrote, "unless there be some dull wits who cannot perceive it." Sor Juana endorsed Father Kino's belief, even writing a sonnet honoring his view of the comet.

The Church approved publication, declaring that it "implants a Holy fear of God in our souls, His comet being something like a lash, or a sword of justice which God suspends from heaven, terrifying all mortals, so that each one may endeavor to improve his habits."

When Carlos de Sigüenza read the missionary's work...he considered it a direct attack on his *Manifest*, and the reference to "some dull wits" to be a thinly veiled attack on himself. Unfortunately Kino wasn't available to clear up the misunderstanding; he had shipped westward to begin his missionary service on the remote and virtually uncharted "island" of California.

A former Jesuit, Sigüenza made a powerful, indeed indignant response to Father Kino's alleged criticism. He wrote another book— bitingly sarcastic—which was subtitled, *"Astronomical and Philosophical Balance in which Don Carlos de Sigüenza ...examines not only the objections to his Philosophical Manifest against Comets raised by the Reverend Father Eusebio Francisco Kino...but also what the same Reverend Father pretended to have demonstrated in his Expósicion Astronómica de el Cometa."*

Although much of the debate sought justification in the opinions of classic writers and Church Fathers, Sigüenza y Góngora freely quoted the work of Copernicus, Galileo, Descartes and Kepler, and his published writings on the comet are today considered to be the beginnings of modern astronomy in Mexico.

As I reflected on all this, it seemed ironic that the main Mexican observatory should have been located in a mountain range and a national park named after the patron saint of the Inquisition...and I should be camping in a site named after a missionary who, whatever great virtues he possessed, was averse to seeing astronomy as a purely empirical, scientific endeavor, and took issue with Mexico's first scientific astronomer.

However, to be fair, Kino's and the Jesuit position were by no means antiscientific. The Jesuit contribution to astronomy has been enormous. By 1750, 30 of the world's 130 astronomical observatories were run by Jesuit astronomers and 35 lunar craters had been named in honor of Jesuit scientists.

Bonni with garter snake

Chapter 20

Forest Fare

They shall strike at your head,
And you shall strike at their heel.
— Genesis 3:15

Alfredo came over with my filled water containers and Baltasar in the back of the pickup. Penny greeted Baltasar and Alfredo by wagging her tail side to side like a slapping car windshield wiper. They both were quite taken with her.

While the three dogs ran happily together, I showed my appreciation for the water by giving Alfredo a large bag of dried fruit and several bars of chocolate. Also we managed to coax him into joining us for a pleasant whisky, beer, Italian sausage sandwich lunch—which we dragged out nearly two hours.

Alfredo told us some exciting news—the governor of Baja California would be visiting the park and the observatory in the next few days, and hinted that he might visit the Padre Kino campsite.

Then the conversation turned to the local wildlife and Alfredo repeated that he had never seen a rattlesnake "at this altitude in the park." "Or any type of snake," he added.

Not many minutes later, Bonni spotted a two-foot-long garter snake behind the screen house. She bent down, grabbed it and brought it over to Alfredo. He was astonished and judging by his laughter probably a little embarrassed. It was pretty much unheard of for a Mexican to pick up a snake, and quite incomprehensible for a woman to do so. And then to lovingly release it—these *gringas* are *loca*.

Mexicans often have little more than a superstitious understanding of serpents—and ever since the temptation of Eve, they've all had a pretty bad rap. Most, I think, if they had their way would probably, like good Saint Patrick, destroy the lot of them and feel like they were doing God's work. Of course, the subsequent explosion of rodents and other potential pests would constitute an ecological disaster of almost Biblical proportions.

Bonni and I enjoyed taking the dogs on several long hikes, then one morning we drove over to a canyon three miles inside the park where we had found scores of mushrooms the previous summer. In spite of the recent rains, there were just a few small, shriveled specimens. As we were returning empty-handed to our vehicle we saw what had to be the governor's white Chevy Suburban going by—it was full of guys in suits and sported what looked like the state seal on the door. We hurried back to the campsite.

By the time we got back it was sufficiently gray and threatening to induce me to cover the tents and tables with tarps. While doing so, a white Suburban approached and then drove slowly around the ring road. The governor! We managed to grab and secure the dogs. I dug out copies of my books and the letter from the Secretary of Tourism, and waited excitedly for the vehicle's return. I had my speech ready.

As the Suburban pulled into my camping area, I looked in vain for the state insignia on the doors; and it dawned on me that the faces of the two men up front were rather familiar. It turned out to be a couple of friends and old Baja aficionados—Bicycle Baja Bob Vinton, M.D. and "Mission Trail" David Richardson—who had come up together in David's newly acquired vehicle. We laughed at the coincidence! They told us that three other mutual friends were camping a few miles away in the *Tasajera* valley. We agreed to go visit them on July Fourth. The rain held off, and Bob and David set up their campsite 100 yards away in the valley bottom.

July Fourth got off to a bad start. Pedro woke me twice in the night whimpering to get out of his kennel to go potty. He had diarrhea. Then it started raining at five o'clock—a big surprise that early in the day. So I had to go outside again and re-cover the tents and tables. I was tired from the get go, and so was Pedro who was reluctant to leave his kennel. Penny was trying to drag him out to play, but he wasn't thrilled about it.

The *Parque Nacional* was almost empty. In my mind I compared the peaceful scene before me with what one could expect in say California's Yosemite Park on July Fourth. Both parks are incredibly rugged and beautiful; both are roughly equal distances from Los Angeles. Yet in Yosemite, the visitor would be faced with a steep entrance fee, long lines, parking problems, crowds, and for most not much chance to relax or commune with the wilderness or feel any kind of special connection to the place.

After breakfast, we drove out in David's Suburban looking for the three friends who had gone to Tasajera to photograph and enjoy nature. We stopped at Alfredo's cabin to find out if the chain that normally hung across the road was in place, and if so whether he could open it for us. He was not at home. So we headed down the Tasajera road anyway.

Drat! The chain was in position and locked. That meant if we wanted to see our friends, we'd have to leave the vehicle and walk three or four miles. While we were deciding on what to do, Bonni and I looked for mushrooms in an aspen grove surrounding the gate. We found a few small specimens—and in the densest thicket the skeletal and sinewy remains of a calf, torn apart, with legs hanging off. I did not want to think what the story was on that.

Still undecided, we drove half a mile back down the road to a sunny clearing for lunch. While Penny and Pedro ran free, Bonni and I did some more mushrooming, and then by chance Alfredo happened by. He gave us the key to the lock on the chain, but declined to come with us in his 2WD Dodge pickup because of the rough road. So we set off, all four of us with the two dogs in the Suburban. We had a watermelon and some beers, and were primed for a July 4th party. "Traitors' Day," I jestingly called it.

About a mile beyond the gate, David started having trouble turning the steering wheel—something was catching as the wheel turned with a click and a clunk. The problem grew worse. David stopped, crawled underneath the front of the vehicle, sprayed the steering joints with WD40 and then poured oil liberally over the entire steering, suspension assembly—springs and axle too.

A surprise storm was moving in fast. It was getting grayer by the minute and thunder was resounding through the dense forest. We all agreed to go back. David skillfully turned the big vehicle around on the narrow single-track road. Then lashed by sheets of rain, we were bouncing our way up a steep rocky hill, when there was a sudden horrible shuddering and scraping noise. In spite of the storm and the tall pines and firs all around, we all jumped out and saw that the front tire on the driver's side had somehow moved back and become tightly wedged against the running board. It would be impossible to drive much further without gouging the tire apart.

David and Bob got underneath with water streaming down the road and figured out that the front axle had shifted back several inches along the leaf spring on that side, presumably because the U-bolts weren't tightened down enough. Pouring oil on them hadn't helped; in fact it had probably accounted for the sudden dramatic movement. David managed to coax the vehicle twenty yards up the hill to get off the road and on to a relatively flat area in a little clearing among the trees.

As the rain diminished, I offered to hike out to get my truck and tools, and inform Alfredo of our plight. Bob came with me. I left the dogs in Bonni's care. We walked back through the gate—left it open in case David somehow managed to fix the problem—took a trail through the forest and meadows over to Aguaje del Burro, and then across the ridge to our campsite, a distance of about 3 or 4 miles. After partially unloading my truck and gathering up some essential gear in case we had to spend the night, we drove out, racing the dark, looking for Alfredo. We met him on the road. He couldn't come with us as he was expecting some "official" visitors, but he lent us some blocks of wood and a chain suitable for towing.

By the time Bob and I drove back to the Suburban, David and Bonni had the front of the vehicle jacked up and they'd had plenty of time to ponder the problem in our absence. David used my jack and one of Alfredo's blocks of wood to try to push the front axle horizontally back into place. With time and patience and some effort, it seemed to be working. Satisfied that it was more or less in position, we took turns tightening down the large bolts that held the axle in relation to the springs. It was a painstaking task with vice grips, as we didn't have a big enough wrench to fit. It was getting dark. Hoping it was sufficiently tightened, David attempted to drive out.

I put the dogs in my pickup. Then I went in front in case the Suburban ground to a halt again on the narrow road. After we got through the "gate," I locked it and returned the keys, chain and blocks of wood to Alfredo who was still waiting by the main park road in his vehicle for his visitors to arrive. We drove back to our campsite. We skipped lighting a campfire. Bonni and I had a quick meal of canned menudo, and then went to bed tired. It wasn't what we'd planned, but it was a really memorable July Fourth.

Next day, Bob and David left; but they first headed to the observatory looking for a mechanic able to more securely tighten those U-bolts before hitting the long washboardy road down to the highway. David had generously left me two full, very much appreciated, seven-gallon water containers and some food. What an off-road brotherhood. They made it safely back to San Diego where David faced a bill for several hundred dollars to repair the damage.

Bonni and I were back to being alone, relying on our feet to get us about—something that was much more healthy and relaxing, and enjoyable for the dogs. While hiking over towards Art's Canyon we spotted our first "real," toadstooly-type mushroom poking through the pine needles on the forest floor.

"Ah-ha a bolete!" Bonni said with her "we've found supper" look on her face.

The handsome three-inch wide cap was brownish yellow on top and bright lemony yellow underneath; it had pores rather than gills.

"Is it safe to eat?" I asked.

"Boletes are hard to misidentify, and they're a relatively safe family. Even the poisonous ones aren't likely to kill you," she said reassuringly.

We found a bunch more (they looked like the same species) at the entrance to Art's Canyon. Some had been chomped on by squirrels. Bonni gathered the untouched ones and carried them back to camp.

While eating wild mushrooms was now the most natural thing in the world to Bonni, for me the experience usually set off a terrific battle between the rational and the deep-seated prejudicial corners of my mind. I could be looking at the same facts and be following the same line of reasoning as Bonni, and yet in the final analysis, thoughts would be sprouting in my head that had little to do with facts or reason. Eating wild mushrooms is, for folks like me, an almost religious experience—the Last Supper readily comes to mind.

While Bonni cheerfully prepared the boletes for dinner, I wracked my brains to be sure I hadn't recently upset her in any way. She cut away the spongy pore tissue and any part of the remainder of the cap or the stalk that she thought was wormy. "Boletes can get maggoty very quickly," she explained. I couldn't see anything except mushroom, but with her educated eye she could see the dark telltale pinprick tunnels.

"Shouldn't we try these on the dogs first," I half-heartedly enquired. Bonni answered with a very piercing glance.

While Bonni sautéed the hopefully maggot-free remains of the mushrooms in butter, I comforted myself that I had sampled and survived several mushroom dinners that Bonni had plucked from a variety of cemeteries in San Diego. I also checked and rechecked our mushroom field guides. I noted that many of the most poisonous boletes tended to be reddish and stain blue when bruised—the Satan's bolete was a prime example. Our boletes remained bright yellow.

Noting my sudden intense interest in the subject of bolete identification, Bonni exclaimed helpfully, "I think they're in the genus *Suillus*, possibly *pseudobrevipes* or *kaibabensis*." I flicked the pages of several mushroom guides and found my attention being grabbed by a string of references containing words such as lethal, deadly, and fatal.

...the deadly poisonous Amanitas usually produce no symptoms till 6–24 hours after ingestion...and then it may be too late...the toxins enter the bloodstream and cause sufficient damage to the liver, kidneys, and other organs to be fatal.

Having read that I got sidetracked from boletes and started homing in on Amanita horror stories, rather like I'd been doing with lightning deaths and mountain lion attacks. As author David Arora said, Amanitas are "the deadliest of all mushrooms...Learning to recognize this genus should be an overriding priority for all mushroom hunters, since Amanitas are responsible for 90% of all mushroom induced fatalities."

I fixed in my mind the characteristics of Amanitas: Typically medium to large...with white or pale gills...gills are usually "free," they don't reach to the stalk. Develop in a "universal veil" which breaks as the stalk elongates...remains of the universal veil are present both as a cup like structure (volva) at the base of the stem and some kind of remnant on the cap such as scales or patches. The scales or "warts" are usually white, gray or yellow and are relatively easily brushed off. It is important to dig up any unfamiliar mushroom so as not to miss the volva...Most Amanitas—including the most dangerous ones—also have a partial veil protecting the gills under the cap. As the mushroom develops it breaks leaving a distinct ragged ring (annulus) near the top of the stalk. Many taste good.

Amanita phalloides (Death Cap)—"the most deadly fungus known"—and *Amanitas virosa and ocreata* (The Destroying Angels) are perhaps the worst in the family. The Death Cap is mycorrhizal with pines, and widely distributed in Europe and North America. The Destroying Angels, strikingly beautiful white mushrooms, are reputed to taste good, and the *ocreata* species "recently caused several deaths near San Diego. The victims were apparently starving illegal aliens who ate the mushrooms out of desperation." *Arora*

An average fatal dose of *Amanita phalloides* is about two ounces of the mushroom. The effects of the toxin—amanitin—are centered on the liver and kidney, but amanitins damage tissues throughout the body by inhibiting RNA synthesis within each cell. All the organs may be damaged directly by the toxin and indirectly by damage to the liver and kidneys. "It is a slow and painful way to die." *Arora*

Treatment is largely supportive through mineral and fluid maintenance and dialysis. As the U.S. Food and Drug Administration puts it, "victims who are hospitalized and given aggressive support therapy almost immediately after ingestion have a mortality rate of only 10%, whereas those admitted 60 or more hours after ingestion have a 50-90% mortality rate."

"This couldn't be an Amanita?" I asked as the delicious smell of butter-sautéed mushrooms drifted through the trees. The question came from that irrational prejudiced corner of my mind—all other corners felt a little foolish.

"No," Bonni chided, "you have to be pretty dim to mistake a bolete for an Amanita. Amanitas have gills for a start."

As Bonni started spooning out the bits of fried mushroom from the frying pan and putting them on our plates, I called out, "Not too much for me."

"How much do you want?"

"Somewhat less than two ounces," I quipped.

After I'd worked up the courage to try a few morsels Bonni asked, "What do you think?"

"Hmmmm. They taste good," I caught myself saying.

Weren't the deadly amanitas supposed to "taste good?" No matter what my rational mind was telling me, that deep-seated irrational fear again seized my soul.

I thought of the beginnings of ethnomycologist R. Gordon Wasson's interest in mushrooms, which stemmed from an incident experienced on his honeymoon.

> Late in August 1927 my bride [Valentina Pavlovna] and I took our delayed honeymoon...in the Catskills. She was a Russian born in Moscow of a family of the intelligentsia. Tina had fled from Russia with her family in the summer of 1918, she being then 17 years old. She qualified as a physician at the University of London and had been working hard to establish her pediatric practice in New York. I was a newspaper man in the financial department of the Herald Tribune. On that first beautiful afternoon of our holiday in the Catskills, we went sauntering down the path for a walk, hand in hand, happy as larks, both of us abounding in the joy of life. There was a clearing on the right, a mountain forest on our left.

Suddenly Tina threw down my hand and darted up into the forest. She had seen mushrooms, a host of mushrooms, mushrooms of many kinds that peopled the forest floor. She cried out in delight at their beauty. She addressed each kind with an affectionate Russian name. Such a display she had not seen since she left her family's dacha near Moscow, almost a decade before. She knelt before those toadstools in poses of adoration like the Virgin hearkening to the Angel of the Annunciation. She began gathering some of the fungi in her apron. I called to her: "Come back, come back to me! They are poisonous, putrid. They are toadstools. Come back to me!" She only laughed the more: her merry laughter will ring forever in my ears. That evening she seasoned the soup with the fungi, she garnished the meat with other fungi. Yet others she threaded together and strung up to dry, for winter use as she said. My discomfiture was complete. That night I ate nothing with mushrooms in it. Frantic and deeply hurt, I was led to wild ideas: I told her that I would wake up a widower. She proved right and I wrong.

A little thing, some of you may say, this difference in emotional attitude toward wild mushrooms. But my wife and I did not think so, and we devoted most of our leisure hours for decades to dissecting it, defining it, and tracing it to its origin...we found that the northern Slavs know their mushrooms, having learned them at their mother's knee; theirs is no book knowledge. They love these fungal growths with a passion that, viewed with detachment, seemed to me a little exaggerated. But we Anglo-Saxons reject them viscerally, with revulsion, without deigning to make their acquaintance, and our attitude is even more exaggerated than the Slavs'.

Such discoveries as we have made, including the rediscovery of the religious role for the hallucinogenic mushrooms of Mexico, can be laid to our preoccupation with that cultural rift between my wife and me, between our respective peoples, between the mycophilia [those who had a great love of eating mushrooms] and mycophobia [those who had a dread and fear of mushrooms]...that divide the Indo-European peoples into two camps...There did not seem to be a middle ground.

I have to admit the mushrooms were delicious. I relaxed and was tempted to eat more than I intended. Once the titillation of my taste buds passed, I began to wonder and worry and wish I'd eaten just a little less. It was weird hoping your dinner wouldn't dispatch you in agony. Every little sensation in my body seemed like the harbinger of the end, the prelude to a bottomless perdition—otherwise we had a pleasant relaxed evening. Penny stayed with us by the fire, but Pedro wanted to go early to his beloved, cozy, secure kennel.

Sunny Benedict with rescued dog at the Baja Animal Sanctuary.

On the way to the mountains we find Sparky.

Pedro of the pines.

The valley where we camped. Looking north —
"Observatory Ridge" is on the other side.

Lightning reamed pine tree.

Snow plant.

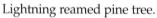

The view from "Observatory Ridge" across Cañon del Diablo to
Picacho del Diablo — Baja's highest mountain.

Bonni seems happy to be leaving me in the mountains for four months.

On the way home, Bonni finds Tanner.

Graham and Pedro returning to camp.

Campsite after rain and hail.

Park director
Federico Godinez Leal.

Ranger Ruben Góngora.

Pedro hanging out with Jane.

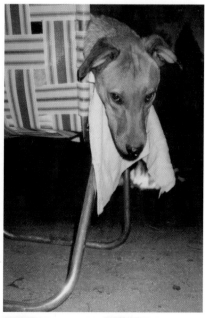

Pedro's favorite fireside chair.

Alfredo and family, Pedro, and new arrival Penny at the observatory.

Penny introduces a fantastic energy.

Encouraging Pedro from his chair.

Chasing a cow.

The great hunter — in her dreams.

Graham inside observatory
main dome.

Outside main dome.

Inside screen house in rain gear.

Armando García at the
observatory

Point of departure for many great hikes.

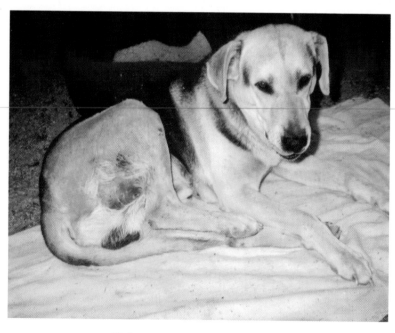

Baltasar nursing a coyote bite.

Penny taking a break from mischief.

Helping Les Braund, president of the San Diego Mycological
Society, with his mushroom studies.

"Half Dome" above, and Picacho del Diablo in background.

Andrew on "Half Dome" with storm brewing over Picacho.

Lightning shattered fir tree.

Bonni and Andrew on tree we watched fall.

A plate of delicious enokis (*Flammulina velutipes*).

Bonni showing Alfredo her *Leccinum insigne.*

Photo by Bonni Mackintosh

September — aspens around camp turning yellow.

Chapter 21

Learning to Live

He who does not imagine in stronger and better lineaments,
and in stronger and better light than his perishing eye can see,
does not imagine at all.

— William Blake

My first reaction when Bonni suggested Penny stay with me was entirely negative: I thought she would be too small and pudgy for any serious hiking, too likely to be eaten, and too rambunctious to train. But the idea of her going home to be confined to the yard and bored all day while Bonni was at work played on my mind. And Pedro had clearly come to love having her around—especially as he could always use his speed to outrun her if necessary. So I decided to let her stay and thought if she gets eaten, my conscience will be clear.

Again, I was kind of sad when Bonni was preparing to leave. It would be another month before she could return. Storm clouds were moving in. I tied both dogs till well after the truck disappeared on the road to the north. "You guys are a big responsibility," I complained.

After tidying and sorting the tents, I took Penny and Pedro for a four-mile walk to keep them occupied, although I didn't really want to. My heart and my feet felt heavy. It was sunny away from camp, but black and gray right above the valley and the campground.

> Pedro is such a polite dog…he just stands back and waits and lets Penny go first if she wants the water, and she'll push her little nose in to get it. She's cute. She just looks up at you with her little brown eyes just full of love…and occasionally you can look right beyond those eyes…

Back near camp, I beat the squirrels to a group of boletes pushing up through the pine duff. They looked like the same variety that we'd eaten so I risked frying a couple of caps. And they still tasted good—perhaps even better than before, as I was less paranoid.

I also found another mushroom growing on a dead aspen stump. Its stalks were a velvety chocolate brown and the caps were a creamy yellowish brown. Although it was a gilled mushroom, it certainly wasn't an amanita. A little study convinced me it was a specimen of *Flammulina velutipes*, the wild cousin of the commercially grown enoki. It typically grew in bunches around stressed and diseased aspens. It was hard to misidentify. After I'd studied a dozen photographs and read a dozen detailed descriptions, I satisfied myself that it was a good edible and I couldn't go wrong enjoying a couple of caps.

To be "absolutely" certain of my identification I needed to do a spore print; that is leave the caps for a couple of hours over a paper plate or piece of paper and examine the color of the usually clearly visible spore deposit. *Flammulina velutipes* has white spores and the only other mushrooms it is likely to be confused with are in the genus Galerina, especially *Galerina autumnalis*, which has brown spores. But as I was sure of my identification I thought it painstaking overkill to make a spore print. So I had a beer and merrily fried up a pair of two-inch-wide, bug free caps.

After boldly relating to my tape recorder how tasty they were, my certainty and courage deserted me a little. To put my mind at rest, I reread some of the mushroom guides, and read a little more about *Galerina autumnalis*.

I was trying to figure out if the sudden churning in my stomach was more physical or psychological when I read that some authors insisted on calling *Galerina autumnalis* the "deadly galerina." And when I read that it had the same toxins as the lethal amanitas, I felt my RNA synthesis grinding to a halt.

As I frantically and tirelessly perused page after page of drawings, photographs, and what might under other circumstances seem like rather boring technical descriptions, it occurred to me that the necessity of eating wild mushrooms was a wonderful way to learn about nature. It's probably the kind of stimulating education that kids in hunting and gathering societies receive. If only we could teach our children through such "learning to live" classes, how quickly we would eliminate Attention Deficit Disorder—either through sheer terror or the wholesome effects of natural selection.

As my liver and kidneys hadn't imploded or my bowels exploded by the time I was burying the coals of my fire, my panic attacks subsided and I was able to partially convince my fungophobic self that I had just eaten a delicious, nutritious meal.

It's hard for we fungophobes to appreciate how important mushrooms were to the native inhabitants…for food, medicine, preservatives, dyes, poisons, and mind altering religious experiences. Hardly any retrospective account of the habits and diet of the natives in the San Pedro Mártir, or anywhere in Baja California, ever mentions mushrooms.

Yet, we can be sure that when hunting and gathering peoples—who needed to be on the most intimate terms with their environment and all the possibilities and dangers it afforded—searched the forests for food, literally everything would be scrutinized and evaluated. Experimenting with tastes and nibbles and modes of preparation must have been a common practice when investigating possible new foods.

It had been a tiring day. I slipped into slumber seconds after sliding into my sleeping bag. But I wouldn't have fallen asleep quite so readily if what was about to befall that night were known to me.

In the blackness of midnight, Pedro woke me, whining to get out of his kennel. I had to exit the tent tense and cold, and escort him around with a shovel. He didn't throw up, but had a severe bout of diarrhea with possibly bloody stools.

At 1:30, another faint whine woke me again. I was quickly outside opening Pedro's kennel and following him around. He had more of the squirts.

Then around four in the morning I was woken by what sounded like a retching noise. I called, "I'm coming," then hurriedly opened Pedro's door and let him out without a leash. He disappeared into the forest, with me scurrying after him to bury whatever was left to evacuate. But all he was doing was running around eating grass. I followed patiently for ten minutes, shivering in T-shirt and underpants, before deciding to retire to my sleeping bag and leave his kennel door open. Through chattering teeth I said, "You can come and go as you please."

Snapping awake at 7:00, I anxiously poked my head out the tent door to see if Pedro was in his kennel. Oh joy, he was fast asleep inside.

I had no idea what was making him sick. He hadn't eaten any of the mushrooms. Penny was fine. After our morning wander in the forest I was back in camp relaxing, enjoying my decaf coffee, and both dogs were basking beside me in the warmth. A pair of western bluebirds frolicked in a pine tree. A hummingbird was collecting nectar from the bugle-like flowers of a scarlet penstemmon. There was not a cloud in the sky; it was picture postcard peaceful.

I knew Pedro was really under the weather when I saw Penny stalking and chasing the juncos by herself. After watching her trying to vainly entice poor Pedro to play, I did my best to distract her with her toys and then elected to cut the hair around her face and rump, and generally trim her coat. She was totally trusting and delighted in the attention, indeed seemed to assume it was her dog given birthright to be so pampered. All done, I could better see her mischievous brown eyes...and the shape of those scraggly ears that had been so much trouble flopping into her food and water bowls.

Pedro's diarrhea went on for another two days and nights. If I woke in the night, I'd step from the tent and pour him out of his kennel. He was not enthusiastic...but he usually managed to do his doo-ty before scrambling back.

When Pedro finally recovered and returned to his old self, I felt like celebrating.

> Pedro did a wonderful firm doo doo. I was so happy. I couldn't believe such joy at seeing it...just a regular, nice, solid, well-formed doo doo...an hour or so later on our walk he did another one, even more pleasing.

One morning Penny starting barking. Her bark was not loud enough to be annoying, but she had great awareness and made a good watchdog. Pedro joined in and for the first time showed his fear by a line of hair ridging along his back. They had spotted a coyote— a big, healthy-looking, yellowish gray coyote. I tied both dogs before they had a chance to go after it. To a background of yapping, I went out alone to scare him away. I was very mindful of a comment author Coppinger made: "coyotes...have bigger more robust teeth than dogs of twice their size." I got within its comfort zone (50 yards) then it took off in an unhurried watchful retreat.

Coming back I was surprised to see a bluebird fluttering inside the screen house. Lucky for him, and for the bug mesh, both dogs were secure on their lines. I was able to gently direct it back out the door.

Around noon on July 13, more boiling energetic clouds appeared. Thunder was echoing around the valley. I prepared for the storm by dressing warmly, covering and putting away what I could, and retiring Penny and Pedro to their kennels in the gazebo. They knew what was coming and were eager to get inside. Pedro was soon asleep; his head pressed against the grill like a waffle. It began to hail hard. The aspens leaves were quaking from the hits. The ground was turning white.

I let the dogs out for a potty break during a lull in the storm. Penny especially loved the rain. She ran and ran and then lay in her characteristic style, flat on the ground like a furry toad, sodden, but joyfully clinging to Mother Earth.

The storm moved on and while it continued to rumble in the south, the warm sun broke through. High above, a rainbow seemed to be cleaving the top of a lustrous pearl-and-ivory cloud, like a heavenly rendition of Saint Peter's martyrdom. We went for a walk. Penny was very affectionate, and stayed close to me. Pedro displayed the lightning in his genes by occasionally racing after something that caught his attention. He was back to his old happy, healthy self.

That night, returning to camp after taking Pedro for a potty walk I had to stop looking at Penny's shockingly green eyes when I directed a flashlight at her. They suggested banshees or gorgons or werewolves, and her unkempt, hairy face added to the illusion.

Two days later, the sun was shining and we were wandering around near camp. I was loudly singing *America the Beautiful* when I saw my first *Amanita muscaria* mushrooms at the base of a ponderosa pine. There were three of them in a wonderful grouping—red caps with white spots pushing up through the soil and the pine needle duff. I wanted a photo, but they were dull and dirty. I tried unsuccessfully to blow and pick the dirt off; then I had the idea to pee on them, and sure enough they cleaned up a very photogenic, shiny, red. While I was down on my knees framing the shots I kept looking up and glancing around, convinced I could hear singing.

Whereas the scientific name for this mushroom *Amanita muscaria*, or its common name, Fly Agaric, won't mean much to most people, its image is familiar to nearly everyone. Its white-speckled, red-capped form has been long celebrated in western popular culture—it is the familiar fairy "toadstool" widely depicted in paintings, pottery, poetry and book illustrations. Many believe *Amanita muscaria* has had tremendous significance for Indo-European cultures for thousands of years, and has indeed been intimately associated with the origin of many of today's religions.

In 1968, R. Gordon Wasson published a controversial book—*Soma: Divine Mushroom of Immortality*—in which he argued that *Amanita muscaria* was the sacred "plant" of the ancient Aryans.

The Aryans were originally a warrior and grain-growing people whose homeland was in Central Asia. Approximately 4,000 years ago, the migrating Aryans split into three distinct groups: European, Indic, and Iranian. The Indics who settled into what is now Afghanistan and the Valley of the Indus possessed a rich oral tradition of poetry and song, which was eventually written down and preserved in the *Rig Veda*—the Sanskrit sacred writings that became the foundation for Hinduism.

The Aryans had a broad pantheon of gods. The Rig Veda contains numerous references to a deity who was the god of inspiration and poetry, and somehow also a plant and a drink which was said to have hallucinogenic properties. It was the mainstay of the early Aryan religious ceremonies. The plant, the drink, the god were all referred to as Soma.

Knowledge of the plant's identity was lost soon after the Aryan exodus from their homeland. The identity of Soma became one of the great mysteries of cultural anthropology. All the candidates met with serious objections when examined in the light of the many references to it in the Rig Veda.

Of the more than 1,000 holy hymns and songs contained in the Rig Veda, 120 are devoted exclusively to Soma, and references to Soma abound in the others. It is recorded that Parjanya, the Aryan God of the Lightning bolt, was the father of Soma, which had been divinely inseminated in Mother Earth. Soma grew in the mountains; it was the sap of life and the life force, the Ambrosia of the Vedic gods. Soma was thus a sacred food, not something to be indulged in lightly or profaned.

The virtually unquestioned assumption of those who attempted to determine its identity was that Soma was a "plant." Then R. Gordon Wasson put forward his startling theory that Soma was not a plant but a mushroom—none other than *Amanita muscaria*. Wasson believed the hallucinogenic properties of *Amanita muscaria* to be the cause of the "ecstasy" and divine inspiration described in the sacred work.

He pointed out that the Rig Veda hailed Soma as a red fruit or a small, leafless "plant" with a fleshy stalk. No reference was ever made to its roots, flowers and seeds. Nor was there any reference to the propagation of this plant. If Soma were indeed a plant, why wouldn't the Aryans, who were known for their skill as farmers, have bought it with them when they migrated from their original homeland and began to cultivate more fertile soils?

One of the most interesting aspects of Wasson's argument can be seen in the rituals and practices of a number of Siberian tribes that long continued to use and venerate the "divine mushroom," seemingly in the same manner as did the Aryans.

Georg Langsdorf, in 1809, wrote about his observations among the Koryak people.

> The Russians who trade with them, carry thither a kind of mushroom, called in the Russian Tongue, Muchumor (*Amanita muscaria*), which they exchange for squirrels, fox, ermine, sable and other furs: Those who are rich among them, lay up large provisions of these mushrooms for the winter. When they make a feast, they pour water upon some of these mushrooms, and boil them. They then drink the liquor, which intoxicates them; the poorer sort, who cannot afford to lay in a store of these mushrooms, post themselves, on these occasions, round the huts of the rich, and watch the opportunity of the guests coming down to make water; and then hold a wooden bowl to receive the urine, which they drink of greedily, as having still some virtue of the mushroom in it, and by this way they also get drunk.

This strange practice, perhaps one of the earliest affirmations of the trickle down effect so favored by Republican economists, was also mentioned by a Swedish army officer, Filip Johann von Strahlenberg, who published a book in 1730 about his twelve years as a prisoner of war in Siberia. He too noted with astonishment that among the Koryak tribe the urine of persons intoxicated with fly agaric is not wasted. He recalled observing people waiting outside huts where mushroom sessions were taking place. When those under the influence came out, those waiting in the cold collected the urine in bowls and gulped it down. He further observed that the drinker himself often drank his own urine to prolong the state of hallucination. Usage of *Amanita muscaria*, in Siberia continued until the Russians introduced alcohol.

According to Wasson, the Rig Veda suggests that Soma could be consumed in two forms: 1. Directly, by either ingesting the raw "plant" or its juices, or 2. By drinking the urine of others who have ingested it.

Amanita muscaria contains the only known hallucinogen—muscimol—that is not metabolized by the body. The psychoactive alkaloid passes largely unaltered through the kidneys. And that, supposedly, is the secret of *Amanita muscaria's* unique ability to transfer its hallucinogenic potency in urine. The muscimol in *Amanita muscaria* can apparently be recycled up to five times in this manner.

Another parallel commented on by Wasson was that the celebrants of Soma spoke of the greater potency and "purity" of the dried "plant." And with the tribes of Siberia the mushrooms were usually not consumed until after they had been dried in the sun. The drying had a purpose.

The fresh mushroom contains ibotenic acid, which arguably produces more unpleasant side effects—nausea, vomiting, and profuse sweating—and certainly less of the mind altering "benefits" of the chemically closely related muscimol. The drying process converts a significant amount of the ibotenic acid into the more potent muscimol.

Wasson argued that all major religions are rooted in psychoactive drug taking. For over 20,000 years shamans and divines around the world have been playing with psychoactive drugs. And those under their influence have universally claimed contact with higher intelligences. As observers like Aldous Huxley have recounted, the mind in everyday life is programmed to awareness of only a tiny fraction of the signals received by our senses; such drugs bring a wider range of signals to awareness.

According to Wasson, *Amanita muscaria* was the most widely used sacred drug in the Old World. And those with an expanded mind have even suggested that the mushroom was a major factor in the rise of Christianity.

In a book called *The Sacred Mushroom and the Cross*, John Allegro proposed that Christianity originated as a fly agaric mushroom cult, which hid its secrets behind layers of puns and allusions.

Allegro was one of a team of researchers hired by the State of Israel and the British government to decipher the "Dead Sea Scrolls" after they were discovered in the 1940's and 1950's. Allegro was hired because he was a respected Biblical scholar familiar with every major historical Middle Eastern language including Sumerian, Egyptian, Hebrew, and Cuneiform.

His ultimate conclusion (and he was asked to leave the team for his unexpectedly radical opinion) was that Jesus was a Mushroom secretly taken and worshipped by the Jewish sect, the Essenes.

Such a suggestion gave rise to scandal... and mirth as revealed, for example, in this ditty floating in cyberspace.

JESUS WAS A MUSHROOM
There was a scholar from England
He got a call from the Pope

He said "Come on down to the Vatican
To analyze the Dead Sea Scrolls"
For twenty years he labored
All alone in a little room
And when he came out he promptly pronounced
That Jesus was a mushroom...

Now as you can imagine
This did not please the Pope
Who said "John M. Allegro
You've been smoking too much dope"
But John, he said "Your holiness
You and I are both adults
And the etymology clearly shows
The apostles were a mushroom cult"...

So how do you think that he walked on the water
How do you think that he raised the dead
It was just folks hallucinating
On the mushrooms they was fed...
[Copyright 1994 by Darryl Cherney.]

Others have taken up the argument and pushed it even further. *In Strange Fruit: Alchemy, Religion and Magical Foods*, (Bloomsbury Press, 1995), Clark Heinrich suggests that *Amanita muscaria* is the key to unlocking not just the mystic symbolism of the Vedas and the Gospels, but also the Torah, Talmud, the Philosopher's Stone of Alchemy, and even the Holy Grail. According to Heinrich it is no coincidence that the chalice can also be seen as mushroom-shaped.

I had washed the mushrooms clean...they were bright and shining like little blood-red, diamond-studded chalices bursting from the earth, or like star-pocked crimson heavens. Now they were ready to be photographed. On my knees, I snapped a series of shots while Penny and Pedro looked on. And again I heard singing! In the warm and welcome sun, blessed by the god of inspiration, I heard singing, and delighted in the moment as my companions ran free.

Was this the forbidden fruit? Was this Soma, the fruit of the storm, the creator of God consciousness, the key to the spirit world, to the mystery of life, and the power of the universe? Was this the divine mushroom of immortality?

I picked up the most perfect of the three scarlet caps and brought it back to my camp to dry. Pedro ran at my side and Penny bounded before me, her ears and red tongue flapping, the essence of playfulness and happiness. What a bond I felt with her—just a few short months ago, alone and bereft of love, a sick and sad throwaway puppy. And now, I rejoiced; she was in doggie heaven.

Chapter 22

Hint of Honey Sweetness

…it is a fact, patent both to my dog and myself, that at daybreak I am the sole owner of all the acres I can walk over. It is not only boundaries that disappear, but also the thought of being bounded.

— *Aldo Leopold*

It had been a warm, cloudless, breezy day. It was almost dark when I heard a vehicle approaching. I grabbed Pedro, but Penny took off to greet it. It was Alfredo, his wife Socorro, their two young children, Isai and Elia, Socorro's brother Andrés, and big old Baltasar. Both Penny and Pedro couldn't wait for anyone to jump down from the truck; Pedro stretched up to Baltasar in the pickup bed and began to lick his face, while Penny, as soon as the door was opened, jumped into the cab to offer her greeting. The children were overjoyed at this friendly little waggy-tailed ragamuffin.

Alfredo's family were such open, warm, happy people. Socorro was a scream. She was the jolliest of all—a buxom smiling woman whose stained and missing teeth merely added to her authentic charm. She had a relaxed, natural dignity that radiated pure contentment. I am sure few millionaires had what she had.

They had brought me a large watermelon as a present. I cut it up, and laid it out with some snacks and drinks, and acted the role of the good host. I brought over some chairs, buckets, and containers, and we all settled by the fire. Three-year-old Elia was a sweetheart; but I watched her closely because she was giggling and walking unsteadily right by the blazing fire. I alone seemed unnerved by what she was doing. I was sitting on the edge of my seat ready to jump between her and the burning logs. If I were her parent I'd have been paranoid, holding her back. At the same time, boisterous six-year-old Isai, was throwing stones into the flames, winding himself up like a baseball pitcher and sending sparks everywhere. It looked like he was going to throw himself in.

When I suggested that might not be a good idea, Isai wandered off and began playing boomerang with a branch by my screen house. After a couple of near misses, I asked him to throw it in the other direction. He had a couple of relapses before he got the idea.

Listening was clearly not his forte. I was showing him a colorful mushroom book, and with boundless energy and enthusiasm he was asking lots of questions, but he had no patience to listen to the answers; he was on to the next question before I could offer even the briefest of comments.

I tried to distract and occupy him by making a game of looking for bats and satellites—both readily seen in the night sky above the San Pedro Mártir. That gave him something to shout about. After hearing him enthusiastically shrieking a score of times, I don't think I'll ever forget the words *murciélago* or *satélite*.

They stayed over an hour. Alfredo took my empty water containers again and said he'd return in a day or two. In spite of the "chaos," I was left with an aura of relaxation. Their company emboldened me for the entire evening. I wandered in a wide circle around my campsite, gazing up into the great clarity of the heavens.

I studied the constellation Scorpio "crawling" up the southern sky. It was easily the most graphic and perfect representation in the night sky. Some stellar intelligence could hardly have arranged the stars better to suggest a scorpion. And Antares, the brightest star in Scorpio, seized my imagination, perhaps because it hung so close to Mars. Antares is a "Red Giant" several hundred times the diameter of the Sun and several thousand times brighter. Although 400 light-years from Earth, its twinkling redness is apparent even with the naked eye. It wasn't quite up to Mars' unusual brightness, but Antares to the Ancient Greeks was the "rival of Ares" (i.e., rival of Mars). And there they were, dramatically juxtaposed in the night sky, like unequal twins or blood brothers, promising who knows what calamities for we poor mortals.

Even though I hadn't nibbled any of the *Amanita muscaria*, and certainly, after what I'd read about its dubious family, had no intention of doing so, I held the plucked specimen before the fire, and meditated on the flame-lit beauty of its red cap and snowy white gills and raggedy stem. It had many of the amanita characteristics—the ring around the stalk, the spotted remains of the partial veil on its cap, the "swollen" base to the stem. How this strange jolly looking fungus, this mycorrhizal fruiting body, had fired man's imagination. I didn't need to risk ingesting any of its dubious flesh to feel under its influence.

As its tiny white spores drifted unseen into my four-foot-wide, glowing bed of coals, the fire pit suddenly appeared like a giant red cap bulging from the earth. Moments later, as I was lost in the illusion, I looked down at the dusty, devastated surface of the Red Planet...then as little jets of flame shot forth, my spirit was whisked light years into space to gaze in awe at the glowing surface of the great star Antares, the Red Giant.

When I raised my eyes to the black silhouettes of the pine trees on the western horizon, by some distortion of time and distance I fancied I saw the setting stars sinking to the earth like tiny illuminated cones dropping slowly from the branches to the ground.

Two days later, after I had just rebuked the dogs for chasing some cows, Alfredo came back with his family and brought the filled water containers. I offered them peanuts and cookies, and shared with them my last drop of whisky and can of beer. I gave Alfredo a box of dog cookies for Baltasar. Isai was nattering away about comic book characters and kids' TV shows; I couldn't understand 90% of it—lots of stuff about witches, vampires, murders, and impaling people with arrows. His sweet little sister hardly got a word in. Alfredo said he was heading down from the mountains and he offered to bring me anything I needed. I gave him money for more beer, tortillas, fruit, and bug repellent. What a wonderful friend Alfredo had turned out to be. He invited me to his cabin for lunch the next day. I accepted and resolved to work on my Spanish before heading over.

I walked the dogs over to Alfredo's rustic shack, which sat among a half dozen other cozy wooden shacks secluded among the tall pines in a little valley just off the road to the observatory. The map described the location as a "forest camp." I had a delicious carne asada lunch with the family. I learnt that Socorro was born in Baja California, but her father was from Iowa, and her mother from Sonora.

Alfredo showed me the one scorpion he'd found in the mountains. He had it in a small bottle of alcohol. It was bigger than and not quite like other Baja scorpions I'd seen. He found it with some construction material, so it might have come up from below. Even so, it made me just a bit more thoughtful about picking up firewood. Alfredo said he'd be leaving the next day and should be back in a few days.

Alfredo drove me back to my campsite in mid-afternoon. Isai rode in the back of the truck with me, talking incessantly, bouncing up and down, and pointing to something new every second. It was worse than with a garrulous English speaker as I still had little idea what he was saying. As best I could, I tried to politely ignore him and enjoy the scenery. Finally exasperated, I made a game of constantly turning his head with wild exclamations of my own. "Look, look, a bluebird...Over there, look, a squirrel." And before he could squawk out two words, I'd be twisting his neck the other way with a breathless, "Look, look in that big tree. That is where the witches live. Up top... look."

"No?" He said, spinning around.

"Si. Si. Es verdad. It's true." I said, enjoying this new game.

The second half of July was warm and sunny—I hardly saw a cloud for two weeks. In such dry spells a procession of bees and wasps were attracted to any water I left out. I had to rescue a few bees from the washing up bowl. And I was amazed to watch one slip into my kettle through the little whistle hole; I never saw it emerge. As it was too difficult to peer inside the kettle all the time and as I hated to waste water, I just accepted that my tea and coffee and soup might have a little hint of honey sweetness. One time I took a swig from an open can of soda and felt a lump go down my throat. It was all part of camping in the great outdoors.

The tiny nuisance flies gradually disappeared as the summer progressed; butterflies, swallows, and hummingbirds took their place. I had to shoo quite a few such intruders from the screen house. The mosquitoes were never much of a problem. I would see and hear a few in the morning and a few in the evening, especially after rain when there was no breeze; occasionally I'd get bitten, but when necessary a timely application of repellent provided ample protection. And Penny and Pedro had their mosquito netting...but it would have been no problem without it.

A quiet afternoon, feet-up, nose in book, was a welcome sequel to a stimulating morning hike or playful romp. Even the chores were a pleasure—feeding, watering, and attending to the dogs, gathering firewood, cooking, cleaning, washing up, washing clothes, keeping coolers in the shade, securing tents—because I had so much time, and I just felt totally organized and on top of everything. And always I was surrounded by a divine uncertainty...never quite sure who or what was going to happen next.

And it was the same for the dogs—from the moment I opened the kennel doors in the morning, and both dogs either emerged slowly with big yawns and stretches, or like greyhounds from the gates, usually because there was a cow or squirrel around, every minute of every day was either exquisite stimulation or down time to peacefully doze and dream. They were both in doggie heaven.

They had favorite chewy/squeaky toys. Digging holes, especially if they thought they might be on the tail of a squirrel or a chipmunk, could occupy them for hours. And a tug of war with an old sock provided endless entertainment. Penny introduced a wonderful energy. She loved to chase and be chased.

One beautiful sunny evening I joined in and all three of us ended up running, rolling, and goofing around. Needing a break, I threw a tennis ball and went to sit down in the gazebo. Pedro picked it up and ran. Penny went in hot pursuit.

I was looking at the sunset, recording, "These guys are great: they make me paternal, maternal, fraternal, and in a way they touch on the eternal." Both of them ran by the door one way, and then seconds later they ran back the other way kicking up a cloud of dust. It was like watching a tennis game. I was about to intervene when Penny, on the next pass, collided with a gazebo guy rope. Such was her speed and mass she almost took the whole screen house with her.

Later, Pedro dozed off in Penny's basket. He was big, lanky and overflowing it. Penny was trying to throw him out, jumping on him and biting his leg. It was so amusing. She knew how to make things happen. He was soon out of the basket chasing her around.

The dogs were running themselves happy, and driving me sane. I watched a number of squirrel chases; and from my vantage point I so often saw the squirrel going one way and the dogs going the other. They never managed to get one. Pedro came close a couple of times with his greyhound-like bursts of speed.

One sunny afternoon, I was reading in the screen house, the dogs beside me sleeping. A junco was hopping and pecking on the ground outside. He chirped too close. Simultaneously, and seemingly in psychic union, Penny and Pedro leapt to their feet and dashed out the door chasing the little bird. The junco was flying just a few feet from the ground emitting a wild series of chirps. The dogs were at first a yard behind. But even when it was hopeless, they continued to follow, apparently just for the fun of it.

Both dogs went for juncos preferentially. For other birds they might raise an eyelid or even a sleepy head, but for a junco they were always ready to explode into the wildest pursuit. I don't think it was just a matter of being into junco food, but rather that little bird's boldness and squirrel-like chirping made them seem provocative and taunting.

Penny and Pedro wandered freely around camp but they never wandered off; I could usually see them and call them in. They only went further when all three of us would go on a hike. I was much harder on Pedro when he very occasionally failed to respond to my calls than I was on Penny—I would force him to sit and berate him in a firm loud voice. I expected more from him, and desired that he give a good example.

It wasn't very often that I felt the need to clip them on their lines. I tried to give them the maximum of freedom. But it was a compromise; I guess it's God's dilemma...a parent's dilemma. How much freedom to give? Shall I let them free to be happy for a while or shall I keep them tied and close and safe...and incidentally spare myself a lot of grief? With Pedro and Penny, I erred on the side of freedom, realizing that they could and probably would get into trouble.

Chapter 23

Pressed to Mother Earth

Rejoice with me; for I have found my sheep which was lost.
— Luke 15:6

On July 22, a lone hiker, a middle-aged Mexican carrying a staff and a backpack, appeared as if from nowhere and went marching up the road to Botella Azul. Both of my barkless watchdogs followed. I called and they came bounding back down. Pedro returned to camp, but Penny stayed in the valley bottom.

The hiker was disappearing up the hill so I went with Pedro to fetch Penny. I last saw her run behind some brush, but when I reached the spot, she had gone. I called and called, but there was no sign of her. I looked back up the road—nothing. My baffled, urgent shouts echoed across the valley. She would be coyote food on her own.

With Pedro in tow, I ran up the steep road, stopping two or three times to catch my breath, call out, and look around. I was shouting myself hoarse. Half a mile from camp, I stopped again to survey all the gaps between the trees and every granite slope. Then it dawned on me, Pedro had disappeared too. I stood alone for minutes that seemed like hours. How could such an ordinary morning suddenly go so very wrong? I mouthed a curse or two, then yelled into the silent forest, "Penny, Pedro, Come."

The only movement, the only sounds came from the birds. And the only comfort I had was thinking that Pedro and Penny might be together. I wondered if they were with the hiker. But he must have heard my voice! Why didn't he call back, or stop and wait, or walk back down the road if the dogs had attached themselves to him? I had no idea how far he was going. He could be a mile ahead by now.

I returned alone to camp to grab my wallet, passport, and other essentials…and get my whistle as I was straining my voice. Hearing the thump of paws and the sweet music of a tinkling chain collar I turned around and there was Pedro…but only Pedro. I hugged and thanked him and while I patted his long, thin head, our eyes searched the forest in vain. Clouds were gathering. A storm was likely. Penny was out there somewhere, alone.

Then I recalled that July 22 was my mother's birthday, or rather it would have been her birthday. I thought back to the afternoon of her funeral. There was a summer thunderstorm and a steady rain. I was back at home with my father and my two brothers looking at photographs and reminiscing. We all felt the same sadness—it didn't seem right, mum was out there alone, in the rain.

I remember looking at that photo of my mother holding her beloved little Bonny, and how, suddenly, in my mind, I pictured that little black nosed, bedraggled ragamuffin stretched out on top of her grave, soaked, keeping watch, comforting her.

And as I recalled the image, I realized how much that conjured dog resembled the little Penny that I had now lost, even to the way that she would lie impossibly flat, almost melting into the ground.

It was horrible to think of Penny falling victim to a coyote or a lion—but at least that would be relatively quick; I was more anxious about her returning to the state in which we found her, full of worms, covered in ticks and mange...alone, sick, expiring in misery. The thought near broke my heart.

After waiting as long as I dare, hoping Penny would appear as she had so many times before, I put a fresh bowl of food and water down just in case she wandered back to camp while we were away, then tightened my daypack on my shoulders and led Pedro back up the road as fast as I could jog. As it got steeper my boots started sliding on the decomposed granite. I fell twice, but what were a few cuts and scrapes compared to the fact that Penny was lost?

We had gone over a mile, when ahead on a straight flat stretch, between the trees, I saw the Mexican hiker striding back toward me. And there—I felt like shedding tears—just behind him was Penny, tongue hanging out, ambling merrily along, clearly enjoying her adventure. Pedro and I were all over her with greetings. The hiker sauntered by commenting on what a cute dog she was. I was sure Penny had followed him the whole way. I asked no questions. I was just glad to have found the "lost sheep."

After we sat awhile reveling in our togetherness, I picked Penny up and carried her a good part of the way home on my shoulder. She was the lightest little burden I ever had to bear.

Even though the hiker had gone and there was no one in sight, just to get my emotions back in line, I clipped both dogs on their cables.

Then I told myself that I was probably overreacting and being too protective, so I let them loose again. They both promptly disappeared. When they returned a few minutes later, I put them back on the cables. They were lucky not to be tied, chained, and nailed down. After we settled by the fire for the evening, I was reading a book and came across a little snippet that I thought might be of interest to my miscreants. "Two dogs were put to death for witchcraft in Salem," I said loudly, trying to sound like Saint Peter Martyr at his best. "They were hung." Penny and Pedro didn't look particularly imbued with salutary fear.

In the rich evening light, although she was just a few yards away resting her head on the edge of her soft basket, I looked at Penny through binoculars. She was larger than life with her sharp, brown, sensitive, orangutan-like eyes. Her hair was definitely "graying." And just for a moment I swore she looked like my old mother, settled by the fire, watching TV, thanking God that all her boys were safely home.

I stayed up thinking about the day, and paid tribute to my mother's birthday by resurrecting a bouquet of beautiful memories and directing a few orisons to the heavens. I saw a spectacular shooting star to the south, twenty times brighter than Mars; it was glowing green, casting shadows and lighting up the valley before fading out towards the west.

Pedro was on his chair, looking at me with his usual full measure of devotion. Penny was in a deep sleep, twitching and faintly growling. I recorded: "It is such a delight trying to make these guys happy. Even though they are just dogs, it is really quite touching, it really changes me."

July 24: I was surprised when Baltasar suddenly appeared in the morning. I speculated Alfredo had left him behind when he left the mountains, and he hadn't yet returned, so the poor dog had got lonely. Now I had three dogs. I fed Baltasar plain dry food so he wouldn't find my hospitality too irresistible.

What a monster. His skin was patchy; his ears looked like they'd been chewed up. He barked too much. He peed on my tents and cooler. Pedro was slavishly deferential to him and was constantly licking his face. In spite of my best intentions, I got irritated and almost despondent about his being there. I worried about not being able to get rid of him and all three dogs acting like a pack and attacking the cows and deer. Ironically, I also worried about losing him—although it was the thing I most wanted to do.

Perhaps sensing my mixed feelings, Baltasar came over while I was sitting and put his paw on my knee as if to say, "It'll be all right."

"You bastard," I said, "why can't you be a horrible dog, so I can just chase you away?"

I tried walking all the dogs. It was too much trouble. Pedro was more interested in Baltasar than my commands. I was shouting too much and needed to rest my voice. So I brought them to the vicinity of camp and was glad when they all settled down to snooze.

Another junco chirped near the gazebo. Again both Penny and Pedro rose from their slumbers and took off in pursuit, this time in the wrong direction. Baltasar looked on amazed as the junco's white-barred tail flashed low to the ground, heading west whereas Penny and Pedro sprinted about 200 yards to the north before they realized they were chasing a phantom. They were not good hunters, but they were excellent entertainers.

That night, Baltasar tried to sleep by my tent door, but he was snoring loudly, and sounded like he was about to expire after each labored breath. I moved him to a tarp covered with old towels about twenty feet away. Baltasar took the hint and stayed there. I prayed that Alfredo would soon come to collect him.

Next day, patience exhausted, I decided to try walking Baltasar back to Alfredo's place. Not sure how I could manage three dogs, I kept one dog on a leash at the beginning, then realizing I wasn't achieving much beyond dislocating my shoulder, I let the three of them run free. Near the Salvatierra campground they all took off after three deer. Penny and Baltasar returned at my calling, but Pedro disappeared for a worryingly long time. It was a hot day and I had to go fetch him. When I finally got hold of him, I threw him on his back, shook him by the scruff of the neck, and did the whole dramatic Alpha routine. After that I kept him on a leash the rest of the way. He was heeling and sitting like his life depended on it.

When I saw cows, I put Penny on a leash too. A little later, I heard barking from the forest. It sounded like another dog. The barking turned to yelping and got louder. Then three large agitated coyotes suddenly appeared on a rocky, wooded slope. I led my guys to a shady spot beneath a tree. Baltasar was happy to stay close. We stood together and watched the coyotes till they slinked away.

There was no one at Alfredo's cabin, but while looking for a water container for Baltasar, I peered inside a blue 55-gallon plastic drum and saw several healthy-looking, big-eyed, bushy-tailed gray squirrels among some corn leaves. I wondered had they got in and couldn't get out? Or were they Alfredo's pets? Did he keep them to show the tourists?

I sat in the shade on a raised concrete slab, which was probably the floor for a new shack, and waited hoping Alfredo would return so I could be rid of Baltasar. After 30 minutes resting, enjoying the peace, the singing birds, and the antics of the squirrels high in the pine branches, I heard a vehicle. Baltasar bounded over to greet it. I was delighted to see it was Alfredo's truck, and in the fully loaded pickup there was Alfredo, Socorro, the two kids…and another dog!

It was a patchy white, black, and gray young fellow with striking blue eyes…possibly an Australian shepherd mix. A rope around its neck served as collar and leash. He was no pampered puppy. He was mangy, with red raw patches. After he jumped down, Penny and Pedro immediately started playing with him; every few seconds the dog would sit and vigorously scratch his head with both rear feet. Alfredo said they had found it on the road between his village of Ejido Sinaloa and the Meling Ranch. Trying to be polite, I commented on what an interesting dog it was, but he was in such terrible shape he made even Baltasar look like a model of canine health and grooming.

Alfredo opened up the cabin and invited me to have a seat inside. After a long silence from the kitchen, he brought out and showed me a large polystyrene cooler, which had been gnawed open. Several cartons and packets of food inside had been half-eaten and scattered all about.

"Was it rats?" I asked.

"No, squirrels," he replied. He pointed to a place where they had chewed their way through the plywood wall of his shack.

There was another long silence. To break it, I innocently inquired, "Do you have pet squirrels in that blue barrel outside?"

"In the barrel?…No," he said, his voice rising.

I wished that I had said nothing as he slipped out with his dark eyes vacant and expressionless like those of a shark homing in on the scent of blood. The two children smiled and started rabbiting on about something I failed to understand. I was concentrating more on a knocking noise outside.

I went out to see Alfredo standing over the drum with a six-foot-long metal bar in his hand. I stepped away silent, wishing I had tipped the barrels and let the squirrels free. It was so ironic—just a few days before I was hesitating to tell Alfredo that my dogs had been chasing squirrels…embarrassed that they were harassing the wildlife in the park.

Alfredo pointed to his new dog and said, "I will call him Zarco. He has fleas and ticks."

"And mange," I added. "It needs to be treated."

He replied, "It'll be OK. In the winter all the parasites will drop off and die in the cold."

I thought his skin would drop off and he'd die in misery long before the winter. As politely as I could I said it was necessary to do something about Zarco.

He invited me to stay for lunch. But I said I had to go...I just wanted to leave. He offered to drive me back; I said I wanted to walk to exercise my guys. He offered me a cold beer, which I accepted...then he said he'd drive over later. I reiterated that I had some chemical solution to clean up the puppy.

It was hot on the way back. Both dogs were inclined to stop at every shady spot, but I managed to chivvy them along. Penny growled at a cow. I stamped my feet and shouted, "No, no, no, no." She rolled onto her back like a little boat turning turtle and thought she'd better placate me by looking as cute as possible. Worked every time. Pedro was as good as well-beaten gold after his chastisement in the morning. We were back in camp around two o'clock.

If Alfredo did bring Zarco, I had decided—all politeness aside and as much as I hated the task (the instructions sounded like you were applying a mix of anthrax and cyanide)—to apply the dip to him.

Sure enough two hours later Alfredo drove the family over...and there was the new dog in the back of the truck. He leapt out. Before Penny and Pedro started playing with him again, I put on disposable latex gloves and examined Zarco who was still scratching incessantly with his two back legs. If you wanted to be sarcastic, Zarco seemed a very appropriate name as he probably had sarcoptic mange. His ears were the worst affected area. With unseemly haste I put on my waterproof rain gear, mixed up the concentrated dip with water and set about soaking the little fellow with an old cloth.

"This is good stuff," I offered.

"Is it as good as used motor oil?" Alfredo asked.

"Not quite as messy," I said.

When I was walking with my burros I remember other Mexicans had endorsed old motor oil as a cure for saddle sores and to protect open wounds from flies. Its use may not be so far fetched! Petroleum has been used medicinally throughout history. North African and Middle Eastern nomads used it to treat camels for mange. Certain American Indian tribes valued it for covering wounds. In 1859,

Robert Chesebrough (of Chesebrough-Ponds fame) watched oil field workers scrubbing a dark waxy substance off their drilling rigs. And when he discovered that many of them rubbed the substance on cuts and burns, swearing by its efficacy in healing, he took a sample back to his New York laboratory where he isolated the translucent material we now know as petroleum jelly. After inflicting all types of cuts and burns on himself to test the stuff, he concluded that they tended to heal quicker and resist infection better when petroleum jelly was applied. He named it Vaseline.

Indeed, as I read the label, I was reminded that the dip contained an "aromatic petroleum distillate." Zarco was compliant at first, but soon started struggling. I got sprayed when he shook. I even got a little pinprick tooth puncture through my rubber glove. Though it drew just a pinhead of blood, I now had to consider the possibility of rabies.

Thinking back to Pedro's early vomiting spell, I hoped Zarco wouldn't react badly to the dip and get sick. Still, it was hard to imagine how he could be worse off than he was. After sodas and snacks, I gave Alfredo a spare collar and leash for Zarco.

When they were ready to go, Alfredo secured Zarco in the truck bed with the leash. Before their truck was out of sight, I heard a horrible yelp. Zarco had jumped from the back of the pickup and had almost strangled himself. Fortunately, the collar was loose enough for him to slip through. Alfredo stopped, put Zarco back in the truck and drove off.

Zarco scratching incessantly

Now happy and healthy

Chapter 24

Coyote Attack

And when I feigned an angry look,
Alas! I loved you best.
— John Sheffield 1701

It was a cloudy evening. At first a wildly gusting wind was moaning through the campground making it too risky to light a campfire. Then an hour after sunset the wind moderated and we could all huddle by the flames to get warm.

I was always tending to my companions' doggie comforts, and watchful for the slightest problem. I moved Penny's basket and Pedro's chair back from the fire when I thought they were too hot, and closer when I thought they were too cold. Not many Mexican dogs would receive such consideration.

It was late. I was reading and thinking about retiring for the night. Suddenly Penny started growling—at first it was a low purring growl, like a contented old tomcat, then she growled louder and louder and lapsed into her short, snappy little bark. Pedro was woken from a deep, twitching sleep. I was chiding her and telling her to shush, when there was the shocking noise of a branch snapping and a chilling screech from the forest. Penny rose from her basket and ran barking into the blackness. While Pedro was just thinking about joining her, I clipped him on a line and called, "Penny, come. Penny. Penny."

She was fifty yards away, barking and growling as furiously as she could. I trained my flashlight on her and shouted again for her to come. She turned around. Her little eyes shot back their incredible hypnotic jade green. I would have shuddered if I hadn't known it was her. She continued to bark and hold her ground. Machete in hand, I walked over and met her half way, bringing her back on a leash.

Unsure what was out there, I built up the fire and sat for a further hour with my machete stuck in the ground between my legs, a sheath knife in my pocket, and the shovel handle practically touching my knee.

Usually I knew exactly what Penny was dashing after. I had grown tired castigating her for chasing cows—it seemed an almost impossible lesson for her to learn that come means come, and cow means cow, and when there's a cow and I call come, I mean come NOW…forget the cow!

But after a number of cows wandered into the camp at night, and began rooting through the trash bins I was increasingly disposed to turning a blind eye to her cowgirl antics. She never did anything worse than drive them a fair distance from the campsite anyway.

As I relaxed about it, I was more likely to laugh when I saw Penny in hot pursuit of some poor animal fifty times her size. She would go "flat out," looking like one of those pre-photographic era paintings of racehorses with their legs splayed hard in both directions at once. Even Pedro seemed amused by her over-the-top, bovine directed bellicosity.

One morning, in early August, Penny was running with a pinecone in her mouth, being chased by Pedro; she ran and ran and couldn't shake him off, so she dropped it, pulled back her black hairy face, showed her white teeth and snarled. And boy could she snarl. What her bark lacked, her snarl packed. I thought back to Bonni's comment about Penny being a chicken on a stick; if Penny was a chicken, she was a chicken with teeth.

I was having breakfast. Penny and Pedro were 100 yards away, still tussling over that pinecone, when I heard Pedro barking and thought someone must be coming. That was followed by loud urgent yelping. I jumped to my feet fearful lest a rattlesnake had bitten one of them. Instead I saw four coyotes bearing down on Penny. She was running, turning, and rolling so fast, they couldn't get hold of her. And when they had a chance, her vicious lunging snarl made them hesitate. Pedro, showing uncharacteristic courage, dashed to her side, distracting the attackers and giving me time to sprint over and chase the coyotes away. Penny was so full of pluck, she was ready to go after them. I had to make a very ungainly tackle as she tried to run past me.

The coyotes disappeared behind a hill. I clipped the guys on their leashes and hurried forward to be sure they'd gone…or to drive them away if necessary. Standing beneath the lightning reamed pine on top of the rise, we looked down to the road and saw the four big-eared coyotes glaring back at us. They were spotted or mottled like African wild dogs and their large erect ears seemed almost grotesque after one becomes accustomed to doggie proportions. Penny and Pedro were emboldened, barking, and straining to get at them. We walked closer—the "magnificent three," chained together. Slowly, the coyotes backed off; we drove them across the valley and over another hill out of sight. I then inspected both my guys. Penny had two streaks of saliva across her face, but I was relieved to find no blood or wounds.

Walking back to the screen house, I was amazed to see a heavyset man down by the trash bins. He was dressed in a blue and white plaid shirt and bright blue overalls, and was easing from his shoulders a large blue backpack with a small blue suitcase strapped on top. Resting on a pair of ski poles, he smiled cheerfully and claimed that he'd just returned from climbing Picacho del Diablo. I invited him up to my campsite for a coffee. He declined the coffee, but accepted an orange and a glass of water.

He said his name was Helmut and he was from Germany. We conversed in English with the odd Spanish word helping us out. He seemed to be a pleasant, humble man. He wasn't much taller than I was, but he was certainly stocky and muscular, and also kind of rounded like he was a few pounds overweight. It was hard to be sure given what he was wearing.

He had hitchhiked up to the park. Tourists in expensive trucks passed and wouldn't stop, but he had eventually got a ride with a Mexican rancher. One of the rangers, probably Alfredo, then took him to the observatory where the administration director arranged for an observatory employee to run him to the trailhead at Padre Kino.

He said he'd left the Padre Kino camping area about noon the previous day—I must have been out hiking with the dogs. He had reached the top of Picacho at sunset, camped the night 50 meters below the peak, started down at 5 a.m., descended to the canyon bottom and then hauled himself back up to the plateau, returning to the Padre Kino campground about nine o'clock in the morning! With no decent maps and following no particular route, he claimed to have picked out the way as he went along.

I was astounded by his claims and had to wonder if he'd mistakenly climbed another peak on the plateau, such as Botella Azul. But it would be hard to confuse that forested high point with the sheer, naked mass of Picacho. Anyone with an eye and a few brain cells to string together would know that Picacho del Diablo was the unquestioned Alpha peak there in the San Pedro Mártir.

"How heavy is your pack?" I asked.

"Forty-five kilos."

"Wow. Did you leave it in Campo Noche at the bottom of the canyon and go light up to the peak?"

"No, I took everything to the top. I wanted to overnight up there and I had some cans of beer I wished to drink in celebration."

"Did you find anything on the peak?"

"No."

Given the fact that he had just about run up and down Picacho with 100 pounds on his back, he exuded a fantastic energy. He was in a hurry to hike and hitch out, and cross the Sea of Cortez to scale another peak near Copper Canyon. He explained that he was in the middle of climbing all of Mexico's highest and most interesting peaks and that he usually did it in half the time that everyone else took. "I ascended Orizaba in a day, most climbers take two," he related. When I asked for his email address he said, "Oh I'm too old for that. I'm 51 and I don't know much about computers." He gave me his card with his address in Mexico City.

He said he'd come to Mexico a few years before with a $100, and ended up staying. "This is my sacred land," he confessed. He had a large crucifix around his neck, and a smaller talisman of the Virgin of Guadalupe. He was obviously very religious.

I was disappointed that he couldn't stay and chat longer. I wanted to know more about how he made the climb and by what route. He had made it sound almost easy and routine. Knowing he might have to wait a while to get a ride out of the park, he picked up his pack and marched smartly away along the road swinging his ski poles. I had to compare the way he looked with the state that Mark and Pete were in when they returned from Picacho—they looked like they'd just scaled Everest, hiked the Sahara, and hacked their way through the Amazon. But there he was, rapidly disappearing beneath his great burden.

Once Helmut left, I was left wondering if I'd met one of the most incredible people in my life or a complete charlatan. To ascend Picacho del Diablo and return in the timeframe he outlined, he would have to be much fitter than he looked, and would need the devil's own luck to find and follow the right trail all the way to the peak and then back across the plateau.

I decided to secure the camp and take Penny and Pedro on a long ramble up to the ridge. Half way up, a family of quail fluttered from a manzanita thicket almost under our noses and retreated in a frenzy of fast little feet across the gorge that we were hiking besides. Penny and Pedro went in hot pursuit. They were scrambling up a steep rocky slope into an extensive patchwork of brush. I called for them to return. At first I called softly, then feeling less and less amused, I called louder and louder. Pedro was the first to respond and come back. But Penny was scurrying through the brush, ignoring me. I kept calling and even hurled a stone at a tree to get her attention.

In the end, I threw down my pack and bellowed her name one last time. Poor Pedro was scared and took off. "This is it," I roared my frustration to the forest. "I don't care if I have to climb Mount Everest; I'm going to get that dog." I'd been too lenient, too swayed by her adorable charm; and every time she sank into her submissive roll I hadn't followed through with any meaningful punishment; there were no consequences for her misbehavior, so naturally she thought she could totally ignore me.

I scrambled up the rocks and crashed barelegged through the thick, scraping brush, following her pine-like tail. When she knew she was cornered she lay down, looked at me and rolled over, no doubt confident that she could assuage me again. I was not assuaged. I was shouting, being as dramatic as I could; my performance merited an Oscar. Not only was Penny on her back, but she was peeing up in the air like a spouting whale, and squinting and blinking as if she expected to be thrashed.

I felt awful—she looked so scared. But I had to make her more responsive to my commands; otherwise, with all the coyotes around she was dead meat. I made a big show. I grabbed her jowls, shook her, dragged her along the ground a bit, lifted her, stared furiously into her eyes, symbolically slapped her chin a few times, then carried her down to the trail and my pack, where Pedro was cowering twenty yards away.

Realizing I had made my point, I lowered my voice. I reassured Pedro, and then with Penny on a leash, I showered all my attention on him and ignored her. I'm sure that hurt me more than it did her because I just wanted to pick her up and cuddle her because she looked so upset. It was necessary tough love, but I fear it was even tougher on me.

Penny was almost human…Imagine finding yourself picking up a cute baby orangutan, shaking it, and shouting at it, dragging it along the ground, jabbering and screaming…and you might be able to feel something of what I felt. Caught on camera, the incident would have blackened my name forever more. There was no defense.

When I heard coyotes calling, I felt even more awful. I knew if anything happened to Penny now, I'd be devastated. I'd never forgive myself. Nevertheless, I carried through with my resolve. I kept her on the leash and took no nonsense from her on the trail. I firmly tugged her leash if she didn't stay sensibly by.

Ten minutes later, I sat down in the shade of a tree and felt my message had been more than well made. I now did everything I could to make her feel loved, while continuing to lavish attention on Pedro, so he wouldn't feel left out.

Even though I knew I reacted so strongly because I was on edge after nearly losing Penny to the coyotes that morning, I was depressed about what I had done, as all theories aside, it just seemed cruel to scare and intimidate her that much. I vowed I would never do it again. If she was going to be eaten by a coyote then she would at least know with her last eager breath that I loved her with all the pieces of my broken heart.

It wasn't an easy thing to do, but I unclipped the leash and let her free. Surprisingly, she came along on the trail inordinately attentive. She followed me closely...much closer than Pedro. If I said come, she came. If I whistled, she came. If I clapped my hands, she came. Even a stare brought her to my heels for a submissive roll.

On the ridge I was still trying to make amends...hand feeding her, holding her water bowl for her, rubbing and reassuring her. And coming down, and all afternoon in camp she remained close and responsive.

I pulled Penny to me by the fire that night and said, "She brings out all my maternal qualities, maybe more so than Pedro." Pedro retired to his kennel early and Penny stayed up with me, her basket right beside my chair. Before retiring, I lovingly carried her to her kennel while some far away cow was mooing the moon.

I was woken in the middle of the night by a wild rushing and crashing in the forest. It sounded like a herd of buffalo—a hundred hefty, hoofed animals in panic flight. They were coming towards me from the direction of the Observatory Ridge. My brain couldn't accept what I was hearing. But when Penny and Pedro started loudly barking, I knew it wasn't a dream. I wriggled out of my sleeping bag and poked my head from the tent door. I could see nothing moving. The stampede seemed to be mostly passing to the north, with a remnant to the south; or maybe that was just an echo. As I was trying to make sense of it all, I had to wonder if somewhere out there a mountain lion was straddling its ambushed kill, preparing to feast.

August 3: I walked the dogs over to Alfredo's. I let them run free but I was being extra protective, and constantly scanning between the trees. While I was chatting to Alfredo in his cabin, Isai smacked Pedro on the head for no reason. Instantly, Alfredo hit Isai in the same fashion. I was impressed.

I told Alfredo about the climber and his claim to have scaled Picacho in so short a time. He was incredulous and said the claim was "bullshit." No one had ever returned that quickly. I tried to keep an open mind, but it was hard not to be skeptical.

Alfredo drove me a mile-and-a-half to the observatory to fill up my water containers. Assuming I would return soon, I left Penny and Pedro tied up at his shack playing with Baltasar and Zarco, who now had stopped scratching and was looking markedly improved.

Unexpectedly, we had to wait a while for someone to open a faucet, but I was not able to enjoy the small talk, wondering if my buddies were chewing through their leashes or strangling themselves.

After 30 minutes I told Alfredo I'd walk back down to his cabin and wait for him to bring the water. Isai wanted to come with me. I suggested it would be too long a walk for him. He pleaded and promised and reassured me that he could do it. As soon as I gave my reluctant approval, we set off with him jabbering again about heaven knows what. I was my usual model of politeness trying to hang on his every word and encourage him to say more. Even so, after ten minutes he went silent, stopped in his tracks and scowled like he couldn't take another moment of this torture. "I'm tired, I'm tired," he declared.

Knowing I couldn't just leave him there, and suspecting he was bored rather than tired, I tried to distract him by initiating a stone-throwing contest. Isai liked throwing stones. There was the thud of many a missile against many a tree. He got more hits than me. And with a few perhaps poorly translated but timely references to murders, mutilations and immolations, we were back at the shack in no time.

Pedro, as I'd feared, had already chewed through his leash and was wandering free. I unclipped Penny, so all the dogs could run together.

Four Mexicans were waiting for Alfredo at the shack—they were educated, well-spoken, really nice guys from Mexicali, probably business types. They gave me a cup of cold beer, which I very much appreciated as I'd run out a few days before.

Fascinated by my Baja travels and adventures, they said they would like to camp with me for a couple of days. I gave them directions to the Padre Kino campground. One of them declared he was a big fan of Padre Kino. He said *Rim of Christendom* had just been published in Spanish, and he had read the entire weighty tome several times.

Alfredo drove down with the water, and then invited me to share a *carne asada* meal with his family. Socorro laid out a superb spread with salsa, beans, cilantro, onions, tomatoes and hand made tortillas. Even Pedro and Penny were given a juicy piece of meat.

It was Friday and I was keen to get back to camp because it was the most likely day that someone would show at the campground. Alfredo offered to drive me. I accepted as it was getting late. I sat up front with him while all four dogs were milling around in the pickup bed. Recalling how Zarco had jumped out from the pickup and nearly throttled himself, I decided not to tie Penny and Pedro. But as we bounced along on the rough road, I kept looking anxiously over my shoulder at Penny, thinking she might be getting carsick.

Sensing that she was about to leap out, I asked Alfredo to stop so I could travel in the back with her. A few seconds after we were underway again, bumping along at 10 mph, Penny indeed tried to jump. I just managed to catch her, then put her on a leash and cradled her in my lap.

While I was stroking and reassuring Penny, Baltasar stood up next to us and peered into the forest; he was big and pushy, and was rubbing against me, with his butt almost in my face. And there, crawling out was an inch-long, white tapeworm. I tried to shove him away but his legs buckled so he ended up sitting on my feet. Then he stood up and backed towards us again. Suddenly, even though she was on the leash, Penny leapt from my lap and jumped from the pickup. Looking at Baltasar's approaching rear end, I felt like doing the same thing.

Poor Penny was dangling by her neck like a fish on a line. Perhaps because in the excitement of the moment she didn't seem "heavy," I decided to pull her in rather than let her drop and risk her going under the wheels. After that she was really subdued and readily settled in my arms.

When we arrived back in camp, I gave Alfredo $10 for the water and the meal and the ride, and was glad to be alone with my guys. After washing my hands and changing clothes, I walked the dogs around the ring road to make sure no one else was camping there. It was a relief to see Penny running around looking as happy and playful as ever. I had always known and assumed Baltasar had worms, so I was not sure why I felt so queasy and disgusted at the sight of that tapeworm.

The following afternoon, the four Mexicans that I'd met at Alfredo's shack arrived at my campsite in three vehicles. They asked to place their tents "somewhere in the area."

I said, "Of course, of course, anywhere." My expectation was they would camp about 100 yards away.

They actually camped right by my campfire! It was so Mexican.

Why be 100 yards away all on your paranoid lonesome when you can all be on top of each other, partying, celebrating life, and listening to loud music.

I took them for a hike up to the ridge. One of the guys was considerably overweight and was soon struggling, but soldiered bravely on with a large beer bottle hanging from his shoulder strap in lieu of a water bottle. In fact, they were all drinking beer to quench their thirst.

They drank more *cerveza* back in camp. And when they found out that I was out of beer, they drained almost a whole liter bottle into one of my large, insulated coffee mugs. They then invited me for dinner. They borrowed my grill and started barbecuing meat and preparing all the fixings for a fine taco/burrito fiesta.

A group of forest workers drove up in a large truck. Then Alfredo came with his family. My humble campground was suddenly hosting about fourteen people. It was no coincidence—the four Mexicans had invited everyone over. They certainly had brought plenty food and beer, and delighted in sharing it with their guests. If my mug got more than a quarter empty one of them would be topping it up before I could raise my hand in protest. Wow—that was a beautiful side to these guys; they were so open, generous and accepting. We all had a blast. I got tipsy and woke with quite a hangover.

Early that morning, a Sunday, with everyone gone, dead, or asleep, I walked Penny and Pedro a mile up the road towards the old cabin. I was feeling rather delicate. The dogs found a pile of white bathroom tissue, and Penny was playing with it and sticking her nose in it. When I whistled and shouted an urgent "come," she came running to me and diligently planted her now distinctly brown nose on my shorts. Looking at the stain, I suddenly felt even more delicate, and hurried back to camp to wash off the spot with water and iodine solution.

In spite of all the park signs in Spanish emphasizing the need to respect and preserve the place for future generations, most Mexicans visitors, I discovered, either didn't bother to bury their human waste and bathroom tissue, or just covered it with leaves and needles.

Also, one of the vehicles, a Toyota truck, had developed a front wheel-bearing problem on the drive up. My guests took the wheel assembly apart, in the middle of my campsite and made the necessary repairs. I gave them some rags to mop up the grease and dripping brake fluid.

While that was going on, they insisted I join them for a special breakfast of tongue and tortillas, followed by an exquisite homemade oxtail soup. Although not particularly hungry, I ended up devouring my share and I must confess it was delicious.

By midmorning the vehicle was back together and after warm goodbyes, and plenty of gracias on my part, they left. I was glad to be on my own for a while. Rain looked likely. My first urgent chore was to wander around with a shovel and bury all the paper and *caca* at least a foot deep, too deep for the dogs to dig up.

Chapter 25

Big Storm

How are the mighty fallen?

— 2 Samuel 1:25

It was August 5th. I was expecting Bonni to bring our son Andrew up on the 8th. For the sake of Bonni and her mushrooming, I had wished for rain...and we got it.

The rain started around 3:30 p.m. The first big drops shook and washed the dust off the tents. Then it became heavier, developing into a full-blown, thermometer-plunging thunderstorm. Over half an inch of rain fell, but the water was quickly absorbed into the dry ground. My headache receded just as fast. The forest had a clean, fresh smell of pine, vanilla, and wet sage. And the warm shafts of evening light sloped through the trees, rich and ethereal like myriad golden stairways to heaven.

The following morning, Penny chased a "speeding" pickup around the ring road, all half a mile of it. Seven or eight beer-clutching Mexicans were in the back whooping and cheering her on. She wasn't barking but obviously just running for the sheer fun of it. After I grabbed her, they drove up the road towards the abandoned log cabin and then everyone in the bed of the truck jumped out. My heart sank. I thought they were going to camp there, but they had exited to push the pickup up the steep hill. I was about to go for a hike but I decided against it till they'd gone.

I clipped the dogs on their lines. Pedro was still able to chase a squirrel up a tree. Penny was further away and howling to get at it. But I dare not indulge her; I knew she'd go visit the Mexicans. I was glad to see them come back down the road and drive out.

Later in the day, certain it was going to rain again, I gathered up some reasonably dry logs, pine needles and other kindling and placed them under a tarp. The sky darkened and the thunder rolled closer. I called the dogs from the forest and they immediately scurried into their kennels. The rain fell till after five. The sky then became sufficiently blue to convince me that the storm was over. But just as I stepped out from the screen house there was a sudden flash and a near instantaneous bang, which made me jump and left my ears ringing.

"That must have hit within hundreds of yards of this place," I shouted into my tape recorder.

I thought back to something I'd read about storm hazards:

> For about 10 minutes or more after the rain ends, even when it brightens and the sun is coming out, lightning is still a threat; in fact, most fatalities occur at the time that the storm appears to be ending. These late lightning strikes can be very dangerous.

That was followed by other nearby flashes and booms. What was left of the storm seemed to have gravitated to my campsite. I nervously looked under the table in the screen house to see a propane gas bottle. That would be ironic, survive a lightning strike and then get incinerated by an exploding gas bottle. I moved it outside.

Even in the midst of this almost personal storm, the pinyon jays were still squabbling and calling, while a score of juncos picked their way across my campground taking advantage of the dogs being locked up.

Again it brightened and I assumed the storm was over. Nearly all the horizon was blue. I was outside washing some clothes in the pools that had formed on the large tarp—all I had to do was add a few drops of biodegradable liquid soap—when another heavy deluge dropped from the small gray-black cloud that seemed to have placed itself right overhead. It was an oddly persistent storm. Against the blue and sunny backdrop, and the inevitable rainbow, the rain came shafting solid and surreal. A fresh golden-yellow pinecone thudded into the ground forty feet away by my campfire. I was hoping a bolt of lightning was not going to follow it down.

Then when it really was over, the spreading blue gave way to a peaceful, bird singing, colorful, purple, pink, buff and beige sunset.

Next morning there was not a cloud in the sky, but there were several cows and calves by the trash bins. While Penny and Pedro were very happy to harass them to a respectful distance, I proceeded to dry out the camp and hang up some washing. However, the clouds started building fast and early. We had two light showers, and then by 11:00 it was raining hard again. I closed both dogs in their kennels outside and covered them with tarps. My laundry was not dry yet so I left it on a clothesline strung between two trees, getting a bonus rinse. During a lull in the rain I recorded, "There's a strange roar off to the south. Sounds like a waterfall. I have no idea what it is." The first flashes and rumblings sent me out to check and secure everything better. The rushing noise grew louder, and then a swirling eddy of wind came blasting through the tops of the trees like an incipient tornado. Penny and Pedro barked at the unseen monster. Most of the laundry was shaken to the muddy ground.

After a much closer flash and crash, I changed into dry shoes and socks, and put on my clownish oversized green galoshes. Before noon, we were enveloped by a storm as black as night while a steady rain fell. "It's early," I recorded, "and this is going to be a long day." The rain grew more intense. The ground was flooding. I had to wait ninety minutes for a relative lull in the rain so I could let the dogs out.

They hardly had time to pee before a sudden violent downpour sent them running back into their kennels. Large pools were forming all around, including one by my feet in the screen house. I couldn't resist dashing out and washing more clothes in the puddles on the silver tarp. There was now no sign of a junco or a pinyon jay, or anything alive outside.

A cold powerful wind swept through the clearing. The sky was all brown and black, and there was a continuous rumbling of thunder. The lightning was reflecting off the clouds. I pushed my fingers in my ears at each flash. I wished I had brought earplugs. I was anxious, but at the same time I was deeply moved by the experience. I found myself tempting fate, calling out, "Man, I am alive!"

The air seemed so charged with energy I could almost see it and taste it and picture the leaders and streamers and collection zones. It was as if the whole world was buzzing with electricity and expectation—almost as if God himself was about to appear. While half-mesmerized by the grandeur of Armageddon, chunks of thumbnail-sized hail started battering the thin nylon above me.

They were the biggest hailstones I'd seen in my life, and I wondered how long the screen house could take such a battering. It was fascinating to think that the hailstone I had just watched bounce off the ground or splash into a puddle was minutes before hovering maybe 20–30,000 feet above the mountains.

Hail forms when strong currents of rising air inside thunderclouds carry water droplets above the freezing level, and there the droplets turn to ice and grow as more water freezes on their surface. When they are heavy enough to overcome the updraft, they fall at speeds up to 90 mph.

Ironically, the noise of heavy rain and hail made the thunder less frightening—like a martial beating of drums desperately trying to drown the unnerving din of battle. The ground was soon flooded. Little rivers were flowing from pool to pool. The water was an inch deep by the gazebo door. The dog kennels outside were in puddles at least half an inch deep; and water was splashing inside them from the hail even though the kennels were covered with tarps hanging a foot over the doors. Although clad in sweat pants, sweater, and rain gear, I was shivering. It was amazingly cold.

The pools outside joined like a concentrating enemy army, at first surrounding then inevitably moving into the screen house. I was standing in a puddle. A slight rise under the table was the only dry spot left. I was glad I hadn't brought the dogs into the gazebo or they would have been floating away.

"Oh my God, I'm just looking out at what was my fire; that's now a lake." With water running in every direction, the slope of the ground was all-important. I peed inside the gazebo. There was no point going outside.

A lightning strike anywhere close might reach me through that conducting sheet of liquid. After a couple of anxious hours, the rain moderated and the "lake" began almost visibly sinking back as the parched soil quickly soaked it up. Judging by the depth of water in the bowls and pots outside, I guessed the storm had dumped close to three inches of rain.

I made a mug of coffee and then went for a walk. The dogs followed eagerly but Penny was jittery and jumped at every sudden clap of thunder. The main arroyo had a stream for the first time that summer; it was a stream flowing between a number of broad pools.

There was a small bird on the ground by a fallen log. I assumed it would, like so many others, fly off if the dogs gave chase; but this time it ran and flapped and tried to fly, but it obviously wasn't going to make it. It was probably just a youngster. Penny pounced and ran off with it in her mouth. Sounding like thunder in my heavy rubberized rain gear, I chased her for 100 yards. She eventually dropped it. It was still alive. It felt strong and warm, and there was no blood. I carried it back to camp in my cupped hands. I thought I could secure the guys and give it a chance. But it died in my hands, a beautiful little black and white bird with a black beak and patches of yellow in front of its eyes. I identified it as a black-throated gray warbler.

We were all surprised to see a group of horses appearing from out of the misty gray. Penny ran at them "flat out," no doubt confident they would scatter before her greatness, but they just looked at her probably more amused than threatened. As she couldn't intimidate them, she came ambling back. Then Pedro and Penny took off together to try the pack approach. I called. Pedro returned straightaway, but an emboldened madly yapping Penny followed the horses into the forest. And when she came back I had no heart to scold her; I showered her with congratulations for returning home...and Pedro for staying put.

It was hard to be sure with so much mist, but there seemed to be smoke on the slope to the southwest. As the air cleared, I could see that there was a fire—just one of the 75,000 North American forest fires started by lightning every year. "Only YOU can prevent forest fires." How naïve Smokey Bear's warning now sounds. In the rush to offer a better Smokey slogan, I don't think anyone has proposed: "Together, with time, we can start thousands of fires to produce a healthy open forest." Fortunately, as the forest was so wet, the fire had as little chance of spreading as my suggested slogan.

About seven that evening, with the aid of the stashed wood and kindling, I got a tentative campfire going. Initially it gave off more smoke than heat. The smoke was drifting slowly towards the clearing western sky, turning the sunset tawny and tan.

Unusual for Penny, but she wanted to go into her kennel at nine. Pedro stayed up in her basket. He had hiccups. I stayed up with him in case Bonni came. Every time Pedro threw his head up, my heart fluttered; I wondered if he'd heard a vehicle.

It was a still night. I could see no stars close to the eastern horizon, so I assumed there were clouds there, a rare occurrence after dark. Mindful of the possibility of more rain, I was looking around deciding what to put away when there was a terrific crashing boom. I thought at first it was thunder, but as there had been no flash I realized it was a tree falling not too far away.

Then as I was putting the fire out, there was a sudden rushing sound above me. Already on edge, I pulled in my head and tightened my grip on the shovel. Thud. Another pinecone hit the ground. The rain and the storm seemed to have weakened and loosened so much in the forest. The moon was just rising, revealing that there were indeed clouds to the east. I retired at eleven, a little disappointed that Bonni hadn't come.

Warming inside my sleeping bag, I listened to the sound of water droplets falling from the aspen onto the tarp still partially covering my tent and the kitchen table. Another tree or big branch fell somewhere in the forest. It was hard to relax and fall asleep.

Thursday, August 9: I woke to find it wet with condensation inside the tent. The humidity and cloud cover meant that the temperature never dropped below 45°F all night. I hoped nothing would spoil in my cooler.

It was a partially cloudy morning. I walked the dogs around looking in vain for mushrooms. It might be a few more days before the recent rains sent them pushing forth. The wet ground, however, accentuated the subtle colors of the fallen cones and needles—red, brown, wine and black. And I was able to pick up a dozen pieces of trash, especially clean and colorful plastic caps that the rain seemed to have washed out.

Hoping for a sunny drying day, I was disappointed to see the thunderheads building early. Yet, the cloud cover fluctuated. When it changed from 90% gray to just 20%, I seized the opportunity to dry my tents, tarps, and clothes in the sun.

By early afternoon the sky was threatening again. Billowing alabaster cumulonimbus clouds ringed the horizon like a celestial city. I brought some lunch items into the gazebo and shut the dogs in their kennels. It rained steadily for about 45 minutes, and then the sun emerged. I took off my raingear, put on some shorts, and took the dogs for another walk.

Hawks and swallows were drifting and circling way up high— higher than I'd seen them before. They were little more than specks against the blue sky and the churning clouds. Hundreds of pinyon jays flitted and squabbled in the treetops.

Half a mile northeast of camp, Pedro jumped on top of a rocky outcrop and looked down at me as if he wanted to jump into my arms. "Pedro on this rock," I quipped. The sky darkened again, the rumbling grew louder. More rain seemed imminent. I called him down, and with a few graceful leaps he was beside me enjoying a good old head rub.

"Home," I said, pointing back to the campsite. We had gone less than a hundred yards when I heard a dramatic cracking noise behind us. We all turned together and watched astounded as a pine tree crashed to the ground right where I'd been rubbing Pedro's head. What a thrill to see it go. I led the barking dogs back over. The three-foot-thick ponderosa pine had simply cracked at the base and had knocked several branches from other trees on its way down.

Chapter 26

Heavens

Zigzag lances of lightning followed each other in quick succession, and the thunder was so gloriously loud and massive it seemed as if surely an entire mountain was being shattered at every stroke. Only the trees were touched…a few firs…were split into long rails and slivers from top to bottom and scattered to all points of the compass.
— John Muir

That evening, a day later than expected, Bonni and our son Andrew came up to visit and bring supplies. They also brought our city dog, Bella, for a romp in the woods. Bella was a border collie mix that we'd picked up in Mexico. It might have been in her genes, but I'm sure her earlier experiences had not been pleasant—she craved constant affection, and deprived of it she could be moody, jealous, and unpredictable. After an unprovoked piece of snarling savagery directed at one of our other dogs—an inoffensive old female chow— she came within a whisker of being put down.

We gave her one more chance and tried to do all we could to make her feel more secure. I took her for more walks, for rides in the car, let her in the house more often, and generally surrounded her with human companionship…and she slowly improved and actually started to seem more like a nice, loving, loyal and obedient dog. She seemed particularly attached to me, but I couldn't say the feeling was mutual.

There in the mountains she looked unnerved by the sudden alien environment she found herself in. She was very standoffish with Pedro, growling at him if he came within two feet of her. She was much better with Penny; every time they came nose to nose, there was a tail wagging rapport.

Bonni made a kennel for Bella by wrapping a tarp around a large sturdy cardboard box. She was not an adventurous dog; there was little chance that she'd wander off, but we decided to clip her on a line at night anyway.

When we were hiking, Penny and Pedro continually climbed up rocks, jumped over fallen trees, and went gleefully after deer and cows, whereas Bella rarely left my side, and stuck with me so closely she kept colliding with my boot, sending me stumbling. She didn't fit in with Penny and Pedro's playfulness. They were inseparable and living their doggie lives to the full. She had an expression on her face like a lost and homesick moray eel. In her mind nothing surpassed the reassuring touch of a human hand.

The day after she arrived, Bonni's mushroom club, the San Diego Mycological Society (SDMS), came up for a "Baja Foray." After they had explored in small groups all around, we paid them a visit to compare findings at their campground just off the observatory road. They all agreed to join us on a hike up to the Picacho viewpoint.

The morning that we were expecting them, just before they arrived, Armando García, the operations supervisor at the observatory, came over with an American couple whose vehicle had developed a serious transmission problem. They needed a ride out. After we'd arranged that with a couple from Colorado who happened to be camping there at Padre Kino, Armando invited Bonni, Andrew, and me over to the observatory for a guided tour. Indeed, he offered to come get us, and the dogs, in his truck and drive us there himself. Such is the incredible atmosphere of warmth and hospitality that can be enjoyed in Mexico.

I found myself leading eighteen people and three dogs along the trail to the ridge. In spite of all the recent rains, the mushrooms weren't yet popping in profusion. But with that number of people looking, there were enough interesting finds to keep everyone going. I thought the final rise to the ridge would be too much for some of the more senior members of the group, but amazingly they all made it— perhaps a testimony to their delight in the forest and the wholesomeness of a diet rich in wild mushrooms. When everyone got their first glimpse of Picacho the gasps were audible. It was a perfect day to be up there—warm, clear, and still.

It had been the grand finale for the group. Back in camp they made ready their departure. Several left me their spare food, water and even such much-appreciated items as a pack of AA batteries. Bonni had brought up several packs but after we'd gone through a dozen in one day—feeding our little two-way radios, GPS receivers, flashlights, and tape players—I was watching the stock very closely. I always had my solar chargers but they wouldn't be quite enough for all my needs if I ran out of regular batteries.

One warm sunny afternoon, Bonni, Andrew and I, and the dogs, were exploring a valley running east from the Padre Salvatierra campground when Bonni noticed several slivers and hunks of freshly shattered whitish wood. They gave off a sweet smell reminiscent of a sawmill or a lumberyard.

Bonni suspected that there was a lightning struck tree nearby. We searched around for more pieces and were surprised to see lengths of limbs and hunks of trunk hanging in the branches of other trees. We followed the debris field up a slope towards a rocky ridge, where a shattered white fir stump was all that remained of a once prominent, perhaps sixty-foot high tree. Standing at its two-foot-wide base, one could see that the tree had literally exploded into hundreds of pieces, which had flown as much as 75 yards in every direction. I was sure it had been hit by one of those dramatically loud thunderbolts from the recent storm—most likely that late dangerous strike that had left my ears ringing.

I picked up a fragrant two-pound piece of the exposed heartwood as a souvenir, gazed up at the stump, and pictured the lightning strike and the explosion. It was so vivid in my mind that I was almost convinced that I had been there and seen it happen. I kept seeing myself ducking as the woody shrapnel shot all around.

Our next hike took us on a mushroom hunt into Art's Canyon. We ascended higher than I'd gone before, above the trickling stream and the mossy pools to where the rocky valley opened to more rolling, traversable country. Suddenly, hearing a loud cracking, all three of us looked up to see, less than a hundred yards ahead, a large pine crashing to earth, and taking with it a number of branches off other trees.

I had become blasé enough about falling trees to shout "timber," but Andrew and Bonni stood astonished as the dogs barked furiously. We ran over and saw how the tree, a ponderosa, had dropped neatly between two other trunks and lay firmly wedged right on the ground. Minutes after it went down, all three of us were excitedly walking along the three-foot-wide trunk taking photos and looking at the little polypore fungi and woodpecker holes that had moments before been eighty or a hundred feet in the air.

On any long hike in the San Pedro Mártir one is going to pass tens of thousands of large mature trees and a few will always be ripe for falling, especially after heavy rain. That's why it's a good idea to carefully examine the state of the trees where you intend to camp.

I knew of the locations of a number of precarious dead standing trees. There was a branchless, two-foot-thick, twenty-foot-tall trunk right next to my Cathedral. It looked impressively solid but it was light and rotten inside. I rocked it and realized it would take just a determined push to send it crashing. I thought I'd use it to surprise and impress Andrew. I planned on one of our walks to feign anger over something, run at it screaming and do a flying kick to knock it down. Instead, I gave that rare pleasure to our eager 13 year old; he floored it while I took a photo.

To Bonni's dismay, Andrew and I enlivened our hikes with other son/stepdad bonding by throwing our sheath knives into some of the rotten old trunks. That provided endless entertainment till both our knife blades snapped with the abuse. Undeterred, we resorted to the machete. Getting that to stick in an old tree was quite a feat, but Andrew managed it several times, and I watched proudly as he, Arthur-like, drew out the long blade.

Another entertainment for Andrew was an old army surplus hammock tent that I'd brought up and never used. After spending hours restringing it and securing it between two trees, he found a fun place to escape to and lose himself in a book.

A radio news report primed me to prepare for the annual Perseid meteor shower the night of August 11. The concentrated array of shooting stars known as the Perseids—they appear to radiate from a point in the constellation Perseus—graces the night sky every year sometime between August 8 and 14. During that period Earth passes through a stream of debris left behind by the comet Swift-Tuttle; at six miles across, the comet is the largest object known to make repeated passes near Earth.

Perseid activity increases markedly in the hours after midnight. I was determined to stay up and see the show, but Andrew had long since retired, and it proved too late for Bonni to keep her eyes open. She drifted off on her cot while I, hot tea in hand, ogled the heavens and occasionally spouted appreciative "ooo's" and "aaa's." There was an added local bonus—flashes from unheard distant storms across the gulf occasionally illuminated the horizon.

Such was the show it was hard to believe that these meteors were light and ashy, and rarely bigger than a pea. They started to burn up over 50 miles above the earth, and almost none ever hit the ground.

The Swift-Tuttle comet was scheduled to return in the year 2126. As I gazed into the heavens, I wondered what the Padre Kino campsite would be like then—would it still be surrounded by an unsullied old growth forest? Would condors grace the sky? Would it look as it does today, or would the San Pedro Mártir and its visitors be unimaginably different? I fancied I might be there in spirit to see for myself, with Penny and Pedro romping beside me.

As promised, Armando García came to pick us up at 9:30 a.m. on August 14. He loaded all three of us and all the dogs in his pickup and drove slowly back towards the observatory.

On the way, he checked out the vehicle with the transmission problem in the Kiliwa Campground. Armando had kindly offered to keep an eye on it till the owners could get back with the needed parts.

We walked the dogs around the observatory buildings for a while then we put them in their kennels and went inside. Standing at the base of the main 2.1-meter telescope building one gets a great view of the mountains and the desert and Picacho, but it's even more heady from inside the structure, especially on the external circular walkway three or four stories up, just under the dome. Armando said the cupola had been struck by lightning the previous Sunday—a not uncommon event. He was inside when it happened and said the noise was incredible. There was no damage however.

I made notes as Armando explained that by the 1960's excessive light pollution made untenable the siting of telescopes in the Central Valley of mainland Mexico. So a search was made to find the best site for astronomical observations in Mexico. An initial selection was made by analyzing meteorological satellite photographs, then field observations were made at the most promising locations. In the end, a site was chosen at 9,280 feet in the Sierra San Pedro Mártir.

A suitable road had to be built into the mountains and everything needed had to be transported to the location except for the clear skies and the starlight.

Today the observatory has in operation three modern reflecting telescopes with main lens diameters of 0.84-meters, 1.5-meters and 2.1-meters.

The 1.5-meter telescope was installed in 1971, in a joint project with the University of Arizona. The 0.84-meter telescope was installed the following year. The largest of the telescopes, the 2.1-meter, was constructed between 1974 and 1979, and dedicated on September 17, 1979. It has been in continuous operation since 1981. The 2.1-meter lens reputedly weighs around 3 tons! Thanks to international cooperation, all the telescopes have been regularly upgraded with the latest instrumentation.

The fraction of nights lost due to bad weather or high humidity in the San Pedro Mártir is a little over 25%, which is similar to that of the celebrated observatories in the Chilean Andes, slightly better than

Mauna Kea on the Big Island of Hawaii—the largest observatory complex in the Northern Hemisphere—and considerably better that the Mount Graham observatory in Arizona. Spring and autumn are the best seasons for observations, with the lowest percentage of cloudy nights. Typically, May and June are the driest months, while July, August and September are the most humid. Winter nights can be affected by the tail ends of North Pacific storms.

Armando gave us a detailed account of the major observatory operations and patiently answered all our questions. We saw the giant telescope close up, the camera attached to it, the computer packed control room, and the electronic repair laboratory—and we talked to a couple of the staff working there. Armando showed us how the great telescope mirrors were periodically cleaned and recoated to enable them to do their job.

We learned that in the near future, an 8-meter (almost four times as big as the largest telescope in place) infrared telescope could be erected at the site—an exciting but expensive joint Mexican-International project.

Before showing us the rest of the facilities, Armando had a lunch appointment, so for about ninety minutes we explored and walked the dogs around the telescope area looking at the two smaller domes from the outside.

We found the site for the proposed new 8-meter infrared telescope and tried to imagine what it would look like. It commanded a fine view of the forested plateau to the south and west, so we enjoyed our own snacky lunch there in the warm sun. We looked down on the main *Vallecitos* meadow area through which ran the road up to the observatory. The most popular campsites were in that meadow, beside the road.

It was cloudy all round except for a big blue break overhead, much like the clear eye of an enormous hurricane. The "monsoon" clouds to the south were billowing and magnificent, and appeared to be sitting right above our campsite.

When Armando returned, he showed us the plant for making liquid nitrogen from the air. We saw a tank being filled and watched the frozen vapor creep along the ground. Liquid nitrogen was used to cool the cameras attached to the main telescopes. With the dogs secured in the back of his truck, Armando then drove us almost a mile down the hill to see the staff accommodation area—including a large, impressive, new building—and the mechanical, electrical, office, and other support facilities.

Then to crown a fascinating, educational experience, Armando drove us back to our campsite, where all was well. Finally, he generously offered any help or assistance we might need, including permission to refill my containers with the observatory's filtered and purified water.

August 16: while Bonni drove out to look for mushrooms, Andrew and I and the dogs went on a five-mile hike that began with a visit to a different viewpoint on Observatory Ridge.

We climbed on top of a majestic granite outcrop that I named "Half Dome" after its look-alike big brother in Yosemite. We both removed our boots to give our sweaty feet a chance to cool. I wouldn't go near the edge, but Andrew and Penny were bold enough to peer over at the 400-foot sheer drop into a tributary canyon to Cañon del Diablo. Andrew had a great head for heights; he crawled forward on his belly and enjoyed dropping stones and watching them bounce on the rocks far below.

Looking east there was an extraordinary contrast between the clear blue sky over the desert and sea, and the black clouds swirling over the mountains. A particularly ugly one had settled right over Cañon del Diablo, between our viewpoint and Picacho del Diablo. The disturbingly close, fast-morphing underside looked laden with thunderbolts; and it seemed to be coming our way like it had taken a personal interest in us. Hoping I didn't sound too alarmist, I urged Andrew to put his boots on, and, "Let's get the hell out of here."

Big raindrops began spattering all around as we started making our way down the boulders and gullies on "Half Dome's" more gently descending west side. Normally the dogs would be after us as soon as we went ten feet, but this time they just stood and stared as we were dropping out of sight. I wondered if the electricity in the air was short-circuiting their brains. Penny and Pedro snapped out of it first, and came hurrying over, finding their own way down. But approaching the relative safety of a saddle between dome and ridge, I realized there was no sign of Bella. The rain turned to stinging hail.

While Andrew held Penny and Pedro, I went back up to find her. She was pacing around looking wide-eyed and terrified in the middle of the curving dome. Once I'd got her started she followed in her usual close position. A couple of the descents from boulder to boulder were too much for her; I had to carry her in my arms.

Thinking we were down and relatively safe, I gently lowered her to the ground. As her paws were scrambling to make contact with the wet pine needles, there was a flash that lit up the dark base of the clouds. I barely had time to say "Oh Shhh"…before that was followed by an almost tangible, breathtakingly loud BANG, and then several booming echoes. As soon as Bella got her paws down, she scurried straight back up the slope in wild panic. I called in vain. Somehow she found the strength and momentum to pull herself up all the drops she couldn't get down.

I finished the "Shhh…" comment, and then feeling like a mobile lightning rod, I climbed up again to fetch her. She was pacing near the edge of the sheer drop looking even more wild-eyed. The hair was rising on her back. I called and slapped my thighs as a signal to come. She didn't respond. I was giving her to the count of five. At four she dashed over and I unceremoniously scooped all forty-five pounds of her into my arms, and carried her down as fast as I was able. She was so agitated, her claws drew blood on my legs and I feared she was going to bite me.

I put Bella on a leash, and then Andrew and I led the dogs north, staying just below the high point of the ridge. The sharp cracks of the storm echoed all around. It was easy to understand how early theologians could believe that the clouds that were menacing us contained vengeful, malevolent gods prone to hurling thunderbolts at offending mortals.

Energized by the storm, we were all briskly stepping and leaping up even the hardest of slogs. Bella seemed to have recovered her composure, so I released her from the leash and let her follow at her pace. Again she chose to stay a foot behind my boots. Collisions were inevitable, but she didn't seem to mind. She would trade a few slaps in the face for security.

I was looking at all the granite caves and overhangs and evaluating them as places for shelter if the storm really overtook us. After resting in one as a shower passed over, we continued hiking along the ridge, towards another aspen grove. The main mass of thunderheads seemed to be drifting away to the south—the time between flash and crash grew longer.

By the time we got to the aspen grove, the sky was 80% clear and we could at last relax and explore a little. The aspen trees in that grove were mostly small, with trunks less than a foot thick, but densely packed together and often flattened in great swathes a hundred at a time. I speculated it was probably due to a combination of wind damage and fungal infection. Certainly there were scores of groups of handsome brown and yellow *Flammulina velutipes* among the trees. I popped a few of the more appealing bunches in my mushroom bag as both a love offering and for dinner. There was also an abundance of wild onions in the grove, so I lifted a handful of those.

We found the new road that had been bulldozed up to a viewpoint on the ridge called *Mirador de Altar*, and gratefully followed it down to intersect the one-track road to Padre Kino. Penny and Pedro ran off into the Salvatierra meadow chasing a squirrel. I couldn't be too hard on them after they'd followed so faithfully all day, so I just sat down and waited for them to return.

Bella, of course, stayed at my feet. Just minutes from the campsite, we heard a truck approaching from behind; it was Bonni back from her mushroom hunting session along the Tasajera road. She had done well. Andrew jumped in the truck and I walked the dogs "home."

We had lots of tales to tell that night by the fire. And Bonni and I enjoyed a few coolish beers—I won't say cold because the temperature never dropped below 55 degrees the previous night. In fact the cooler was so stuffed with perishables I willed a return to freezing nights to really chill it down.

About two in the morning, I stepped out of the tent to check on the dogs. Although the sky was clear and full of stars I saw a number of far off flashes, and this time I heard a few faint rumbles. I went back to bed not really believing that we'd get any rain. At first light, however, I woke to see a black, overcast sky. And soon the thunder came on loud and threatening.

I got everyone up, made the coffee, gathered together some breakfast items, and only just got everything covered when it started bucketing down. The strong gusting wind snapped a guy line and uprooted another. While Andrew and Bonni tried to stay dry in the center of the screen house, I was dashing around fixing and securing everything in my rain gear. I loved it—working in the rain was simply delightful.

The ground was flooding. If it had continued all day, the road out might have become temporarily impassable, but the rain moderated and it ended up being a fairly nice, partially sunny afternoon.

I hadn't seen Alfredo for several days and I was down to just 5 gallons of water. While I still had the truck I decided to run over with Bonni to the observatory, where we spoke to some of the maintenance workers. Armando wasn't around, but the kindly workers helped us fill all my empty containers with filtered safe water. It was a good feeling to have over 30 gallons again.

Knowing Bonni would soon be leaving, I wrote a website update, looked at the photos I had taken, read my mail…and enjoyed one final hike with her up Columbine Canyon. It was a beautiful evening to walk the dogs and enjoy a tepid beer. Bella had started out with us, but before we were out of earshot of camp she, much to my surprise, decided to run back and stay with Andrew.

Rain threatened again next morning. Bonni and Andrew timed their departure to perfection. A few drops began falling as we were saying our goodbyes. I suspect Pedro was glad to see the back of Bella—she even managed to growl at him as she was climbing into the truck. They'd hardly been gone twenty minutes before the rain really started and the road became slick and puddle pocked.

To help me adjust to my abandonment, I focused on the fact that I had my buddies, enough water for two or three weeks, and perhaps enough food and supplies to get me through the summer.

Taking the dogs for a walk in the rain, I looked around at a dripping, gray campsite and some small part of me even relished the satisfying and perhaps selfish feeling that this was now all mine—at least for a while.

That evening, Alfredo and the extended family paid a visit, and we all settled by the fire. What a great bunch—they were still laughing, joking and enjoying life with great dignity and gusto. Alfredo explained his long absence by saying that his truck had broken down near San Telmo and he needed to wait below to get it fixed.

The day after they left I began a long, diary-type letter to Bonni.

Chapter 27

Letter to Bonni

I hate quotations. Tell me what you know.

— Emerson

Sunday, August 19–Campo Padre Kino

Dear Bonni,

I hope you and Andrew got home safely without any problems. Yesterday evening Alfredo stopped by with his wife, two kids, parents, brother-in-law, and two dogs. He said he'd seen you heading down towards San Telmo. Those Sprites came in handy as did the elk sausages, potato chips, and the pie. We had quite a party here. Around 9 o'clock I said, "Bonni should be home by now."

Alfredo said he'd brought me a present but it broke on the way up—he described it as a *"plato de tierra,"* which sounded to me like "a plate of earth." My best guess after many embarrassing tries was that he'd brought me a ceramic bowl!

Anyway, not long after you left, it started raining and blowing hard. I had to dash to cover/secure everything, especially Andrew's tent as I'd filled it with most of my bags. It was gray and depressing at first with you guys gone. Even Pedro and Penny seemed unusually quiet.

By evening all was clear and blue again. I was cooking my salmon veggie delight when Alfredo arrived. Had to shelve it till today— delicious lunch and dinner.

Well, as you can imagine, the mushrooms were popping—I'm looking forward to the next few days. It was a warm 80% clear day today, so after drying out and getting organized I walked towards Art's Canyon to see what there was.

I hadn't even reached the cathedral when I saw a grouping of bright yellow 'shrooms by the road. Some were babies; some were two inches across. There seemed to be at least twenty scattered on the open ground. Being so close to camp I decided to leave them till I returned to take photos and pick the best ones to study (and maybe eat). In the arroyo before Art's Canyon, there were several puffballs. They were white and undifferentiated inside so I brought one back to eat. When I sliced it I saw tiny elongate jelly-like blobs along the cut. I don't think they were maggots—they certainly weren't moving—but the sight of them put me off frying a hunk.

I also found in the arroyo a beautiful little cup-like polypore? It was about the size drawn here:

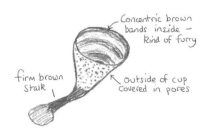

Concentric brown bands inside – Kind of furry

firm brown Stalk

Outside of cup Covered in pores

The predominant color was a kind of rusty brown. It was growing out from under a stone in the arroyo bottom, possibly rooted in a mix of wood, soil and pine needles. Because of the obvious pores outside the cup I presume it is not a cup fungus, but a polypore? My best guess is it is in the genus *Coltricia*. I took some macro slide photos.

Anyway, after lunch I walked back over to the yellowish fungi, camera in hand. I was sure they were the shaggy stems—*Armillaria straminea*—they had yellow and white shaggy stems and a scaly cap. Well I never got to discover if they'd be good to eat. They were all gone. Just four hours after I'd seen them, every one had disappeared. There was just a little hunk of yellow flesh on the ground. No doubt the squirrels scoffed or stored the lot! I won't make that mistake again.

Later in the day along the trail to the ridge I found half a cap of a bright yellow bolete—naturally it bore teeth marks. I think my best bet is to go searching early.

However, the best 'shroom of the day was brought to me by Alfredo in mid-afternoon. Again his truck was loaded with all the family. The kids were shouting "Mac-keen-toshy" as they drove up. I thought the party was going to be early today, but Alfredo just wanted to present me with a monster 'shroom. It was almost six inches across the cap, and the stalk was over an inch thick. The gills were white and ran down the stalk a little—decurrent? The cap

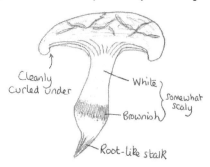

Cleanly Curled Under

White

Somewhat Scaly

Brownish

Root-like stalk

was like a round loaf of bread—yellowish-brown and cracked, more smooth than scaly or warty. The cap was perfectly curled under:

Alfredo found it near the visitor center. I'm not sure what it is. I'm trying to take a spore print without removing the stalk. I can't see anything on the plate yet—so I guess the spores are white. It looks a bit like *Lentinus ponderosus*, but I wouldn't bet my life on it.

Well, I'm by my fire here with the *perros* asleep on chair and basket, the new moon eluded me this evening, ash is raining from my fire. It's getting cold. Got down to 40° last night. I'll retire early and try to rise early to beat the squirrels to what's-a-popping.

Monday, August 20

Well, my early a.m. walk around camp and over to Art's Canyon wasn't very productive—just a few puffballs. But it promised to be a good day so I secured the camp and hiked up Columbine Canyon, to the Aspen Grove. Never saw a mushroom on the way. It was hot and dry—a nice change.

At first, the only thing I encountered among the aspens were mosquitoes. Luckily, I had repellent. But the warm, dank, shady grove was promising, so I kept looking…and, suddenly BINGO…fungi. There were several small delicate specimens and numerous *Flammulina velutipes*. There was running water and a pool for Pedro to splash in. Then I found a mushroom I'd never seen before. It was sticky all over—shiny and slimy. There were several. The cap was white to cinnamon. The gills were white. From *Mushrooms Demystified*, I think it might be in the genus Limacella, possibly *Limacella illinita* (close relative to an Amanita). It was like this:

Then I found a mushroom a minute. The best find was on the side of a little gully snaking through the aspens. I suddenly saw a bunch of bright yellow discs. They looked like amanitas. But when I pulled one up it was a bolete. There were at least a dozen in various stages of emergence from the leaf litter. And not a squirrel in sight. They were pretty much bright yellow overall; the flat caps were slightly rosy tan. I took four of the biggest, meaning to have them for dinner.

My mushroom bag was soon full with about 15 different species of 'shrooms. I found another different bolete—the cap was more tan and rounded rather than flat—otherwise it was yellow. It was probably the best day's 'shrooming I'd ever had.

I returned to my camp ready to fry and identify but no sooner had I got the books open when Alfredo and his family came over. So I had to break off my work and hand out cookies and melon, crackers and chocolate. Alfredo's jolly old dad enjoyed a drop of whisky.

Poor Baltasar—last night he was sleeping out and was attacked by a pack of coyotes. He was bitten on the meaty part of his rear leg. You know how big he is…As I write I can hear a pack of yelping coyotes somewhere in the direction of Aguaje del Burro. I'm by my fire and Penny is tied. Pedro is on his chair looking up.

I took several photos of the 'shrooms but I didn't get a chance to spore print them. I hope they don't deteriorate too much overnight.

There's another specimen I want to ID. It's a grouping of three 'shrooms with lightish decurrent gills.

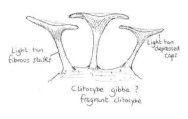

Light tan fibrous stalks

Light tan depressed caps

Clitocybe gibba ?
fragrant clitocybe

I'll try to ID as many as possible tomorrow.

Alfredo's new dog looks much better now—no obvious mange. I gave Alfredo a bottle of made up dip to bathe him again. It was very effective last time. His name is Zarco! Nothing to do with sarcoptic mange, Alfredo assures me.

Well, good night from me and the sleeping beauties by our roaring fire. It got to be 38°F last night. Cold spell or maybe summer is slipping away.

By the way, I sliced the boletes, ready to cook them, when I noticed they were in large part shot through with little maggot tunnels, so I lost interest in trying them. I chucked them away, so the squirrels got them after all.

Instead, I enjoyed another wonderful veggie (chicken) stew with all the fixings. Delicious!

Wednesday, August 22

Around lunch time yesterday an older guy pulled up near the trashcans in an old Toyota car. After a while I went over to introduce myself. It turned out he was a quiet guy, a botanist from Australia. He was up here for twenty-four hours to take photos of some of the plants to illustrate a book on world flora or some such thing. He was about to head towards Blue Bottle to get some photos with his very expensive Leica equipment. He wanted to have Picacho as a backdrop. I offered to guide him up to the ridge viewpoint. It was a glorious blue-sky day.

He knew just about every plant we passed—at least to genus. I was making notes on my tape recorder. It was a super learning experience. And I was able to make a few suggestions thanks to Dick's list.

And on the way up we came across 3 or 4 nice boletes just popping up by the trail. I took a couple of fatties. And nearby were two *Armillaria straminea*, or something very similar. I also found two more boletes up on the ridge. So lots of action.

The Aussie—Tony—was from Sydney. He camped here with me and I cooked him a hot meal. We had got back to camp almost at dark. Interesting guy. He'd rented the car "informally" from a Colombian American he'd met in Ensenada.

This morning I took him up to Art's Canyon, and without a cloud in the sky, we both shot the wildflowers there. I took my tripod and again learned so much. The mimulus looked great by the pools and trickling streams. At one point, Tony lost a $1,000 lens for his Leica. We went back up the canyon to find it. Anyway, he left at noon leaving me all inspired about macro shooting the beautiful Epilobiums and Erigerons, Plantagos and Silenes.

It was cold last night, 0°C. But today was sunny and hot. I cut up one of the boletes and again thought it looked a bit "wormy." So that went to the squirrels, and the other I've dried. Hardly had time the last few days to ID the mushrooms.

Thanks for bringing all the supplies down. It has been gratifying to share my bounty with the likes of Alfredo and Tony. If anyone is coming down the only things I need are more film (especially slides) and maybe a little more beer.

I think I'll go for a sunny evening walk with my camera and tripod. Just call me Macromac!

As I returned to my camp—about 6:30 p.m.—the dogs ran off; they heard a truck. Alfredo's entourage was back. I kind of wanted a quiet evening to cook and read, but no such luck. And Alfredo has a shocking cold—he looks very poorly. Even the other folks complained about his sneezing in the truck.

Zarco jumped out and played with Pedro and Penny—hope he's clean. They frolicked while I passed out the chips, cookies and watermelon, and got the fire going. Zarco fell asleep in Penny's basket.

Baltasar's leg wound looks a mess. Alfredo had shaved the wound area—and there were two clear, deep puncture wounds. One was bleeding profusely, and Baltasar was continually licking it. He settled on the towel I'd put down for Pedro. I gave Alfredo six *Cephlax* and instructed him to give Baltasar half a pill a day till gone. I also gave him a first aid packet of Neosporin to apply externally.

So a visit from Alfredo is not for the fainthearted. He's heading down tomorrow for something—and he promised he'd return the following day with some *elotes* to bake on the fire. I'll *Advantage* my guys mañana. I'm with them by the fire—it promises to be another cold night.

I hope I'll be able to get this letter out soon before it grows too long and bores you silly—you get enough of that when you're with me.

Thursday, August 23
Around 11:00 a.m. today I hiked back towards the Aspen Grove with my SLR camera hoping to get some good mushroom photos. Although it was cold again last night (0°C), the day was hot. Not a cloud. Penny and Pedro preferred to spend as much time as possible in the shade. Back at the Aspen Grove there were some wonderful flowers to shoot, but too many of the mushrooms had dried and shriveled. Nevertheless, I got a couple of good shots of puffballs and flammulinas. The dogs enjoyed romping in the little pools and streams there. Pedro really becomes animated when wet!

I've just put them in their "boxes" for the night. Time for me to retire. Hoping for a quiet domestic day tomorrow. Good to see the moon growing.

Saturday, August 25 (Half a Moon)
I got my wish—washing, showering, tidying, reading, etc. And it was another blue sky "scorcher"—just like today. It was so hot today I'd given up on 'shrooms and planned a trip up Art's Canyon to macro all the flowers I'd become familiar with before they all disappear. That changed at 11:00 this morning when two nice Mexicans from Sonora drove over intending to hike up to the [aspen log] cabin. I persuaded them a hike up the canyon to the ridge would be more scenic. Of course, I joined them, at least up to the climb around the side canyon where all the onions are. They carried a small bottle of water and a cooler stuffed with Tecates. As they went on, I enjoyed a beer—ice cold—then set about with camera and tripod. I took photos of pinks, locoweeds, monardellas; then I encountered a great patch of boletes—big ones—poking up. Got

some nice pictures but I only took one, as again they were maggoty inside. In fact, I sliced one open and took some pics of the maggots. I found another bolete on the way down. The Mexicans showed up in camp two hours later. They told me there were some mushrooms fifty yards from the camp. Sure enough, two photogenic bunches of flammulinas had recently sprouted—one on an aspen, the other seemingly on the ground.

The Mexicans obviously appreciated the view from the ridge; they brought me a bag of ice, some tomatoes, and five gallons of water, including the container.

They told me they'd spoken to a ranger who said the army had found a marijuana plantation yesterday and destroyed it. I remember an army helicopter was "searching" yesterday. Maybe that's why I haven't seen Alfredo since Wednesday? He sure left me with the impression that he would soon return with corn for baking on the fire.

Two other points: a huge branch crashed down in the Cathedral this afternoon, big enough to floor an elephant. It landed right where Andrew pushed over the tree. Also, walking around this evening I found another couple of fat, juicy boletes close to camp. They're just popping through the dry needles—surprise, surprise…but no sign of a fly agaric.

Wednesday, August 29

The gorgeous weather continues. I've forgotten what clouds look like. And still no sign of Alfredo. I wonder if his parents took ill and he took them home to Sonora?

That five gallons of water those Mexicans left on Saturday is turning out to be very precious. I haven't obtained any other water since we went to the observatory—but Mister Frugal here still has a total of about 12 gallons. I can probably stretch that to the weekend. Otherwise I need something or someone to turn up.

The dogs are still enjoying themselves immensely—that little Penny never stops running. She's so funny. And Pedro remains the dependable, obedient one that helps keep her in line. He still insists on his chair by the fire.

I've been up to the ridge twice since Saturday and I've been amazed by the number of boletes. Also, higher up the less maggoty they seem to be. I took one nice clean cap down and fried it with a few wild onions—lots of vitamins I'm sure.

Down closer to camp, I've found a few mushrooms, but now it's so hot and dry I've almost given up till the next rain. I did find a group of medium sized mushrooms crisp and dry under a pine. They have black gills and white stalks. The caps are gray but suggest they were at one time brown and "shaggy." I'm inclined to think they are shaggy manes—*Coprinus comatus*.

But my only reservation is I wouldn't describe the gills as packed like pages in a book. So it might be something else in the inky cap family? The gills don't quite reach the stalk, but end in a smooth ring.

Chapter 28

Golden State

…our life, exempt from public haunt,
Finds tongues in trees, books in the running brooks,
Sermons in stones, and good in everything.
— Shakespeare – *As You Like It*

Late August was a delightful time in the mountains. It had taken a while but I felt as if the journey was coming to fruition—as was the season. I seemed to be physically and mentally sharper. The dogs were more under control, trying real hard to be accommodating. I was less uptight about them harassing the cows, or any other wildlife—their sins were venial. I felt trusting about my situation and relaxed with everyone I met. The nuisance flies had disappeared. The storms seemed to be diminishing. I was convinced that there were few if any serpents in my Garden of Eden, at least not rattlesnakes.

I relished the peace of the forest and the sense of the sacred it conveyed. I relished the company of my companions. Beyond all ambitions for writing another book and thoughts of tomorrow, I just enjoyed our times together, simply living for the moment in camp and on the trail.

I loved the energy of the cold, clear mornings when we'd run around to keep warm and follow the paths of morning light through the trees into the sunny meadows, frolicking over the early frost on the fallen pine needles.

It was usually a healthy start to the day. I'd cover a mile and a half while drinking from my large lidded mug of decaf coffee. Penny probably covered twice that distance and Pedro three times as much as they chased one another and whatever grabbed their fancy, and jumped over everything in their way.

When I stopped to take a sip of coffee, I would look around, scan the forest, the meadows, and the slopes…not in the tense, semiparanoid way of earlier days, looking for coyotes, mountain lions or whatever—but simply glorying in the fact that I was happy, healthy, and alive. I was watchful and alert at some level, but those feelings were now deep down and not intruding on my joy.

Penny and I were losing weight—as we both could afford to do—without the least effort because of our active lives. Pedro—how proud I was of his speed and athletic talents—could eat heartily and stay the same old slim, sleek, tight muscled self.

I started picking up objects of interest such as skulls, other bones and horns and taking them back to decorate the trees and bushes around the camp. It was a rare excursion into the woods that didn't result in a few trophies.

Wealth was everywhere. For a pittance I'd found paradise. It was the same with all my long lonely journeys—the point would come when having gone though the stresses and trials, fears and doubts, I'd at last feel whole, complete, relaxed, tuned-in, needing no one, but basking in every warm and giving human, animal, and spiritual encounter.

With mind uncluttered, and heart untroubled, and no one pressuring or haranguing me, I found it so easy to drift into dreams and meditations, and to commune with the vibes of the forest.

As I was walking today, I was spontaneously singing, 'America the Beautiful,' really sincerely, in a meaningful way.

Sitting beneath the large aspen partially shading my sleeping tent, I closed my eyes in the warm soft breeze and listened to the movement of the leaves and saw their shadows dancing before my lids. It seemed almost like a movie, an unfolding story that I couldn't quite understand.

Every sound leapt from the great silence like shooting stars in the dark: the odd bee droning by, the far off cawing crow, the buzz of a hummingbird drawn to the red bandana around my neck—beak almost in my ear.

Then as the wind rose gently, the aspen leaves sounded like a babbling fountain—so, so peaceful. I found myself whispering respectfully like I was in a church. And again I thought I heard singing! I opened my eyes and all the leaves looked like little quaking hearts shot through with a green and golden light. What home or palace or mall could be more beautifully decorated or filled with lovelier music…what drug-induced trance could be more satisfying?

I saw a bright green fly silently hovering two inches from my wristwatch. I moved my hand slowly toward it and it backed away;

then I pulled my hand away and it came forward, as if it were attached to me. It was a healing joy to have time for such simple observations and meditations; to be so, so relaxed.

The wind gusted up producing a wild vortex of air above my campsite. A hawk appeared ("not a red-tailed, it was whiter and lighter") gyrating and diving and rising. One of its large feathers came floating down into the clearing. Pedro seized it as cleanly as if I'd thrown a dog biscuit.

Hardly had his paws reached the ground when Penny showed her own skillful timing by snatching the feather from his mouth. She then ran up to him, practically tickled his nose with it, and sure enough the chasing began. Penny dropped it and Pedro picked it up, pulled back a little, and invited her to come get it. As so often it all got resolved in a tug of war.

> These are delightful times—moon big, sun warm, fresh air, no sign of a storm, even my shortages are a delightful challenge. Idyllic.

> When Penny thinks life is getting a bit dull she'll just run right up to Pedro and launch a sneak attack, jumping on his back or grabbing a leg in her mouth. Sometimes she'll go running at Pedro full speed, head down, charging, and just bowl him over; then she'll grab his leg or tail and get all growly. She is a terrier, she may be little but she's not going to give up. It's in her genes, and Pedro is a wonderful foil for it. He takes it in good grace.

One night by the campfire, Penny became the "victim." She was clipped to her line and slumbering soundly in her basket. I stood up from my chair to dash back to the "kitchen" to get something and my foot accidentally caught the line; poor Penny was dragged from her slumbers in shock and bewilderment. I had to laugh even as I was trying to comfort the poor girl and get her back into her basket. As I looked into her bemused little eyes I had one of those tender, joyous, "living for the moment" moments. She is such a sweetheart. From her basket, she was watching my big feet very carefully when I came back to the fire.

Hiking was our shared joy. Few sunny mornings passed without us ranging far off into the forest—usually up towards the eastern ridge. We tried a few different, speculative routes and found some great new viewpoints of Picacho. It was challenging but not impossible off trail. Time after time I led the guys up into a maze of granite outcrops, fallen trees, and seemingly impenetrable patches of manzanita, ceanothus, and scrub oaks; although we had to think about it a few times, we always found a way through or around.

I learned to be deliberate and careful of each step when walking sideways on the steep slopes. Not only were the dry pine needles treacherously slippery, but my boots would sometimes catch in bushes whose thin branches were as tough as string, and I would find myself falling with a sensation of having my bootlaces tied together.

Many of the more open slopes were a mass of fragrant rose sage. Traversing one, with locoweed bladders popping beneath my feet, I turned around and there was Penny, eagerly panting, tongue out, sun shining on her little happy face, tiny and adorable amongst the big trees.

A short while later I watched Penny coming down a slope after a lizard, running through some snowberry bushes, twisting and turning like a crazed skier on a downhill run.

I didn't need to give too many verbal commands anymore. I preferred to whistle instead. When I did so, they knew I was asking them to come or change direction. Usually they figured out my intention; a wonderful rapport had developed between us.

I watched Pedro and Penny taking off up a rocky slope into the forest and disappearing. In the early days I would have assumed they would never come back. Now I just walked on and sat on a warm rock and whistled for them and they came romping enthusiastically towards me. Penny climbed up on a rock, real high, and was about to jump down; I just grabbed her around the chest and dropped her to the ground. She is such a tactile little thing, it is kind of fun to pick her up and hold her.

We passed a two-foot-deep rock pool. Whereas Penny was careful not to get her little pink claws wet, Pedro would happily walk in up to his neck to take a drink. And when wet, he got real frisky and playful and would throw his lanky limbs all over the place in an effort to corral and drag an uncooperative Penny into the water. It was as if he sensed that water was the great leveler between them.

A deer appeared 75 yards in front of us. The dogs gave chase. I called and whistled them back. Pedro came first, then Penny in her own good time—the normal pattern. As they couldn't catch the deer, they weren't averse to sampling a little fresh deer droppings, which looked like slightly larger rabbit pellets.

Thirty minutes later, I saw another deer 100 yards in front; I didn't want the dogs to spot it and run off, so I held their attention by suddenly stepping to the side, shouting, and flapping my arms like a deranged condor.

> Sometimes these guys surprise me. I was walking along, eyes fixed on the ground, with the dogs twenty feet in front, then I looked up at a woodpecker; by the time I looked down again both dogs seemed to have gone an impossible distance away and be standing on top of a log. How did they get there? Did they fly? At such meditative moments, time itself just seemed to fly and reality appeared disjointed.

> I am looking at a fir that has fallen and it's wedged between two other firs; so many trees don't make it to the ground, they are supported by others in a precarious state.

As soon as we reached the ridge Pedro would 'excavate' a place to lie down and sleep; he would typically lie on his side and be dead to the world in no time. Whereas Penny would stare seemingly in wonder across the canyon intrigued by the violet green swallows cutting, turning, and swooshing along the canyon sides. She always sported the most thoughtful, philosophical look on her wind blown face. Then when she decided it was time to rest she would just stretch out and lower her belly to the ground, and when she tucked her little front paws under her chest she looked amazingly like a sea lion basking on the rocks.

Her tail now looked less like a branching pine tree, and was more full and autumn fluffy. She was also going gray on her legs and the top of her head and tail—belying her mere ten-month earthly existence. She was almost looking as much gray as black in places.

Surveying along the ridge, I could see little autumn patches of gold where the aspens were thickest. And the shady rock faces, certainly the north facing ones, were generally luxuriously covered and decorated with lichens. When I rested beside one, I found myself drifting into its mural of yellow, green, silver, and brownish red. I readily identified with the tiny bugs crawling in those colorful mountains, canyons, and forests. What worlds there were all around...all I had to do was knock and enter.

Penny got up with me to go, whereas Pedro being Pedro was less keen to interrupt his break. We had to walk forty yards before he raised more than his head and came after us.

On the way down, Penny jumped up on to the four-foot-wide fallen trunk of a tree; you wouldn't have thought it possible. She just managed to claw her way on top and run along it. Pedro and I joined her, then all three of us skipped down a slope of fallen trees like life was a jolly game of snakes and ladders.

It was always good to return to camp, to grab a cold soda or make a mug of tea, then sit among the dry golden pine needles on the forest floor, admiring the yellowing aspens against the blue sky.

It was a magical time. And at its magical best, I had no more ambition than just to camp and walk for the rest of my life, to find home and companionship on the spiritual trail, to die with my boots on.

Chapter 29

With the Worms

Beast, brute, bastard. O dog my God!
— George Barker

Bonni and Andrew came back up just before sundown on Thursday, August 30. They came with our friend Suzy, her fourteen-year-old son Zak, and their boxer-mix dog, Coco. Suzy had driven up in her new silver Subaru all-wheel-drive station wagon.

While the dogs got to know each other, and Andrew showed Zak his campsite home for the next four nights, the ladies handed me a can of Dutch beer and filled the campsite with a beautiful, bubbling energy as we settled by the fire.

Suzy's journey up had not been entirely smooth, but she told of her difficulties with great humor. She was following Bonni's truck through the main drag in Ensenada and not wanting to fall behind and risk being separated, rolled through a stop sign as just about every Mexican north of the South Pole was doing. Then by some miracle of national selection a police car with flashing lights appeared behind her—the poor "gringacita" in her shiny new Subaru. As Suzy pulled over, Bonni realized the situation, parked in a restaurant parking lot and walked back with a copy of the letter of support from the Secretary of Tourism.

The policeman, a polite portly fellow, stepped out of his car and asked for Suzy's license and registration. He then got back in his car, called her over, and began chastising her for breaking the law, emphasizing what a serious thing she had done by not coming to a complete halt at a stop sign. He offered her a choice—"follow me to the station to pay a fine," or for convenience she could put the money into a blank business envelope, put her name, address, and phone number on the outside, seal it, and in two weeks she'd be sent a receipt.

"How much is the fine?"

"$35."

At this point Bonni politely interrupted and showed him the letter from the Secretary of Tourism, and said they were on their way to the San Pedro Mártir to re-supply me. The letter had already got her out of a couple of military searches on the highway. Unfortunately, the smiling officer insisted that justice needed to follow its sometimes painful course and, if she didn't want to put the $35 in the envelope, she would have to follow him to the station and deal with it there. It was a choice most American tourists wouldn't think twice about.

Bonni, however, was inclined to go...but Suzy wanting to have done with it, preferred to pay. She found $30 cash in her purse and got $2 from her son, then asked, "Is this okay; it's all I've got."

"Sure, sure, just put it in the envelope," the policeman said while gesturing that he didn't want to touch the money.

Suzy sealed it, wrote on the details, and handed the "fine" to the officer. He smiled and while he was wishing her a safe and pleasant journey, Bonni leaned into his car and asked if she could write down his name and number. The cop gave a different name and number from that on his badge. When it was obvious that Bonni was writing down his real name and badge number, he went tearing off into the traffic with his lights flashing and his siren going.

Suzy lamented, "I got freaked out; I could have just given him $10 or $12, and said 'Señor this is all we have.'"

Bonni added, "I think that the karma he paid that evening worrying about what we were going to do with his tag number was probably worth it."

Bonni recalled that the officer had said that he loved the San Pedro Mártir and commented about how precious and wonderful it was. Bonni joked, "He has got something in his favor, he does appreciate nature. He's probably one of those guys who comes up here, craps all over, and throws toilet paper on top of the ground."

Suzy had also had a flat tire just inside the park. The tire had been cut through the main tread area by a sharp stone. Zak had been able to temporarily fix it with Bonni's plug-in-the-dash air compressor and one of those inflation/self-sealing sprays—"elephant snot," Suzy called it. The repaired tire just managed to carry them the ten miles to my camp—no wonder they were celebrating.

Coco seemed to enjoy bounding around with Penny and Pedro, but after dark she started obsessively chasing any moving flashlight beam. Luckily, there was an almost full moon, so we needed less light. Otherwise I think I would have been driven nuts by this Gollum-like companion constantly scurrying before me.

Suzy had brought up a small tent, which her son put up for her; but Andrew and Zak slept that night in the station wagon rather than in Andrew's tent, which was still up awaiting him.

Next morning, while the teenagers slept, we adults walked the dogs and saw all the local sights. Then, after breakfast, we set off up to the ridge with Andrew—Zak wasn't quite ready to leave the car. But after five minutes Andrew dropped out with a sore ankle. Bonni sent him back to Zak with some ibuprofen.

As we hiked on, Suzy said, "Zak had some qualms about coming because he's so used to playing with his computer all the time. He has built a computer. He is on line all the time with his friends; it's his lifeline, he lives a virtual existence. The night before we left he stayed up all night on his computer. Next morning he said, 'I don't know how I'm going to survive without a computer. Maybe Graham has one?' I warned him, 'I don't think so.' So he decided he'll just hang out and read a book on cosmology. He's into physics and theories of the universe."

Half way to the ridge, Bonni suddenly screamed and dropped to her knees. "It's *Leccinum insigne*," she shouted.

"What!" I replied, unsure whether to whip out my machete or first aid kit.

"It's *Leccinum insigne*…an aspen bolete."

A handsome mushroom was poking through the pine duff. It had a relatively small orange cap on a long, brown-scaled, whitish stalk, and was a good edible that Bonni was sure she'd find there among the aspens. She was looking forward to trying it.

Suzy showed great determination in making it to the ridge, and we shared her excitement at the stirring view of Picacho del Diablo and beyond. Although it was entirely gray over the mountains, we looked down on blue skies over the desert and the sea, except where a towering, billowing cloud seemed to be melting into the ground as a column of water was falling in flash flood quantities beneath.

When we returned to camp, Zak was still asleep in the car. He spent most of the day in there. Suzy said, "I think that is where Zak feels most comfortable, in the car. It's his connection to civilization."

I added, "We might all be in the car later if there's a big lightning storm."

Bonni drove Suzy, Suzy's tire and my empty water containers to the observatory where she solicited help from one of the mechanics that we'd met with Armando. He permanently plugged the damaged tire and helped them fill about six or seven five-gallon containers.

Although he didn't want to take anything, Bonni thanked him profusely, shoved a 12-pack of Pabst beer in his arms and a 100-peso note in his hand, and insisted he have a great weekend with his friends. On the way back, Bonni had pulled over at a promising mushroom spot. A little while later, Alfredo and his brother-in-law Andrés happened along. Alfredo had brought a huge sack of corn that was grown on his *ejido*—and was coming to offer it to us as a present, suggesting that we cook it up. Bonni invited them over to join in our barbecue.

They'd also brought Baltasar, and he was soon harrying Coco trying to assert his dominance. She was having none of it and started growling at him. We needed to keep them apart. As Baltasar was wandering freely, that meant Coco had to spend a lot of the evening in the Subaru.

Suzy took some of the corn from the sack, shucked the leaves, and then saw that nearly every one she opened had two or three fat, half-inch long, slug-like worms astride the kernels.

I brought one over to Alfredo and Andrés. They said we didn't need to peel back the leaves; we should just put the corn on a grill over the coals and let it cook.

"With the worms?" I asked.

Alfredo replied, "The worms, the corn. *Es lo mismo*. It's the same!"

Now in one sense that was a great truth—but they certainly weren't the same in my mind.

While Suzy placed the unopened corn on the grill, I stripped, de-wormed, and carefully washed my corn, and grilled them "naked." But I had to confess the stripped corn cooked up hard and dry, while the corn in fat worm juice was much more succulent and flavorful. The worms had miraculously disappeared beneath the charred leaves.

I alone seemed to be squeamish. I ate just a symbolic nibble of the good stuff then hid the uneaten portion thinking it would make a great dog chew in the morning. I made up for my loss by tucking into the other items the ladies had worked so hard to prepare—chicken, carne asada, fish, potatoes, and salad.

I offered Alfredo some wine. He was reluctant to have any, but nurse Bonni said it was medicine for his lingering cough. In deference to medical science, and no doubt influenced by the way we were chugging back the beer, he then slowly worked his way through much of the bottle.

When I asked about an army helicopter I had seen a few days before, Alfredo confirmed that the helicopter had spotted seven pot plantations on the other side of Venado Blanco, a high peak north of the observatory. Soldiers had then come in, uprooted and supposedly burned all the plants. I was cynical. Alfredo and Andrés joked that the diligent Mexicans were growing all this pot in Baja, and most of it was bought by Americans and there was none left for the Mexicans. So it seemed to me, the soldiers might rationalize not burning the entire crop and keeping a little for themselves.

Suzy mentioned the extent of marijuana cultivation in northern California, how it had become an industry and a problem—and I joked that all that crop was being bought by the Mexicans so there was none left for the poor Americans. They laughed. But at Suzy's tale of paying *mordida* in Ensenada, they were seriously saddened and said such corruption affected Mexicans too.

Alfredo and Andrés left us looking like they'd had a very jolly evening and said they would try to be back soon.

Saturday afternoon, we left the teens—who seemed to be finding their forest feet—gathering firewood around camp, while we went looking for mushrooms along the Tasajera road. We parked among the aspens by the locked gate, near where we had seen the remains of the calf. How wonderfully different it was from July 4. Almost everywhere we walked there were red-capped fly agarics popping up—many in little photogenic groupings. There was no need to pee on them for photographic enhancement as it was soon pissing down with rain. I didn't hear any singing but the emergence of this crop merited a full choir.

There were other mushrooms pushing up on trees, beneath trees, in the meadows, everywhere we turned. Bonni was ecstatic. What a pity her mushroom group hadn't seen this bounty. Bonni and I searched diligently for the best specimens to take to camp to identify and taste. We were too wrapped in our 'shrooming to care about the torrential downpour or the odd crashing message from Parjanya—the god of the Lightning-bolt.

But poor Suzy looked very unenthused under her umbrella. She had that "I've been kidnapped by maniacs" look. She couldn't understand how we could be so relaxed, picking mushrooms to eat, in the middle of a storm, with the road flooding, and the kids back in camp alone.

When we returned all was well; our campsite had hardly received a sprinkling compared to what we'd experienced three miles away.

Suzy was probably even more horrified when Bonni, consulting her books to identify a large brown mushroom that we'd found growing on the ground, decided to try a taste. "It's okay as long as you don't swallow," she said.

After confidently declaring that it couldn't be a lactarius or a russula, she studied the gill pattern and concluded that it had to be a "Poison Pax" (*Paxillus involutus*). David Arora described its edibility thus:

> Not recommended. It is poisonous raw, and people who have eaten the cooked mushroom for years can suddenly develop a serious allergy resulting in kidney failure or even death.

The next day, Sunday, Suzy took the boys over to see the observatory, while Bonni and I stayed in camp, enjoyed a shower and a little time alone. I was amazed to see that right where my shower bag had been watering the ground, another *Leccinum insigne* was confidently thrusting up from under a reclining trunk. I thought of plucking it and bringing it to Bonni as a gift but instead I led her over and she had the thrill of seeing it in its natural glory…and I relived the joy of hearing her squeal with delight.

Later that afternoon, we found several fly agarics around the campsite, including one magnificent eight-inch specimen, and some more flammulinas growing in cute little matchstick-like bundles perfectly reminiscent of their cultivated enoki cousins—they ended up decorating and flavoring a delicious miso soup.

Bonni, Suzy and the others were leaving the morning of September 3. I got up at dawn to let the dogs out and pack some things for Bonni to take home. With less than a month left, I had a good idea what I could do without.

It was a bright sunny morning, and by seven everyone was up busily packing and loading. A hectic two-and-a-half hours later I was once more "alone" in the whispering quiet of the forest, my usual temporary sadness alleviated by two coolers full of bread, beer, milk, fruit, meat, chocolate and other treats. I was determined to make the most of the next three or four weeks.

Chapter 30

Like Orion

...the autumnal star, whose brilliant ray
shines eminent amid the depth of night,
whom men the dog-star of Orion call.

— Homer — *The Iliad*

It remained a gorgeous blue September day. The temperature climbed to 80 degrees. I derived considerable satisfaction from simply tidying, rearranging, and drying out the camp...and watching Penny and Pedro, of course.

When Pedro is content to be lazy and enjoy the sun, Penny can sure entertain herself; she'll just run and throw a ball...she doesn't need to play fetch, she throws it and fetches it herself, and inevitably she'll get Pedro's attention, and then the two of them will be at it. It's funny how they look at each other...and one of them will suddenly charge.

It was usually Penny. Then they'd race together on a collision course like two fearless jousters...and if Pedro wasn't nimble enough to step around or leap over Penny there'd be quite a pile up. Penny was a smashing dog in more ways than one.

Alone again, I was looking forward to recovering the delightful, meditative mood I'd experienced just a few days before. During the day I came real close, but after dark, for no particular reason, I found myself assaulted by increasingly serious thoughts.

One night, prior to falling asleep, with several owls hooting and a cow mooing like a distant foghorn, I recorded:

I've been up here 3 months, but now I can see the end of this journey I'm beginning to worry about maybe a late summer tropical storm or hurricane coming up the gulf, and what that might do up here in the mountains. There is no evidence or sign of it, and the more time passes the less likely it is to happen.

Later that night, I woke around 4 a.m. from a weird but disturbingly vivid dream—a crazy man had set off a nuclear explosion. It seemed an odd and incongruous intrusion into my world there in the mountains. Given the way that the thunderheads had been mushrooming like nuclear detonations, I wondered if the sight of those clouds had percolated into my brain...or if the dream foreshadowed a mighty storm to come.

Whatever tension I had felt in the dark night had previously served to accentuate the glory of the morning, but that morning as I watched the bluebirds catching the sunlight high in the pine trees and glimpsed the orangey-red flash of a red-shafted flicker flitting between the trees, I sensed something was missing...something indefinable had left the forest, or at least my appreciation of it.

The evening of September 6 was unusually windy.

It's totally dark now...suddenly the wind just kicked up and I can hear it ghosting through the trees. And the smoke from my fire is going along the ground hitting poor old Pedro mostly; he's up on his chair. I just threw my head back to look into the sky to see if it was cloudy...and as I looked up I saw the stars and then some really bright clouds that were just glowing. 'What's that?' I thought. I can't believe it's anything natural—it's too unreal. As I stood up and turned around I could see the moon peeking above the ridge, and its light had obviously caught those thin wispy clouds.

On the afternoon of September 8—another beautiful, sunny, invitingly meditative afternoon—a group of four people arrived in a blue jeep. They started setting up camp a hundred yards away. Before I spoke to them, my first reaction was a kind of territorial resentment that strangers had encroached upon my space, but the three guys and a gal turned out to be friendly, fascinating, informative people. They were young University of California, San Diego, post grads and lecturers who had come up to climb Picacho del Diablo. Two were fellow Brits, and two were Americans.

The research interest of one of the Americans was ants. He said that the vicious two-tone red and black ants that both Penny and Pedro had learned to be wary of were probably western thatching ants,

Formica obscuripes, which are fairly common in coniferous forests from Canada to Baja California at elevations between 5,000 and 8,500 feet. They bite rather than sting, he explained, and the mounds of pine needles overlaying the nests serve an important regulatory function—worker ants move larvae and eggs up and down inside the mound to keep them at the optimum temperature.

Always glad of an excuse to hike east to the ridge, I led them up the trail to one of my favorite viewpoints and caught up on all the news from San Diego and Britain. As they surveyed the canyon, and the mighty twin 10,000 feet peaks, I could see that they were impressed if not overawed by the climb they were about to undertake. I lent them my detailed map of the peak and the plateau, and suspecting they might encounter more insects down in the canyon bottom, I offered them some repellent.

We raced the dark back. After feeding my guys and grabbing some snacky food, I took the dogs over to their camping area to chat some more. And by the time I led Penny and Pedro back "home" it was too late to bother with a fire. The dogs were in their kennels by 9:15. Thirty minutes later, after paying my respects to the night sky, I jumped into my sleeping bag. Considering what the next few nights would bring, I did well to grab a good night's sleep.

After breakfast next morning, I led the dogs and the four climbers south along the trail through Columbine Canyon and up into and a little beyond the aspen grove. It was hot with a cool breeze—too dry for mushrooms, but otherwise the most perfect day. When it came time to part, Penny was rolling at the feet of her new friends, enchanting them, and reveling in their belly rubs. Pedro was less forward, but happily accepted a few goodbye head pats.

I worried about Penny going after them, so I put her on a leash and retreated more than half-a-mile before daring to release her. It was a delightful excursion, but I was glad to be back in camp, alone again, reading and trying to relax.

An hour later, Ruben came over to inform me that a Mexican construction worker had gone missing from the observatory. He conveyed the sketchy details: the man was maybe 40 years old, wearing a white T-shirt; he disappeared at night, he could have been drunk, he might be a little crazy, he may be injured. A helicopter would fly up tomorrow to begin searching for him.

Even though I spent the rest of the evening alone, my longed-for solitude was now somewhat vitiated by finding myself on edge thinking about the missing man. I had been left with a disturbingly vague picture—I didn't know if he was a poor lost soul wandering out there in need of help, or a madman to be feared.

It was windy and cold. I was staring into the small, burned down fire, studying its pulsing glow like a crystal ball.

It was a losing battle with the frigid wind. I buried the coals and hurried to my sleeping bag. My fingers and toes were so cold I couldn't warm up even with an extra blanket on top of me.

Eventually I fell asleep and at two in the morning I was woken by the noise of the wind raking the treetops. And as I listened, I was sure there was something else outside, something sizeable moving about. Penny and Pedro hadn't raised a bark. Safe and warm inside their kennels, they probably considered themselves off duty, but I had to know who or what was out there.

I went out wearing just a sweater and flip-flops, and clutching a hammer. There was half a moon. It seemed to be "misty" in the forest—not something one could see, but rather a thing subtle and intangible, like heavier air close to the ground.

Turning around by my tent door, I was shocked to see right in my campsite two cows and a large, white bull. The bull was just twenty yards away, nostrils spewing steam. I walked slowly towards him, flashlight beam in his face. His reflective eyes stared back. I shouted and threw my arms up and started hitting a fallen tree with the hammer. The two cows hoofed it up the hill, but the bull just shuffled nonchalantly twenty-five yards, and then stood his ground among the small aspens.

Not wanting to push my luck, I retreated to my tent hoping that was the end of the matter. Sleep had barely claimed me before the sound of invading cattle woke me again. I stepped out dressed as before. And there was the bull, back grazing in my camping area. I went running towards him shouting and waving the rock hammer; this time he took off more purposefully. A fifty yard chase ended when I put my foot in a rotten tree stump. Wearing just flip-flops, I had to shake off all the cold, damp, crumbly, wood chips from my toes. The bull stopped when I stopped. I ran at him again, hissing and slashing with the light beam. As he trotted away, it seemed reasonable to assume that at last he'd got the message.

Back inside the tent, I listened to the radio for a while…and then I couldn't sleep. So I just kept on monitoring the news and the talk shows, and periodically pulling off the headphones and listening.

At 3:45, I was surprised to hear more munching from outside. "Bollocks!" I shouted. I knew it was the same bull. Frustrated and angry, I scrambled out of the tent, picked up my walking cane and threw it at him. It swished through the air like a boomerang. Unfortunately it missed. Then, getting an insight into Penny's mentality, I found myself shouting and running at that bull not caring about anything except him leaving my territory. It took off galloping to the west. As my anger subsided, I could hardly believe I was doing this at almost four in the morning. I was tempted to release the dogs if there was a next time.

Above, in the heavens, as he'd done for countless eons, the mighty hunter Orion was rising in the southern sky to battle his own fierce red-eyed bull, Taurus. While at his feet crouched his two faithful dogs, the constant companions of the chase: Canis Major, the big dog and Canis Minor, the little dog. Sirius, the brightest star in the heavens, is the adamantine nose of the big dog. It is not only intrinsically a bright star, but also one of the closet stars to earth, and it is often called the Dog Star, after Homer's reference to it in the Iliad.

Returning to my tent, I shone the light on Penny and Pedro in their kennels; their big tired eyes seemed to be saying, "You're on your own pal. See you at sunup." I caught a couple of hours sleep and woke with corpse-cold toes. I never really got warm the whole night.

September 10, 2001: I stuck my head out in the morning and there was that chunky white bull just forty yards away. Exasperated, I chivied the dogs out, and after a couple of curving stretches they both immediately gave chase. They were now very much on duty. I never recalled them. Pedro stopped and came back of his own accord, but Penny kept going, chasing that bull, like Orion himself, right across the arroyo, snapping at its hocks.

The bull eventually kicked like a horse and turned around to try to strike Penny with his horns, but that didn't deter her; she kept snapping and harrying till the obdurate creature decided he'd met his match, and if he wanted any peace he'd better hoof it over to Campo Salvatierra. Penny ran proudly back to my open arms, panting, tongue hanging, eager to receive my copious congratulations.

After a well-deserved breakfast, Penny stretched out to glory in the morning sun. She was my Canis Minor, my little Miss Martial, my Nergal, my she-wolf. As I looked at her in her basket I thought that she had come to me like a boisterous bouncing daughter of Mars drifting on the Tiber, or an effervescent baby Moses eagerly rowing his basket down the Nile.

I recorded:

> If anything happened to Penny I would be so upset…I would
> be upset if anything happened to Pedro of course. But I see
> him more as an adult, a soldier taking his chances, but with
> Penny though, I see her more as a fun loving child and a
> sweetheart, like a beautiful daughter, so it would be more
> tragic for that reason, although in some ways she is more
> martial and aggressive than Pedro, but nevertheless that's
> how I see them.

I paid my respects to my sunlit cathedral, then led the dogs east to
the ridge and the canyon overlook to see if the UCSD guys were
visible on Picacho. I trained my binoculars on both summits and all
the approaches but there was no sign of them...and no sign of the man
missing from the observatory. I was particularly watchful for vultures
gathering in the sky. It was a beautiful cloudless day. "Sad to see the
sage so shriveled…red has become the predominant color up here
with monardellas, paintbrush, and pinks."

We got back to camp and instead of lying down as they usually do
after a long hike, Penny and Pedro were sniffing around as if
something had really got their attention. And I noticed that the water
I had left in their bowls had almost all gone!

They began staring at a nearby hill. I looked over and was amazed to
see two other dogs. They were about the size of Pedro. One appeared to
be a small-eared, German shepherd mix; the other was a white
nondescript mutt. I looked through my binoculars—they had no collars
but they didn't look particularly flea bitten or famished. Neither Pedro
nor Penny barked or moved, but Pedro's fur rose along his back till the
dogs walked off south in the direction of the road to Blue Bottle. I had
no idea what their story was, but I was glad they had disappeared.

A couple of hours later, however, the "wild" dogs returned,
ambling across the valley, heading towards us on the ring road. I
managed to clip a snoozing Penny to a line, but Pedro bounded over
barking furiously, looking like he intended to attack them.

I shouted, "Pedro…Come! Come!" At which, both the "wild" dogs
took off back up the road.

If they had to pass my camp to return to wherever they'd come
from, I hoped they would detour around us and I'd never see them
again, but having seen them twice, and mindful of how hot and dry

it was, I began to worry that they might be desperately thirsty.

It was a fine evening; I secured the camp a little more than usual then took Penny and Pedro for a walk in the opposite direction from where we had seen the dogs. Back in camp, still tired from my exertions of the night before, I was happy to sit awhile and listen, and look at the bugs in the evening sky—the sunlight caught them like little forest sprites. I could hear voices in the wind, human voices, but there was an ethereal, unreal quality to the sounds, like in a dream. I doubted there was anyone out there.

Events were conspiring to keep me ill at ease. As well as the missing man, I now sensed the presence of the strange dogs somewhere close by. It was hard to know how to react. I decided to wander out a way and leave water in a bowl, but back by my fire I wondered about the wisdom of attracting unknown dogs in case they got into a fight with Penny or Pedro.

I should stop looking around; it's making me paranoid. In the last light I was looking at a fallen tree that had been cut up to clear it from the road to Blue Bottle, and there was something white in among the pieces; I wondered if it was that poor white dog, but looking through my binoculars I could see it was a boulder.

Around ten o'clock, I was drawn up close to the glowing remnants of the fire with Penny hooked to a line beside me. Pedro was already in his kennel.

I'm just about ready for bed...I didn't get much sleep last night. Looking up at the magnificent stars and the Milky Way, I feel glad I got through this evening without dogs and bulls...and just hope I get a peaceful night because I am tired and I had visions of going home. Instead of enjoying this experience I started thinking, "O man I've got to deal with all this stuff"...No way can the dogs harm me, they're too timid, but even so it's draining, like an unknown factor out there.

Inside the tent, I covered my sleeping bag with even more blankets and jackets, so I wouldn't get as cold as the previous night. Under all that weight, I could hardly move.

It's about 11:30...I was woken from a deep sleep by what sounded like the sound of chopping, like chopping wood...and I woke up thinking was that a dream? The wind was kind of gusting in the treetops and I wondered if it had clouded over and some weather had moved in. But it was all starry as far as I could see.

Chapter 31

September 11

Whosoever ye be, death will overtake you, although ye be in lofty towers.

— The Koran

I woke at first light, thankful to have slept well. There were cows outside judging by the sound of twigs snapping and hooves meeting logs. I was glad they hadn't come in the night. The pinyon jays were screeching "like little devils;" it sounded like there were dozens of them doing their early dawn chorus. I unzipped the tent and stepped out. It was 37°F. Penny began making a few halfhearted runs at the cows. They had no intention of messing with her and hurried away.

It showed every sign of being a warm, dry day. After breakfast and walking the dogs, I settled down to read a book called *In the Company of Mushrooms* by Elio Schaechter, a fascinating author who I had the good fortune to meet at the San Diego Mycological Society. He bore a strong resemblance to the older Einstein. I started to make notes— "Pliny the Elder mentions that boletes cure 'fluxes of the bowels,' remove freckles, help with sore eyes, and alleviate dog bites."

Occasionally I would look up and survey the forest—listening, aware, gaining a little intimacy with the wildlife. A woodpecker was tapping loudly half way up one of the pines. A squirrel was throwing himself around with his every chirp.

Suddenly I heard the sound of barking. The "wild" dogs had returned. Penny and Pedro sprang up and sprinted towards them. I was shouting at the top of my voice, "PENNY, PEDRO, COME. COME."

The wild dogs ran. My guys went after them. I found myself wandering northeast through the woods, leashes in hand, alone, with no sign of Penny or Pedro beyond their occasional distant barking.

For several minutes, I was shouting in vain, feeling helpless, vacillating between anxiety and anger. Eventually Pedro returned. Monks of New Skete notwithstanding, I grabbed his collar, threw him on his back, slapped his muzzle, and shouted at him. I was most angry with him because I expected that he at least would respond. I put him on a leash and went looking for Penny. Several minutes later I saw her 200 yards ahead running between the trees with the other dogs who were keeping their distance from me.

Realizing that I was simply driving the wild dogs further away, and Penny with them, I decided to return to camp. It occurred to me that I might never see her again. My voice was strained from all the shouting. I was approaching the campsite, full of self-recrimination, when Penny came bounding up behind me. Although enormously relieved, I threw her on her back shouting, "Come." I chained both my guys and then I went back into the forest looking for the other dogs. Penny and Pedro howled and whimpered to join me, but for once, I was not moved by their entreaties.

As I thought about it, Penny seemed to have befriended those dogs; they seemed to be more interested in playing with her than hurting her. My first reaction had been to wish that they would just disappear, but now after seeing them three times and sensing no danger from them I felt involved and concerned.

If I befriend them, I have enough food, I have plenty of medications—worming tablets, dip, Advantage. If they're friendly guys, I could possibly help them out without compromising my guys. Maybe Penny could bring them in.

We started for the ridge later than I intended—just before noon. I left out a bowl of dry dog food and a bowl of water. We ascended, off trail, along the sunny north slope of one of the valleys running due east. We walked through manzanita and yuccas, climbed over lichen-covered, reddish, gold, and silvery metamorphic rock. It was a struggle, but it was more rewarding than following the same old path. The air was perfumed with the lemony scent of poléo, *Monardella linoides*, and there was a profusion of goldenrods, Mexican pinks, and *Linanthus melingii*.

The final ascent was steep enough to help me appreciate how the UCSD guys might be feeling if they were climbing Picacho at that moment. We reached a great viewpoint atop a magnificent rocky spur. I took a series of panorama photographs of the scene before me, from the desert and the head of the Sea of Cortez in the north, along Diablo canyon, up to the twin peaks, and over to Blue Bottle.

These dogs must think I'm some kind of mountain worshipper because every time I come up here, all I tend to do is look at the peak.

While I was doing that, Penny started growling at something on the forested slopes below. She could see something I couldn't. There was a dizzying hundred-foot drop before her. I held her in case she was tempted to jump off.

Before heading back down I picked a handful of poléo plants to make tea—I was running out of milk and didn't much like black coffee. Approaching the tents we were greeted by a terrific buzzing, and found ourselves engulfed in a passing swarm of bees. Otherwise nothing was amiss in the camp; the food and water were still there; nothing had been touched. After Penny and Pedro settled for their afternoon nap, I made my late lunch and continued reading my mushroom book.

The evening was warm. Penny, Pedro and I walked together towards the Salvatierra campground. A host of unusual wispy clouds drifted high above—they were boiling inside and the wind smoothed over their tops producing an impression of flowing hoods or veils, and some looked like white angels in flight. It was enough to make me feel a change in the weather was likely.

I returned to camp with a couple of large crooked logs balanced on my shoulders for firewood. In a moment of frivolity I held them, one in each hand, above my head like Thor or Parjanya about to unleash his bolts.

Even as we settled for the night, Penny was still growling occasionally, seemingly at nothing. We were all on edge. At one point, both dogs took off barking, searching in vain for the source of our malaise.

I was sitting by my fire reading; it was probably about 8:30 p.m., when there was a terrific crash. It sounded like from the direction of the road or the valley slightly to the west. You can probably hear the dogs still barking away. It made me jump and it certainly made them jump. I'll see if I can find out what it was tomorrow, but certainly something, a big tree…or a meteorite…came down. Boy, we were all jumping out of our skins. And we've got old Penny growling away—she's still growling. You tell 'em Pen. I think I'll put more wood on the fire in case there are aliens coming towards us; Penny certainly thinks so…Well all's quiet now. A little bit ago, I looked up into the sky, and immediately I cast my eyes up, there was this shooting star, and it was just drifting slowly across the sky…leisurely in its course across the heavens.

After the scare with the falling tree, I couldn't relax and concentrate on reading, so I picked up my Walkman and began scanning the airways.

Well, I've just been catching the news on the radio about the attacks on the Pentagon and the World Trade Center…just amazing the consequences and ramifications of what seems to have taken place. Just like Kennedy being shot or Pearl Harbor or something on that scale…Pedro is in his kennel; I'm going to put Penny away, and then I'll get into the tent and listen and catch up on what's happening.

It's just so shocking and sobering; it kind of makes everything else, my life, this trip, my [residing] in the United States, everything, suddenly seems in a new light; I feel such a great sympathy for the country to have been so attacked. It's just terrible. I was listening to the radio and suddenly Penny started barking in her cage, and that's something she doesn't often do; in fact I don't remember her doing that at all. So that got me out with the light, looking around….There was nothing out there I could see, so I've come back into the tent to listen to some more news. The time now is just gone midnight, and I'm sure this analogy to Pearl Harbor is going to be overblown. In some ways it is such a different thing, but in one way it is a day that will live in infamy…September 11, 2001.

After falling asleep about 2:30, I slept right through to seven o'clock.

What an incredible night…the world is not quite the same today as it was yesterday morning…What a calm and peaceful day it was here, and how beautiful it was at times; and I was ignorant about what had happened…The only good thing that might come out of this is that everyone is going to come to their senses and solve this Middle East situation. It seems ridiculous that squabbles about territory between Israel and the Palestinians can bring in the United States and make Americans so vulnerable...and I hope the U.S. puts pressure on both sides...we can't just give Israel a blank check. This has to stop. It makes me so angry to think that the United States has made all these enemies in backing Israel and if Israel is not going to act sensibly then the United States as far as I'm concerned once they bring the people who did this to justice and any countries that supported them to some kind of justice then Israel needs to be told to compromise and settle. I'm not sure Sharon is the guy to do this, but that's my feeling at the moment, that there is a bigger question here and once justice has been rendered to the unspeakably evil people who did this and the people who are behind it—the financiers and master minds like Bin Laden or whoever—then there is a bigger question: the conflict in the Middle East has to be solved. If that means putting pressure and a bit of reality on Sharon and Israel, then so be it. Last night I listened to both Sharon and Arafat offering condolences...and I must say with both of them it sounded extremely hollow, and I was not convinced by either side...The other thing I thought about was the failure of intelligence on this and all that money that Bush and his government are proposing to spend on this missile defense scheme. And when you build this Maginot Line in the sky, people are going to get around it however they can, and if that involves putting nuclear weapons on Jumbo jets and flying them into New York it will be done, so this whole business is very questionable when you consider how that money could be better spent on intelligence and other aspects of the military and a thousand other great uses. I hope that policy is going to be reassessed.

I took the dogs for a walk to find the fallen tree—there were several candidates. The most likely one was a giant ponderosa that had started to fall but had dropped against another giant—their branches intertwined like locked arms—it looked like a wounded soldier held up by his straining comrade.

Covered spring at Aguaje   Storm over camp

Graham and Bella

Chapter 32

Accelerating Anxiety

Nothing is apt to mask the face of God so much as religion.

— Martin Büber

Wednesday, September 12: Fortunately, I couldn't get any radio reception during the day, so I had time to digest events and mentally return to my little mountain world. I found a thread-waisted wasp inside the gazebo and resorted to my insect field guide to make my best guess that it was probably a species of *Ammophila*.

Later that afternoon, the UCSD party came back from their attempt on Picacho del Diablo. They had gone up the wrong canyon on Monday, and ended up south of the main approach where they had come across "a pool full of shrimps" and a plaque to a dead climber. After picking up the right trail on Tuesday, they all made it to the peak, where they found, among other things, some cigarettes, a large fishing lure, and a plastic jug of water. They reached the summit around noon and were still up there as I was observing from that rocky overlook.

They said the hardest part had been climbing out of Cañon del Diablo and back up to the plateau. After hearing their stories and sharing in their triumph, I reluctantly broke the news about the terrorist attacks. I invited them over to my fire. I remember telling them that one radio commentator claimed that more Americans had been killed on September 11th than at either Gettysburg or on D-day. As so many of the victims at the World Trade Center weren't Americans, I wasn't absolutely convinced, but to even think in such terms brought home to us the magnitude of the loss of life. Sadly their triumphal return degenerated into a solemn evening.

Long after we had all retired to our sleeping bags, another party came in around midnight, made camp beside the main arroyo and went through all their racket of setting up.

Next morning, the UCSD group left wondering what kind of situation they would encounter at the border. I got chatting to the arrivals; they were Southern Californians who were also attempting Picacho. They tried to convey what they had seen on television, then warned me that rain was coming. When they began putting on their backpacks, I clipped Penny to a cable.

I brought over her soft basket so she could stretch out in comfort. She wanted nothing to do with it until Pedro came over. He's got every place in the forest to settle and he plunks right into her basket. That was enough for Penny—she was immediately on top of him trying to kick him out. And it's the same with both of them. When one notices something—be it a ball, pinecone, stick, or whatever—the other decides that they want it. Penny is probably the worst culprit. "She has her head down to the ground and her butt up in the air in her kind of 'I want to play' gesture. She's a bad girl, but she's a cutie."

Later that day, two hikers with minimal daypacks approached the Padre Kino campsite. They stopped by the wooden signs as if trying to make a big decision. I went down to talk to them. They were a young couple from Belgium. I told them about the ridge viewpoint and then guided them to the trail. It was clouding over; the wind was kicking up in sudden gusts. Rain was very likely. There was an almost electric buzz or hum in the air, like the sound of distant power lines. I advised them to retreat if they heard thunder or if the sky got too black.

I prepared the campsite, securing the tents and gazebo—but the rain held off. I took another hike towards the observatory, looking in the sky for vultures and thinking that Pedro and Penny might be able to find some sign of the missing man. A helicopter was searching the same area. When it passed low overhead, I hid from it and tried to keep the guys still and out of sight. At one point, as we tackled a tough slope, two juncos flashed around us, flying low, corkscrewing through the air like dueling F-16 pilots. Even Pedro and Penny realized that there was no point chasing them.

Returning to camp in the evening, we were overtaken by a large pickup truck full of Mexicans. I thought they were forestry workers or road workers. One of them spoke English, and said they were a mountain rescue team looking for the missing construction worker, who hadn't been seen for five days. They filled in the details of the story. The man was from mainland Mexico. There was a party at the observatory; the man got drunk. While alone at four in the morning he jumped or fell from a second story window. There was blood beneath the window and a trail of it into the forest, but then it disappeared.

After they drove off, I was looking forward to dinner and settling by my fire for the evening listening to the radio. It looked like it was going to be another calm, still night but the wind suddenly picked up sending sparks and hot embers flying from the campfire. I watched them drift into the air like seeds seeking fertile ground and realized I'd have to bury the fire.

To keep warm I led Penny and Pedro through the forest, boldly spiraling away from the campground, edging ever further from my comfort zone, eyes raised to heaven.

> Immediately above there's Arcturus and Spica, and further south there's Mars leaping right out...very bright, and there's at least one bat flying around between the trees.

At last the wind died down and I was able to return to the center of my little galaxy, and spend the evening warming with my buddies around the much-appreciated crackling flames.

Inside the tent, I continued listening to the radio till well after midnight. I nodded off only to be woken at two by the sound of the wind gusting and Penny barking. I heard on the news that there was a storm in the mountains north of the border. Even though the sky was clear in the San Pedro Mártir, I went outside to cover and better secure the tables and tents.

About seven o'clock I was wrenched awake by what sounded like snoring. I stuck my head outside to confirm what I suspected and dreaded—the monster had returned. Baltasar was back. He must have walked over in the night. By the time I emerged from the tent he was up and about, lifting his leg and marking his...or rather my territory. I was caught between my usual sympathy and irritation.

Sensing rain was likely, I made a cozy shelter for him next to the kindling and firewood stashed under the tarp-covered kitchen table. He settled there happily.

By 10:30 it was raining hard, and as the thunder boomed I was scrambling to put on my rain gear, get my dogs in their kennels, and get in the gazebo. I wondered about the guys on Picacho. We had almost half an inch of rain, but the ground was so dry and absorbent it left little evidence beyond the pools on my tarps. When it seemed to be over, I led the dogs into the misty forest and came back to find a junco in the gazebo. I "escorted" him out. He was fortunate the dogs hadn't seen him first.

About 3 p.m. the sky brightened. I filled a bag with some dry dog food and tried leading Baltasar back to Alfredo's shack. Sure enough, he stuck close to me the whole way, more so than my guys who were incessantly chasing the squirrels that were chirping all around. I put Penny on a leash after seeing a coyote bolt across the road. It began to feel like a military operation getting the big fellow safely home and trying to keep everyone in line.

There was no one at Alfredo's. After making sure Baltasar had plenty of water, I put Pedro on a leash too, then scattered all the dry food behind the shack. While Baltasar ran too and fro like a frenzied chicken, I hurried away hoping he would be too occupied to notice that we had gone, or that he would be too tired to follow. I urged the guys up the steep track back to the observatory road, whispering for them to hurry, even dragging poor Penny at one point.

I only allowed them to rest after we'd gone almost a mile. Ranger Ruben drove up while we were sitting under a tree. He was still searching for the man who had disappeared. He explained that Alfredo had temporarily left the San Pedro Mártir, having been assigned to complete some construction and maintenance tasks near Laguna Hanson, in the *Parque Nacional* to the north. He would be gone for ten days. I mentioned that Baltasar was at Alfredo's shack, and asked Ruben if he could watch out for him.

I returned to my camp to find the Belgian couple in the process of leaving me some coffee, oil, and sugar. They said they had to head down to the highway as they were out of food and water. I offered them my water and supplies. Given the momentous events in the world, I was glad of their company; and they too had felt isolated and alone. They said that everywhere they'd been in Baja after September 11 was deserted; they'd hardly had a chance to talk to anyone in the campgrounds and tourist spots. Even so, they couldn't be persuaded to stay. They were packed and ready to leave.

> Being on your own in these circumstances is difficult. You really want to be with your friends, your group, to share the experience and…alleviate the impact of it…but I can see the temptation to jump into jingoism and lord it over the perpetrators and make them regret it.

That night, the dogs were eager to get into their kennels, so I retired early to my tent to listen to the radio and express my feelings to the tape player:

I was thinking about the comments of Christian fundamentalists like Jerry Falwell that the events of September 11 were God's punishment on America...That is so ridiculous...maybe we should send them back to God for a consultation...and we should send some of their brother Islamic fundamentalists back to their God for a consultation too...

Obviously a firm, dramatic response is necessary... With Bush in control people think he's likely to really overact...It's scary for sensible people to step back and think about where this could go. But in a way it has to be. We should be scared, because it should be so credible that the people who did this and the governments that supported them should be scared...I think it's good that there's a guy who scares us a little bit in the White House.

After tuning into the news and talk shows for several hours, I ventured out at 2 a.m. to give the dogs a chance to stretch their legs and go potty, but they were too cozy and comfortable in their kennels to bother. It was cold and damp. When I shone the light around, the wet bushes seemed to glow, especially the little aspens. It was surreal, like there was a light inside them. The forest looked Christmassy.

The next day, Ruben came by and said that the observatory water truck was two miles back down the road filling up at the well. He took my empty water containers and soon returned with about thirty gallons, giving me a very comfortable total of fifty—which ought to be sufficient to get me through till Bonni came to get me.

I gave him more than enough food to sustain Baltasar till Alfredo's return—what an investment to keep him there guarding Alfredo's cabin. We discussed the fate of the missing man. There was still no trace of him beyond the bloodstains and footprints beneath the window.

I was beginning to feel increasingly tired and hangovery, and wondered if the extra drink or two I'd been having every evening since September 11 was accentuating my sadness about the events, depressing me in a kind of downward undulation of mood. I was concerned about a small scab on top of my left ear that refused to heal. It had been there 3 months, and half way down the same ear there was another little thickened scabby area. They both felt warm like they were sunburned or infected. I feared it was some kind of proto-skin cancer. In spite of my best intentions I kept scratching off each scab...and they kept growing again. I toyed with the idea of removing them with every burning, bleaching, caustic thing I possessed.

When the climbers returned late afternoon, the dogs ran to greet them. They had been stormed off Picacho. A mist had descended as they neared the peak, and they thought it imprudent to push on with rain and lightning all about. They were preparing to leave immediately. I wrote a quick note to Bonni saying that I was ready to come home if anyone happened to be coming up with enough room for the dogs and me. She would have the letter in a day or two.

By that action I felt like the end had come, my days were numbered; it was time to use my film and eat and drink as well as I could.

September 16—Mexican Independence Day—I woke and recorded:

It is a time of great danger for the United States and the civilized world, but also a time of great opportunity. More attacks will come if the United States is not resolute and determined. The U.S. should be dangerous; every country in the world should know that if they thwart the United States in its righteous anger at this moment then they are in trouble…And I think we should see it through whatever it takes; the time has come to eradicate this kind of terrorism, and at the same time I just hope that the U.S. says to Israel we need you to compromise and work for true justice and peace. Our backing is going to be dependent on you making a determined effort to make peace and address the grievances of the Palestinians.

More storm clouds were building. Again I felt tired and sluggish. I went back up to the Observatory Ridge anyway—more to burn something from my soul than for the joy of hiking. On top of the ridge, looking at the great thunderheads gathering immediately to the north, I decided to quickly get back to camp. Penny and Pedro hardly had time to lie down and munch a dog biscuit before they were following me in full retreat. The thunder rapidly grew from growls to booms to tangible BANGS. Lightning lit rainsqualls drifted down from the dark bases of churning clouds. I urged on the exhausted dogs. Poor guys…it was like the Bataan Death March. I allowed no stops, no rests, and we only just beat the rain to my campground.

After the rain passed, a red Isuzu Trooper appeared towing a trailer full of carousing Mexicans. Their loud voices penetrated the forest. I secured the dogs. They drove up and asked me if I had seen any deer—but stressed they didn't want to shoot any—and then asked where was the best place to walk. I recommended the ridge hike; they balked at the idea of walking over a mile to get there. One of them raised a liter bottle of beer and declared, "I'm drunk. Everyone in the park is drunk. That's why everyone comes here, to get drunk." They were amazed I'd been there for 3 months…mostly sober. They tried to park down below, next to the arroyo but I heard a loud crash, and then a series of "thunderous" bangs, like they were hitting a rock. Eventually they gave up and went to park what was left of their vehicle and trailer back down the road. They staggered towards Aguaje…voices strident, discordant, funny. I ached to be with people who understood. I was glad when they left forty minutes later.

Monday, September 17: In the morning, before radio reception faded, I listened to the ceremonies on reopening the stock exchange, and to the singing of God Bless America from the floor. Inside the tent, snug inside my sleeping bag, I started singing it too. I stepped outside, still singing. Penny and Pedro were in their cages, beneath the mosquito netting, looking at me very doubtfully.

Next morning, Tuesday, September 18, I heard on the radio that the Dow was down 600 points.

All around the camp the aspens were yellowing in earnest and beginning to shed their leaves. The "wild" dogs hadn't returned and I had given up thinking about them, but I was still too uneasy to sit for long, too in need of action to help still my agitated soul.

After our morning hike, I washed the dogs, wormed them, brushed them, and clipped Penny's coat a little. The little princess basked in all the tender attention.

September 19, I recorded:

> I must come back here with the dogs…This is a spot that will be special to me all my life…And if the world does go to hell in a mushroom basket, what a lovely place to come…I could summer up here and maybe winter down below in the remote San Antonio valley. It will be a good place to ride out Armageddon.

Inadvertently, I started walking the dogs in the direction where some coyotes were silently watching us. I had no idea they were there—neither did Penny and Pedro—till the coyotes suddenly started howling. I counted six of them but I suspected there were more.

Penny was ready to chase them off by herself, but she hesitated long enough for me to unceremoniously grab a big hunk of hair and flesh as she tried to run past me. Pedro had his fur up and started barking. After clipping them both on leashes and hoping we looked more formidable than we were, I walked my guys over to try to drive the coyotes away. One coyote was not inclined to yield an inch till we were close enough to see the points of his teeth, then he skulked away to join his comrades in sullen retreat.

Because coyotes were around, I continued to walk Penny on a leash. She grabbed it in her mouth and ran ahead as if she were taking me for a walk. She was such an irrepressible, exuberant little thing, I'm sure she had convinced herself that the poor man had to stay on his leash today due to those dangerous "dogs."

When I finally did relax enough to unclip her, Penny picked up a piece of dried coyote poop and started running around with it sticking out of her mouth like a caricature capitalist with his big fat cigar.

How my opinion of President Bush was changing. I had always thought of him as a few heifers short of a full herd—a strutting, inarticulate, lightweight propped up by conservative financiers who could rely on his promoting the sectional interests of big tax cuts and removing all regulation and restraint from his big business buddies...while simultaneously foisting on the majority of Americans all the religio-regulations and restraints that right wing Christians advocate.

Even though I still fundamentally believed that, I found myself taping:

> I was just listening to President Bush's speech, looking up at the stars...and it was like his voice was booming throughout eternity...excellent speech. I've been very critical of Bush in the past and wondered if he was the right man for the job, but I certainly think he's going about this the right way, so far, and it gives me hope that something really great will come out of this...the hand was forced, to do nothing was a greater risk than to take action.

Chapter 33
Winning Hearts

*Go ye into all the world, and preach the gospel
to every creature.*
— Luke 16:15

I felt I was being torn apart. On the one hand, I was restless and wired for action. On the other, I was disturbed to see how quickly I tired. My somber, serious mood made all activity, especially hiking, seem more difficult.

While cooking immediately after returning from a long, hard traverse towards Blue Bottle peak, I had a sudden lightheaded feeling and a numb sensation in my left arm. That was followed by a vague sense of indigestion and chest pain. Reflecting on those symptoms brought a surge of shock...and yet further symptoms.

Sitting down, I told myself it was nothing—I was famished, dehydrated, had pulled a muscle, the overloaded daypack had pinched a nerve—but mindful that I was now 50, I started to think the unthinkable. Was I experiencing some kind of heart problem? If I had a car and any decent medical coverage in the U.S., I might have jumped in and headed for the border. As I didn't have transport and my best health insurance was living a healthy lifestyle, I had no choice but to face my fate there in the mountains with the companions that had nuzzled their way into my heart.

The "war on terror" suddenly seemed a few degrees less important. As Penny and Pedro ran to and fro behind me filling the forest with their eager panting and the thump, thump, thump of happy paws, I walked in a large circle around the four trees of my cathedral. Then in the very center, in the spot excavated by Pedro so many weeks before, I sank to my knees, pulled Penny and Pedro to me, then stared up at the mighty horizontal limbs of the biggest of the ponderosas.

The yellowing of the forest and the low angle of the sun cast everything in a warm and glorious light. Pinecone seeds fluttered down in the breeze. The squirrels were busy chewing off the young cones and gathering for the winter. Pygmy nuthatches abounded. Pinyon jays were flocking in the air and on the ground. The scene probably hadn't changed much through ten thousand autumns. I was comforted by its continuity.

With a quarter moon slipping to the west, I recorded that I loved my family and special friends...and then silently recalled my shocking but sincere declaration that I loved Penny more than anything in the universe. Sure, I loved her unbearable cuteness, the way she ran, her joy in freedom, her carefree, courageous sense of fun...and I loved the way she had transcended her miserable start in life, but my feelings went beyond the sum of all that. The rapport with her was a mystery that I couldn't begin to explain, even to myself.

And in the great healing silence of the forest, with the moon dipping gently into the trees, and my body literally tingling with love, there remained one more step on my journey. My heart was opened even to those I least understood and felt the greatest antagonism towards.

I reexamined my gung ho, hawkish leanings. I had no more anger at Bin Laden or anyone. There were enough angry, vengeful people in the world...enough injured seeking to injure...enough aimless souls seeking stature in violence, strife, and conquest. A better side of me proclaimed, "there's a universe of understanding and forgiveness." I was struck by the might of the moral force of magnanimity—to love your enemies, to walk in their shoes. Always to ask: what is the cross I must bear to be a Christian? To ask the question is to know the answer. Do I have the strength and the courage to retaliate with love? Am I ready to risk losing the battle to win the war? Or am I...are we...doomed to find defeat in shortsighted victory...or perhaps even worse, find ourselves in a position of perpetual war—every cheered blow serving to create more enemies and fuel more fanaticism, and bring a little more Hell on Earth. Once firmly planted on that proud narrow road, genocide is, so often, the only and final solution.

If ever a man and a people were chosen to illustrate the futility of such an approach, one need only look at the understandable but shortsighted *real politick* of Sharon and the Israeli security forces in dealing with the attacks of Palestinian zealots and suicide bombers. Meeting every outrage with retaliatory strikes, curfews, assassination, destruction of property, collective punishment, a desire to inflict more pain on guilty and innocent alike than that which you have been subjected to has brought nothing but more anger and violence. No wonder Jesus wept and said to his people during his triumphal entry into Jerusalem: "If only you had known…the way that leads to peace! But no; it is hidden from your sight."

Back in camp I watched a fly in the bowl of soapy water under the fauceted five-gallon water dispenser. There were always dead flies and other flying bugs in there. It had seemed like a good way to keep down their numbers. I'd rescued a few bees and butterflies and pretty moths, but this fly, this "enemy," caught my eye; it was sending out waves like desperate prayer. I watched a few moments, and then I was involved. I lifted it out on my finger, gently washed away the soapy water and left it to dry in a safe place.

The time came to retire to my tent. Realizing that I was alone and might be days without a visitor, I shuddered at the thought of Penny and Pedro being trapped in their kennels if death claimed me in the night. I decided to leave their doors open but placed one-and-a-half-gallon water containers in front of them so they at least seemed closed.

Next morning, the rescued fly was still there standing on the table. As the day warmed, it gained strength and flew off.

I set off on another photo shoot, this time west towards Aguaje. Approaching the ridge between the two valleys, I saw a wonderful composition. On the lower reaches of a slope to my left was a collection of aspens turning golden yellow; above them dark green against the blue sky, the pines and firs leapt out solid and indubitably real compared to their quaking, ephemerally clad brothers. And the mighty sugar pines on the highest granite peaks stood with crowns spread like arms, sheltering and gathering in those below. The wild unsullied scene conveyed a mood of sweet, angelic, God-like protection. Penny and Pedro sat patiently beside me while I sought to capture it on film.

Beyond Aguaje about 300 yards, with scores of jays and crows calling in the tree tops, a mottled bobcat stepped out from behind a rock. Because of the racket from the birds I'm sure it didn't hear us coming. It certainly looked plenty surprised as we all came nose to nose. Luckily Penny was already on a leash as I'd seen a group of cows at the muddy Aguaje spring. Pedro was sensible enough not to give chase; he just looked on.

Back in camp, I was standing naked under my solar shower bag, getting ready to enjoy a hot shower when the dogs started barking. A party of about seven or eight hikers with large backpacks was coming down the road from the direction of Blue Bottle. They plunked themselves down in the shade beneath a couple of trees about 150 yards away. My guys ran over. I had to get dressed and go fetch them. My ambassadors prepared the hikers for my approach. Penny in particular had thrown herself at their feet, wagging her tail and winning hearts with her cheerful favors. The hikers looked to be mostly in their late teens or early twenties. The girls in the group reacted like they'd found a cute little forest teddy bear—they couldn't resist rubbing her offered rounded belly and shaking her stubby little paws. Pedro took a little more convincing—he hung back, never really trusting those big backpacks leaning against the trees and rocks. At least he didn't bark.

These young people were on an extended *National Outdoor Leadership School* (NOLS) course. Founded in 1965 as a private nonprofit school, NOLS operates wilderness expeditions and "outdoor leadership training" in dozens of locations around the world; more than 50,000 students have graduated from their widely respected wilderness education programs.

They were waiting for another section of their party to catch up, and were expecting to be re-supplied there in the Padre Kino campsite in two days. I noticed they were all wearing protective leggings above their boots. "A precaution against rattlesnake bites?" I enquired.

One of the instructors answered, "No, I don't think they'd be much good for that; they're meant to keep out stones, gravel, and sometimes snow from our boots."

He asked me if there was water at Aguaje del Burro. I told him it was green and muddy, and offered them a few gallons of my water if they were desperate.

After chatting a while, I left them to it and returned to my camping area with Penny and Pedro on leashes, then did my best to unobtrusively finish my shower behind a tree as their missing colleagues came in to join them.

Cleaned and almost dressed, I was about to release my guys and go chat with them again when they all picked up their packs and walked off to the west on the trail to Aguaje. I suspected they were going to practice their wilderness skills by treating some of that water and then camp somewhere in the forest.

The group had indeed set up camp just out of sight about 500 yards away. In the early evening, when the wind died, I started to hear their voices...and so did Penny. She took off to pay a visit. I had to grab a leash and go fetch her. Pedro stayed loyally by my side. Sure enough

I found her in their camp playing, being petted, and generally winning hearts.

The NOLS group were scattered around three or four tiny campfires. There was not a tent in sight; it seemed they slept on tarps and used other taut, tree-tied tarps as covers. The instructors stressed "bomb proofing" their camps for all contingencies, so that nothing was likely to rip free or be blown away.

I got talking to the half-a-dozen people whom Penny had latched on to. They were cooking their evening meal of what looked like macaroni and cheese, and said they'd been out in the mountains for almost two weeks. When I asked if they'd heard "the news," they said they had no phones or radios.

"Are we at war?" one of them asked.

I replied, "Well you could say that." Then I told them what I knew about September 11. I first mentioned the plane crashing into the Pentagon. At first, they were joking and didn't think I was serious. But when I became emotional recounting the details about people trapped on the upper floors of the World Trade Center and jumping to their deaths, they knew I wasn't kidding and the word spread around the camp. The others came over to listen and peppered me with questions.

Again, I found myself in the position of apologizing for spoiling someone's wilderness experience. However, they thanked me and then invited me to have dinner with them, but I declined because I had to get back to my untended campsite before it was completely dark. I invited them over to visit me and listen to my radio and share my fire.

Not long after I'd got back and got a warming fire going, a truck approached in the near darkness; it stopped below by the trash bins and the sole occupant walked up to ask if I knew where the NOLS group was. He explained that he had brought mail and supplies for them, and had been due to arrive the next day, but under the circumstances had come a day early.

It was now totally dark and still, and from my slightly elevated campsite, his answer came in the form of a procession of lights slowly snaking through the forest towards us. It was mesmerizing and surreal.

There was a serious conference by the trash bins. The students were told that NOLS had contacted their families and all had sent messages of reassurance, advising them to stay on their courses. An hour later they started to drift up. I soon had a group of about 15 guests around my roaring fire, patting and fussing over Penny and Pedro.

The National Outdoor Leadership School was one of the first schools to promote techniques for treading lightly and minimizing impact on the outdoors. Their wilderness philosophy advocates keeping fires small and only burning sticks from the ground that can be broken by hand. They were very tolerant of my heretical huge fire pit and my six-inch-thick logs.

Two of the guys had family in New York City, and friends and relatives who worked in the vicinity of the World Trade Center. They asked if there was a way to call or communicate with their families. I suggested the observatory. They went over in the truck about 8:30.

I needed milk powder and these NOLS students, heartily fed up of a diet heavy with macaroni, rice, corn meal, grits, and oatmeal, were craving meat. I soon had a few trades organized. The group returned to their camping area about ten o'clock. One of the instructors left me with the newspaper and website accounts of 9-11, and confided that a student on a NOLS course in the U.S. had lost his father on one of the planes and had to be removed by helicopter. I was moved and shocked by the photos, and surprised by the blue sky at the World Trade Center. Although I had imagined the scene so often, not once did I paint in a perfect blue sky.

When the guys who had gone to the observatory hadn't returned by midnight, I crawled into my tent eager for the warmth of my sleeping bag.

I enjoyed a good warm up walk in the morning, just staying in the sun. The NOLS students again gathered down by the trash bins to pick up their supplies and discuss their plans and experiences. Of course, Penny and Pedro went down to join them. And over the course of the morning, I was swapping cans of chili, Spam, beef stew, and Vienna sausages for bags of dry milk, powdered chocolate, grits, and oatmeal.

With the group still sitting around "in conference," I walked the dogs up Columbine Canyon. The aspen leaves there seemed more golden and coppery red than the bright yellow leaves on the trees near my campsite. I climbed up the steep western slope of the valley and over to the Blue Bottle road. Every five or ten minutes, courtesy of the squirrels, another pinecone came thudding to the ground, giving the dogs ample opportunities to run and bark. Mid-September struck me as the ideal time to visit the San Pedro Mártir; it was neither too hot nor too cold, and the worst of the "monsoon" storms seemed to be past.

As we approached the Padre Kino campground again, Penny ran over to the NOLS students, who were still sitting together in a circle, and got loved to death. She was making them laugh so much, I had to fetch her away or none of them would have been attentive to their classes.

The supply truck left and the NOLS party retired to their forest camp. It was a peaceful evening. The comforting sounds of talking and laughing wafted from the west. Wary of Penny's wanderlust, and worried about the bad example she might have been on Pedro, I kept both dogs on their lines as we huddled by the fire. When it came time to retire, I put them in their cages and locked them in, saying reassuringly, "I don't think I'll drop dead tonight."

Penny ever vigilant

Storm clouds over the desert

Chapter 34

The Smell of Death

He deserves paradise who makes his companions laugh.

— Mohammed

September 23: It was a cold Sunday morning. I enjoyed my first milky coffee for a while, not minding that it was made with powdered milk. We headed east for our morning walk. Penny and Pedro had oodles of energy, jumping in unison over rocks, trees and other obstacles. They made me laugh even more than usual. We checked out some cattle bones by a shallow pool in one of the canyons. The victim of a lion? I brought back the horns and a leg—complete with hoof—to add to my campsite decorations.

Approaching camp, Penny, big surprise, broke ranks and took off to the west to visit again with the NOLS group. Pedro stayed with me as I went to fetch her from her new found friends who were in the process of packing to leave. They all seemed in good spirits—especially the guys with their cans of sausages, sardines, and stew. We laughed and joked through a goodbye photo session. They planned to descend into Cañon del Diablo and, weather permitting, climb Picacho; then they would try to follow the canyon all the way down to be picked up in the desert. After marching my little miscreant back to camp, I clipped her to a cable. Given half a chance she would have gone with them.

It's about 2:30 and it's a dreamily unreal Sunday—a beautiful day, cloudless…I was reading intently and suddenly I heard this piercing call above the rustle of the leaves. It seemed like it was somebody calling. I wondered if it was one of the NOLS group, or maybe the whole group, coming back…I stood right over Penny so if she was going to run I'd be in a position to grab her. A little while later I heard another cry…and this time it sounded more like an animal. I thought maybe a cat! And then I saw a large brown hawk or eagle flying down by the signs, close to the ground. It flew up into a tree. My first thought was maybe it will grab Penny. If it did, it will get more than it bargained for. Penny would go nuts...she would certainly put up a good fight.

It was a magnificent fully grown golden eagle. Again, I temporarily clipped Penny on a cable to keep her in protective custody till the danger passed.

Monday, September 24: A windy morning and surprisingly mild— the temperature never dropped below 50 degrees all night. A few clouds were moving up from the south. Alfredo came by with a healthy-looking, boisterous Zarco, and confirmed that he had indeed been posted away from the park to finish a construction job at Laguna Hanson. He explained that Baltasar was now being fed and cared for at the observatory, and that he had taken Zarco to a vet for rabies and other shots and a check up. I was impressed.

And I was impressed with my prescience when Alfredo informed me that there was a major hurricane off the southern tip of Baja, and it was expected to reach the peninsula in a day or two.

That night I heard on a Los Angeles radio news broadcast about the hurricane—Hurricane Juliette. It was described as a dangerous "Category 4" hurricane packing winds of over 140 mph. The storm grew out of the remnant of an Atlantic tropical depression that had moved across Central America on September 19 and 20. In the Pacific, drifting northwest and paralleling the Mexican coast some 200 miles offshore, it intensified and became a hurricane on September 23. It continued to grow rapidly throughout September 24, all the while its track shifting ominously to the north, towards the southern tip of Baja.

Next morning, I began searching around for a safer, more sheltered place to ride out the storm if it made it that far north. Unfortunately, all the alternative sites had too many drawbacks with flooding possibilities and dangerous unstable-looking trees. I had chosen so well, it was going to be hard to beat the campsite I already had. In the worst-case scenario, the bottom line might be just grabbing a few important possessions, squeezing beneath a boulder and simply trying to stay alive. I examined every cave-like overhang among the house-sized granite outcrops, assessing its shelter potential.

Penny and Pedro had things other than hurricanes on their minds. I was watching my "Category 4" Penny about to attack Pedro. She was staring him down, holding one of her front legs off the ground, moving it in little up and down circles as if she was getting ready to charge, as if she was already running in her imagination, and her mouth was opening and closing as if she was already chewing on poor Pedro's throat.

When she pounced, it looked like she had gone berserk. I moved to intervene when it seemed Pedro was really getting savaged. Then my erstwhile pliant Pedro decided he'd had enough of the little idiot and started to give as good as he got. He was chasing Penny, snarling and snapping and spewing saliva like he was going to rip her apart. I silently cheered him on. She surrendered by going into her submissive roll; and as soon as Pedro granted mercy and was distracted, she launched a joyful sneak attack and clamped her jaws on one of his back legs. They were an endless source of entertainment.

Later, I went for a hike up to my favorite Picacho viewpoint. I wanted to get a good "continental" perspective on the weather and see if any of the NOLS group was on the mountain. For the first time I left a note in camp saying where we'd gone. I led the dogs on a challenging route, off trail, over alternating outcrops of granite and metamorphic rocks, crunching over pine needles, pinecones, dry manzanita, scrub oak, and other shrubs. The sky was soon entirely gray but a thunderstorm seemed improbable. I was happy to experience a different energy in the forest, even while attributing it to the effect of a potentially devastating storm.

Although the floral high summer had passed, and most of the rose sage, asters, and wild onions were shriveled and brown, I photographed some fine examples of Mexican pinks, Indian paintbrush, locoweed, wild geraniums, *Linanthus melingii, Ipomopsis effusa* (that pink half-flower phlox), and bunches of poléo, *Monardella linoides*.

Then ambling along, looking for more subjects, with both dogs behind and off to one side, I froze in my tracks when, fifty yards in front, a large, tan-colored animal blurred from one manzanita clump to another. A mountain lion? It was running too fast for me to be sure. The dogs gave no indication that they had seen it.

I gave it a few minutes to get clear if it was so inclined, then duly energized set a vigorous pace using my long machete as a walking stick and loudly urging Penny and Pedro to stay close to me. I checked often that my knife was in its sheath, and thought of the camera and tripod on my shoulder as a club.

The final rise to the ridge was a killer, but on top I recovered my breath, and felt the ache dissolve from my legs as my buddies spread themselves on my offered jacket.

Between wary glances over my shoulder, I noted the unusual mass of cloud edging slowly over the mountains from the south, and peered through binoculars at Picacho del Diablo and the awesome expanse of ridges and canyons leading to it. Some of the now yellowing aspen groves close to the summit leapt out like veins of gold. There was no sign of the NOLS group. I was concerned they may not know about the hurricane. It seemed a strange oversight that they didn't have even a small lightweight Walkman radio to listen to the news. Perhaps that was taking the purity of the wilderness experience a little too far?

While stroking the sleeping dogs and beginning to relax, I discovered that Penny's right shoulder was matted with something damp and dirty and putrid smelling. It looked horribly like a bloody wound. I examined her carefully but it seemed her skin was unbroken.

After pulling Penny off my jacket and away from my backpack, I cleaned the matted part of her coat with baby wipes. Did she roll on top of a partially buried lion kill? I thought of the man missing from the observatory!

Heading back down an hour later, I felt obliged to try to retrace our steps and find the cause of the stench. However, I took a wrong turn, and we ended up on a novel but equally challenging descent. After scrambling her way down a steep cliff face, Penny appeared on a rock at head height to me. I inclined my head to hers and said, "Give me a kiss Penny." I was surprised when she obliged by licking my face.

Halfway down, it was a great temptation to throw Penny in a pool that Pedro was frolicking in. But, as if she read my mind, she kept a safe distance from me and the water.

We got back to camp to see a rogue cow rooting around in the trashcans, tearing open bags and scattering litter all over. In unison we chased it away. Penny did a super job, bravely getting right up to it in spite of its viciously swinging horns. I gathered up and re-bagged the trash, then Penny got her much needed wash. I lathered her coarse, matted coat with scented shampoo till she came up lovely and clean, and smelling like lavender.

My hurricane preparations continued. I took down Andrew's tent and brought up more rocks for weights. I burned papers and boxes. Feeling like a soldier left behind in a hasty disorganized retreat, or like a sailor marooned on a doomed ship, I began eating all my best food and special treats as if there were no tomorrow. I shared a can of salmon with the dogs. Penny loved it, and fully appreciative of the fact that it's an ill wind that doesn't blow somebody some good, was now hanging around my kitchen, brown eyes gazing up from her unkempt face, eager for the next delight.

The sky cleared. The wind gusted. There seemed to be a mass exodus from the mountains with hundreds of pinyon jays and other birds flocking together and heading east. It was as if every living thing was cognizant of the threat posed by that unseen monster to the south.

Mártir mushroom madness

Bonni and Suzy

Chapter 35

A Celestial Alpha Roll

Strike the tent.
— Last words of Robert E. Lee

That night the wind was blasting in a series of tree bending, tent tugging gusts that gave me an inkling of what we might be in for if a 100 mph hurricane came sweeping through.

A hurricane needs to be over warm water to maintain or increase its strength. The waters of the Pacific Ocean off Baja California are relatively cool, so if Juliette drifted northwest into the Pacific it would probably weaken rapidly. If it came straight up the landmass of the peninsula or veered east over mainland Mexico it would also likely soon break apart and dissipate.

The only way that monster could get to us in full force was straight up the summery warm waters of the Gulf of California—which was rarely more than 100 miles across. The danger seemed as remote as a bullet entering the barrel of a cannon and blasting it apart. But even if the full-blown storm didn't reach us, I doubted that we would be entirely spared its ill effects.

Just before dawn, I emerged from my tent with the tall pines still writhing and creaking in the cold wind. Hundreds of aspen leaves bounced along the ground like a plague of frenetic frogs. And high above that earthly agitation, beyond the half-stripped aspens, the constellation Orion and the "Dog Star" Sirius commanded the twinkling, velvety blackness. It was a view more familiar to the winter sky, and left me with the feeling that I should have been long gone from those mountains.

By midmorning, calm had been restored. It turned into a perfect sunny day. Armando García came over from the observatory with a party of backpackers—a group from NOLS that included a cute young lady from Ireland, and another from Australia. They were checking out the place in preparation for supplying a second NOLS expedition coming through in a few days. I told them about the hurricane which was growing in fury by the hour.

On September 25, a U.S. Air Force reconnaissance aircraft flew into Juliette's nine-mile-wide eye and measured a minimum sea level pressure of 923 millibars, or 27.25 inches of mercury. It was the second lowest pressure ever recorded in the eastern Pacific.

They were all surprised to hear about it and Armando kindly offered to bring me to the observatory and shelter me there if necessary. His cell phone rang. He had to leave. The NOLS group went with him. I was disappointed. I'd enjoyed talking to them.

> It's four o'clock and I was just changing into long pants and, as I was doing that, I unconsciously muttered, "Will I be alone tonight?" And I thought of all the wonderful people I've met up here and all the great relationships I've had, and I don't think I've had an unpleasant experience with anyone. How many people could say that after a four-month summer? It has just been a joy meeting all these different people, and perhaps Armando García is right up there at the top.

I was taking Penny and Pedro for the day's final walk. It was quiet and peaceful beneath the big trees. Looking around, a mile from camp, with nothing manmade in sight or impinging on any of my senses, it struck me that I could be in Alaska or the north of Canada. I had to almost force my mind to accept that I was in Mexico, in Baja California.

For two nights I heard no more mention of the hurricane on the radio news. I began to hope that it had swung away from the peninsula; but I was also mindful that the story might have been lost with all the preoccupation with the aftermath of September 11.

Knowing Bonni could come for me any day, for old times sake, and as a duty to the dogs, I knew that I should go for as many "final" walks as the weather allowed, and say my goodbyes to all the familiar places I wouldn't see again for a while.

I squeezed in one more journey to the west, beyond Aguaje del Burro and over towards Tasajera. The wind was blasting again. I needed to secure everything in camp before we left. The sky was totally blue. It was maybe 70 degrees—an ideal hiking day. I walked purposefully more-or-less in a straight line, while the dogs orbited, and figure-eighted almost the whole way.

Penny and Pedro just play, play, play. A junco—Charge. A squirrel—Charge. Cow—Charge. Whatever—Charge...I could easily shed a tear when these guys go back to the city, and in a way I'll be crying for myself.

Out in a meadow, I could see the main telescope's white dome clinging to Observatory Ridge like a delicate little puffball, and Picacho Diablo peeking over that ridge as if the mountain were standing on tiptoe. Fine curtain-like clouds were now drifting in from the south and hanging aurora-like above the trees. Concerned that Bonni might drive right into the hurricane, I was praying that she was aware of it and would leave me there in the mountains a little longer, if necessary.

I started eating an apple. I offered Penny a slice; again she ate it greedily—whereas good old Pedro couldn't bring himself to eat any. He let it slip from his mouth and looked at me as if to say, "How could you?" Penny snatched that piece too.

It made me think that Pedro was like a "respectable," obedient, slightly dull Adam, whereas Penny was more like a wayward, lovable Eve. I walked on recording:

> I'm probably asking for a celestial Alpha roll, and I'm sure Peter the Martyr will be wringing his hands at my heresy, but I think we have it wrong to assume God wants total obedience from his creation. I think God delights in that part of creation which just can't resist a little willful fun. I know Penny wouldn't be Penny without that part of her personality. I'm sure even El Diablo can't help but look down and smile at her antics. And if it's true that God is surrounded by cherubs and angels, I'm sure they all bear a remarkable resemblance to Penny.

Suddenly, just ten-feet away, a coyote rose from behind a fallen tree and used it as cover to bolt away. Luckily, Pedro and Penny didn't see it. Pedro had found a large rib bone, and Penny was busy chasing and harassing him. As ever, she ended up with it.

We made it as far as the gate on the Tasajera road. It was raining aspen leaves and pine seeds but I couldn't find a single mushroom. We started back with the sky getting grayer by the minute. I willed it not to rain—a downpour would complicate my job of packing and breaking camp.

The wind moderated. I got an early fire going and began burning more papers, unneeded packaging and cardboard boxes. Penny and Pedro were soon stretched out asleep on the ground. Then about five, I heard the jubilant tooting of a horn. Penny and Pedro sprinted to the road. A white pickup! It was Bonni. I was ecstatic. She had beaten the storm. She could hardly get out of the truck without six eager paws jumping all over her. She offered me a cold beer and said that she'd spoken to Alfredo on the way in, and he'd be over shortly.

Sure enough, half-an-hour later, Alfredo came by with Zarco and the news that, "The hurricane is veering into the Pacific and isn't a threat anymore." I was at first greatly relieved…and then just a tiny bit disappointed to be spared the experience.

Alfredo stayed with us for a couple of hours. The dogs played their hearts out as we sat around a wonderful warming fire enjoying a delicious Italian sausage dinner and a little wine.

Bonni and I retired to the tent about eleven. It no longer seemed important to monitor the news.

However, if I had been listening, I might have heard that the Mexican government had, that night, issued its first hurricane warning for Baja California. By dawn, the very unpredictable Juliette was just fifty miles west-southwest of Cabo San Lucas, subjecting the southern part of the peninsula to violent winds and torrential rainfall.

I spent much of the following morning going through my supplies and equipment, deciding on what to take or give away. And looking at all the recent photos I'd shot I thought about any others I might need, especially as Bonni had brought up several rolls of film. I took a bunch of Penny and Pedro dressed in some of our "sponsors'" T-shirts and baseball caps. Both dogs were commendably cooperative, and endured the indignity with great composure.

In the afternoon we walked the dogs up the sandy, boulder strewn narrows of Columbine Canyon and paused beneath the outrageous red aspens at a spot where Bonni had earlier that summer scattered some of her mother's ashes among the columbines. After partaking of the peace there for forty minutes, I tapped a dry flower head and shook some of the small black columbine seeds into my hand. Further up the canyon I blew them around to give Mother Nature a helping hand.

Five hundred miles to the south, Mother Nature, in the fierce form of Juliette, was still stalled just west of Cabo San Lucas and, although downgraded from a hurricane to a tropical storm, didn't need any help smashing docks, destroying boats, uprooting trees, downing power lines, washing away bridges and a golf course, and leaving thousands of people homeless.

Still believing that the storm had gone careering harmlessly into the Pacific, Bonni and I decided to linger throughout the following day, a Saturday, and leave after leisurely packing up Sunday morning.

When Saturday came we were looking forward to our final communing with the forest, and to vicariously enjoying the happiness and freedom of the dogs. However, it was not to be. Midmorning, three Mexican vehicles arrived and pulled off the road near the trashcans. There must have been about five or six adults and an equal number of children. They set up their tents, including a bathroom tent, just yards away from my camp. I was amazed and disappointed, especially as I'd have to secure Pedro and Penny more than I planned.

Again it reflected the difference in attitudes to the great outdoors between Mexicans and gringos. Mexicans so often go camping to party and socialize and play loud music, whereas gringos are more likely entering the wilderness to enjoy nature and get away from their fellows.

As a guest in Mexico, however, it seemed the least I could do was to be understanding and cheerful about the locals and their cultural quirks. Indeed, it turned out to be no problem. They were polite, fascinating, intelligent people, and were very tolerant, indeed welcoming of the dogs, making it clear that we were just part of the family.

Bonni and I grabbed showers when they all took off to the observatory. As we toweled ourselves dry and frolicked naked in the forest, Juliette was re-intensifying to hurricane strength and began thrusting northward from the tip of the peninsula. Satellite images suggested that the storm intensified even as it was mostly over the rugged backbone of Baja. The National Hurricane Center was surprised and declared its motion anomalous. And beneath its sway, the parched desert was everywhere relieved by impressive rainfall amounts—the total for two or three normal years falling in a matter of hours.

We took Penny and Pedro for a long afternoon romp. While traversing the sunny meadows around the Salvatierra campground, a middle-aged Mexican couple drove up in a new Ford pickup and introduced themselves. They were from Tijuana, and on their first ever camping trip. He was an accountant. They were obviously nervous about the mountains and, given their mindset, incredibly brave. It seemed ironic to me, they lived in a dangerous city—some might argue the most violent city in Mexico, and they were anxious about being in the forest!

As we already had such a large extended family, I invited them to camp next to us; they pulled in just forty yards away on the other side of the ring road. To help their wilderness adjustment, they had brought tequila, vodka, and beer, and a determination to drink as much as possible.

So there we were enjoying our campfire, surrounded by people, and in the end, as was so often the case, going with the flow and very much appreciating their company. And the more the merrier—I was glad when Alfredo drove in to join us for the final evening. We had quite a party, and when it was over I loaded Alfredo's pickup with bags and boxes of surplus food, supplies, and equipment.

After we retired to our tent and into the early hours of Sunday, September 30, Juliette passed over Bahía Magdalena on the west coast of Baja California, and began a rapid, meandering track northwestward just offshore; then, like a battleship slowly bringing its big guns to bear, turned ominously towards the peninsula.

We woke to the sound of the wind. Huge dark billowing clouds were racing in from the southeast. This was no local front or monsoon. It was like nothing I had experienced all summer. This storm had height, and breadth, and depth to it. The hurrying clouds looked more menacing by the minute. We were now fully aware that Alfredo's belief that the hurricane had weakened and turned away had been too optimistic.

In fact, the storm center was moving across the peninsula 100 miles to the south, swirling and stalling over the midriff of the Gulf of California, drawing renewed vigor from its warm waters. Seven inches of rain had started falling in coastal areas of Sonora, where over 30,000 people were being driven from their homes.

The wind was flailing the treetops, stripping the aspens of all their leaves. It was a wildly autumnal scene. Everyone wisely left before us. The forest floor was covered with a moving sulfur and copper-colored sea. Bonni and I battled to take down the screen house that we had so tentatively erected four months before. There was a temporary leafless clearing where it had been and where I had sat through so many storms and rested after so many hikes. But the yellow leaves lay thick everywhere else—in the vehicle, the boxes, in my pockets.

All the tents were down, and all my camping gear and possessions boxed and ready for stowing. Penny and Pedro were curious, running between the boxes and sniffing around the places where the tents had been. They had done their bit to call attention to the sad situation of so many Mexican dogs, and to direct a little wholesome shame on the pride of *la raza*. I willed them to run far off, to chase each other across the clearings, to run free while they could, but they were too enthralled by what was happening to the place where they had spent the last three and four months of their short lives.

Everything was packed in our little Nissan pickup truck—only just; it was a tight squeeze. And there was more stuff to give to Alfredo strapped to the roof rack on the camper shell.

We were ready to leave by 10:30. Penny was up front on Bonni's lap, looking at me with her trusting eyes while I stroked the coarse scraggly locks of her head and neck, and gently tugged at one of her long flappy ears. Pedro took first turn in the back, in his well-padded kennel. Fearing rain and wash outs, there was little time for reflection or sentiment as we hastened out to the observatory road and then west out of the park.

I stopped at Alfredo's "office" trailer near the park entrance gate. It was cold and growing colder. Alfredo thought it might snow. We gave him the extra items, and I gave him a hearty handshake and a polite but sincerely meant Mexican hug.

Ruben had been there for me, Federico had been a kind, gracious, and informative host, but Alfredo was the person who I had come to know best, who had given me the most help, and who more than anyone had facilitated my stay. But all three were wonderful ambassadors for the park and for all that's good in the Mexican character.

Hurrying from the forested plateau and steeply down towards the sun-dappled foothills, I finally eased up on the gas and started to relax, and reflect. There was much to give thanks for. The ridges, meadows, and forests of the San Pedro Mártir had been great places to sojourn with dogs. We didn't have a single encounter with a rattlesnake, scorpion, tick, cactus, or poison oak. I vowed to bring Penny and Pedro back soon and often.

Our ever-curious Penny was standing on Bonni's lap, reaching up, paws and nose to the side window, looking out at the great and troubled vista stretching to the north. It was the same to the south. And Pedro, if he was peering out the back window, would have had the finest view of all.

Like the final curtain on our show, seemingly solid sheets of rain were dropping from the black clouds shrouding the mountains. It was easy to imagine the wild winds and ferocious deluge attacking our abandoned campsite. After four months in the Sierra San Pedro Mártir, it was a timely exit.

Postscript

Hurt not the earth, neither the sea, nor the trees.
— Revelation 7:3

No one knows for sure how much rain fell at the Padre Kino campsite, but over eight inches were recorded at the coastal resort of San Felipe, just thirty-five miles east of Picacho del Diablo.

We ran beside and ahead of the storm all the way to San Diego. There was dramatic lightning, hail, and a colorful rainbow-enhanced sunset as we approached the border. With the increased security, what would normally be a 15–30 minute wait to enter the U.S. at Tecate took over two-and-a-half-hours.

North of the border I was moved and astounded by the great post-September 11 patriotic display of flags, banners, and bumper stickers. I had indeed come home to a different world.

I took Penny and Pedro back to the San Pedro Mártir for two weeks in September, 2002. [And for a week in early June 2003] When they saw the Padre Kino campsite they exploded with delight. Zarco remembered them, I'm sure. Every time Alfredo brought him over, he'd romp playfully with his old buddies. Zarco is still accompanying Alfredo on his rounds, being well cared for, and enjoying his time in the forest.

The search for the man missing from the observatory was called off after ten days. A month later, a biologist conducting research in the park spotted the remains of the man's legs sticking out from a rocky extrusion on top of a hill overlooking the road to the observatory. It looked like he had crawled into a crevice in the rocks to sleep or find shelter. One of his arms was broken, presumably due to the fall from the window, and animals had eaten much of that arm and parts of his legs.

Baltasar also disappeared from the observatory one day; he was never seen again.

Sparky and Tanner turned out to be two healthy, happy, loving dogs. A few months after my return from the mountains I found a home for Sparky through the local humane society. Tanner grew up very pitbullish in appearance, but he is our softest, sweetest, most compliant dog. Like so many Mexican mutts who started with so little, he made a darling of a pet, desperately grateful for everything he has. He manages perfectly well with his single good eye. Perhaps his large frog-like mouth helps, but he catches cookies better than any of our two-eyed dogs. Knowing he'd be less adoptable, we decided to keep him. When Penny isn't chewing on one of Pedro's legs, Tanner's make a good substitute.

We always assumed after her impoverished beginnings that Penny was a plain old terrier mutt; but while browsing through a dog book I spotted a picture that could have been Penny herself—it was of a Glen of Imaal terrier, a rare Irish, badger hunting breed. Every aspect of her shape, size, coat, and temperament fitted the characteristics of the breed. And ever since that realization I have treated Penny even more like the little princess that she thinks she is.

When I'm home in San Diego, I try to take Penny, Pedro, Bella, and Tanner to Dog Beach at least once a week so they can run free and splash about in the surf. And, boy, can Pedro run. I've never seen a dog that can match his speed. With Penny always happy to chomp down on his leg, he needs all the speed he can muster to escape her badger crunching jaws. Maybe I'm biased, but to me she's still the most loving, fun-loving, personality-packed, dumpy princess in the world; and as with our other dogs, I've fallen completely under her spell—I'm always way too tolerant of her cheeky craziness.

I spent the summer of 2002 working on sections of this book in a cottage on Lake Huron, at the eastern end of the Upper Peninsula of Michigan. Ironically, after researching and writing much of the lightning component of the story, the cottage was struck by lightning. Pictures and lamps flew off the wall. A sturdy, wall-mounted, antique mirror exploded across my bedroom leaving a smoking hole above my bed. The computer I was working on was fried, along with other electrical appliances and house fixtures. Fortunately my two backup floppies weren't damaged—otherwise the publication of this book might have been delayed for a few months. And if I'd stayed out on the deck a few moments longer, I might have become part of those lightning statistics, and you might never have had the pleasure of reading it at all.

Although much of the old growth forest of the San Pedro Mártir is protected within park boundaries, a significant portion is owned by neighboring *ejidos*, or communes, set up to provide land to poor peasants after the Mexican Revolution. A change in the Mexican Constitution during the 1990's allowed ejido members, for the first time, to sell their land and land-use rights. Straightaway several American logging companies began making pitches for timber rights.

There were misgivings. Richard Minnich stated the danger:

> Logging could be effective if it were constrained within the natural dynamics of conifer forest ecosystems, i.e., removal of small-diameter stems. However, the experience in California and Mexico has shown that the culling of commercially valuable large stems will result in understory thickening and the potential for extensive stand-replacement burns over long time scales.

With little fanfare and no serious environmental impact study, deals were struck and a new road was bulldozed into the Sierra San Pedro Mártir along the western edge of the park near La Corona. A Louisiana Pacific mill outside Ensenada stood ready to process the logs into boards for a fraction of the cost north of the border. The trucks began to roll; the logging was at first small-scale and tentative.

By 2002, the Sierra San Pedro Mártir was experiencing what was described as "the worst drought in modern memory." And with it came some of the most damaging fires in years. To help circumvent any environmental protest, the land owners and logging companies began to talk up the need for a "sanitation harvest" to prevent a "catastrophic" fire or a fungi or beetle "infestation" of the drought-weakened trees. At their urging, the federal Environment Ministry actually ordered Baja landowners to remove dead and dying trees. Taking that as a nod and a wink from the Mexican authorities, the pace of tree cutting and removal increased dramatically.

As soon as word got out there was an outcry from concerned environmentalists in both Mexico and the United States. Federico, alarmed by reports of park border violations, went to see for himself. He brought a video camera and started to record the felling of the great trees. He taught Alfredo to use the camera, and he too spent hours filming the logging activities.

Not only were the timber companies taking dead and dying trees from wherever they could get their saws and bulldozers, they were as Minnich and others feared systematically felling the tallest, strongest trees most essential to the health of the forest, and were arguably logging inside the park in places by as much as 500 yards.

The videotapes went the rounds of the environmental agencies in Mexico City and were a major factor in the order for the immediate cessation of logging, the closure of the area, and the impounding of the logging vehicles.

With the fate of the San Pedro Mártir in the balance, Richard Minnich and a delegation of other American scientists visited Mexicali, the State capital, in early 2003, to plead for the preservation of North America's "only pristine conifer forest."

The scientists argued that fire has always been the most efficient remover of dead material from the ecosystem and the fires that had burned through those mountains were part of the natural process of "sanitation." The forest's low tree density would protect it during the drought, preventing any major bark beetle, mistletoe or pathogenic fungi damage, while at the same time acting as a brake on the wildfires. They also pointed out that the situation was not nearly as bad as in the managed forests of the Western U.S. where thousands of trees were dying in groups and catastrophic wildfires were raging out of control. As one of the scientists put it, "It's hard to realize that sometimes inaction or careful monitoring is the best action."

The Mexican officials, duly impressed, recommended that the sanitation order be cancelled. One of them remarked, "We don't want to do something that can damage more than it can help."

A delighted American scientist observed, "The whole concern was that the ejidos would pressure the national park to start giving in on the edge, and that loggers could just start wandering inside. I don't think that's going to happen now."

Thoreau once wrote that, "The earth is more to be admired than to be used." And that seemingly radical claim could very reasonably be applied to the precious remnant of America's old growth coniferous forests found in the Sierra San Pedro Mártir. The area would never recover from our abuse.

As I wrote in an earlier chapter, I'd like to think that in a hundred and twenty-three years, when the comet Swift-Tuttle appears in the sky again over these mountains, the giant pines will still be there, offering silent testament to the care that we showed in the first years of the twenty-first century. And I'd like to think that condors will be roaming in that sky...and, above all, I'd like to think that I'll be there in spirit with Penny and Pedro.

In August 2002, on the western edge of the park not far from where the logging had been halted, six California condors were brought to a specially prepared site. The plan was to release five birds ranging in ages from $1\frac{1}{2}$ and $2\frac{1}{2}$ years. The sixth condor, Xewe, was a "mentor" borrowed from the San Diego Wild Animal Park. She was 11 years old and could be clearly distinguished from the dark headed juveniles by her salmon-pink neck and head. She had been recaptured after two years in the wild because she was constantly flying too near power lines. It was hoped that Xewe would teach the younger birds, all raised by keepers at the Los Angeles Zoo, to walk the line (so to speak) in terms of appropriate condor conduct. She would then be returned to captivity after her protégés were released.

An initial release of three condors was planned, with the other two following shortly afterwards. They were expected to be the first of 20 condors set free at the site over the next 10 years.

An elaborate aviary had been designed and constructed by Mike Wallace, wildlife specialist with the Zoological Society of San Diego, and team leader for the California Condor Recovery Program. The spacious, tree-incorporated enclosure of nylon netting and chain link fence was sited to overlook several canyons dropping to the west and allow the condors maximum interaction with the wildlife, but virtually no awareness of their custodians who were separated from them by a blacked out observation "tree house" and an approach concealed by enough natural cover, screens, and camouflage netting to grace a war zone.

After weeks orienting themselves to their new home and feasting on the carcasses of cattle, goats, and the occasional road kill dog "thrown in the trunk" and brought up as a special treat, the big day came.

October 9, 2002: With Mexican and American dignitaries, government officials, reporters and film crews cooing and craning their necks on a nearby rocky outcrop, the door to the aviary was opened and the three chosen birds were invited to reclaim the southernmost part of their historic range. The expectation was tangible. The rhetoric soared.

"This day gives us reason to rejoice," said Dr. Exequiel Ezcurra, President of Mexico's *Instituto Nacional de Ecología*, "Sixty years have passed without condors in Mexico, and today we will see these birds open their wings where their ancestors once did."

"I was an associate solicitor at the Interior Department over a decade and a half ago when we decided to take the last California condors into captivity," said U.S. Secretary of the Interior Gale Norton from north of the border. "Back then there were those who disagreed with our decision, but the approach of breeding them in captivity and reintroducing them to the wild has succeeded. I am proud today to be able to share these magnificent birds with our neighbors in Mexico."

Unfortunately, the rhetoric was the only thing that soared. Unsure what to make of their newfound freedom, and perhaps a little shy of the onlookers, the young condors remained in the pen.

Half an hour later Mike Wallace said, "They're afraid of the door."

Come nightfall, with the cautious condors still huddled deep in their cage, Mike ordered the door closed to keep out any coyotes, bobcats, or mountain lions who might have thought Thanksgiving had come early.

A day later, the three reluctant birds, all bearing small radio transmitters to help monitor their locations, plucked up the courage to "open their wings where their ancestors once did" and immediately strayed beyond their guardians' comfort zone. A golden eagle, a species known to have attacked and killed condors north of the border, nearly knocked one from the sky. The ruffled researchers decided to recapture the birds, thinking they may need more time acclimating and talking things over with wise old Xewe.

A commendably patient Mike Wallace said, "I'm determined to get them out again in the next few weeks," [but] "if we have to chase them all over in deteriorating conditions, I'd rather keep them in here until the weather is better…That may be through the winter, and that's fine, too. We don't lose anything in the long-run. This is a long-run program."

I was reminded of my caution in releasing Pedro. It's hard to hazard your raison d'etre.

A few weeks after the much-heralded San Pedro Mártir "release," the California Condor Recovery Program received a crushing blow with the death of three chicks in the Los Padres National Forest, northwest of Los Angeles.

They were the first chicks to emerge from eggs laid in the wild since 1984. Program officials had been ecstatic. The chicks were closely monitored. They survived the summer, but all three died just as they were about to take flight for the first time. Autopsies revealed their digestive tracts were lined with bottle caps, shards of glass, electrical connectors, washers, and screws.

"We don't know the exact cause of death," said a circumspect condor program coordinator, "but the digestive processes were impaired." Some speculated that the adult condors brought the trash back to the chicks' nesting caves; others, sure that much of it was already in the nest areas when the chicks were born, thought that it had been cached there by ravens or previous generations of condors.

Those working on the program put a brave face on the setback. They pointed out that there were an increasing number of released birds forming breeding pairs and they were looking forward to seeing more chicks hatch in the wild. The old caves and other nesting sites would be cleaned up and there would be even more monitoring of future hatchlings.

Another "great tragedy and a tremendous loss," in the words of Interior Secretary Gale Norton, befell the program on February 13, 2003. In spite of the fact that anyone convicted of killing a California condor could face a year in jail and a $100,000 fine, a condor was found shot to death in a remote area north of Los Angeles. Adult Condor 8, or AC-8 as she was known, might have been the oldest condor alive—she was between 30 and 40 years old—and was the last female condor to be captured in 1986. She had been dubbed the "matriarch" of the captive breeding program, producing 12 chicks in captivity.

In April 2002, after she had stopped laying eggs, AC-8 was released and flew off alone back to her old haunts. At the end of the year she was recaptured and treated for lead poisoning. She had to be force-fed while drugs removed the lead, almost certainly from bullet fragments or pellets lodged in carrion, from her body. She was re-released December 23, 2002 for what turned out to be the final few weeks of her life.

In the light of these blows, some began to ask if the release of condors back into the wild wasn't a fanciful, expensive experiment doomed to failure given the condors' habits and the ever-increasing pressures of human habitation. Others suggested that if California condors are to find homes anywhere other than zoos and wild animal parks, the *Parque Nacional Sierra de San Pedro Mártir* represented their best hope in North America.

(The "initial release" of three condors finally occurred May 26, 2003. Their two comrades were due to join them a month later.)

The road from the highway through San Telmo has in the last year or two been paved for several miles, making the journey to the park that much easier. When the paved road runs all sixty miles to the observatory, it will be just a matter of time before the San Pedro Mártir is "discovered."

Staying in one place helped me interact with the wildlife more than when constantly moving, but there were pros and cons to having the dogs. I probably would have hiked further if I didn't have them, and might have made an attempt to climb Picacho del Diablo. I certainly would have had less work, and more opportunity to sit and be quiet and let nature come to me. But Penny and Pedro turned out to be delightful company, and good little watchdogs.

Through my close relationship with them, I came to better appreciate the happiness and joy dogs can experience, and the tragedy of the needless suffering of these wonderful creatures that are so dependent on us, and yet have so much to offer.

I look forward to a revolution in Mexico, to a time when I can travel the Baja highway and not be troubled by the sight of so many sad and neglected dogs. If my words can in any way help ameliorate their plight, this book will have served its purpose. And Penny will have served her purpose in coming to me that afternoon in January 2001, and propelling this whole endeavor.

Last jaunt among the Jeffrey pines

Assorted Outtakes

When shall we three meet again?
In thunder, lightning, or in rain?
— Shakespeare – *Macbeth*

On my 50th birthday, a friend gave me a comforting present—a sky blue T-shirt trumpeting, "Fifty isn't old if you are a tree." Always looking for signs from above, I realized the place in Baja with the oldest trees was the San Pedro Mártir mountains…maybe up there I would feel rejuvenated.

Kino might have proven that Lower California wasn't an island, but in one sense it remains an island of mystery, an island of anachronisms, a slowly disappearing island of wilderness.

As I get older I'm more and more convinced that we act first and then we explain our actions to ourselves and others. I see it all the time in those instant decisions I have to make…and in those terrible moments of temptation when, for example, I'm dieting and I see chocolate, and even though I tell myself to resist, some stranger within me, some lamentable weakling who clearly has another agenda, walks over, unwraps the delicious morsel, and downs it before my astonished eyes… Sometimes, when what I've done truly astounds me, I need to write to "shed light" on the mystery. And most of my inexplicable actions seem to take place somewhere on the spectacularly beautiful 800-mile long Baja California peninsula.

Wolves, toadstools, fire, and Inquisition—some pretty profound Anglo prejudices?

Excess wariness leads to excess weariness. If the reader follows me into my mental state, worrying about mountain lions, I apologize. It is not my intention to eviscerate the enjoyment from anyone's wilderness experience.

An upside to anxiety is the need to allay it. Lest we fall victim to booze, drugs, insanity, we must turn to spiritual alleviation—trust, acceptance, faith, obedience, love: these "dog-like" qualities are great anodynes.

Alfredo came over early one evening. While we were chatting we heard what sounded like three rifle shots a mile or two to the south. As Alfredo listened with a sudden, serious look on his face, I asked, "Is that someone hunting?"

He nodded.

"Do you think they are Americans?"

"They are Mexicans, hunting deer," he said, confidently.

"Where is their vehicle?"

He gestured towards the corrals at Aguaje del Burro.

We listened in silence for a minute or two. Then Alfredo picked up his hand-held radio and made a call to the army who were stationed sixty miles away down near the highway. He said that the soldiers would either come up to investigate or attempt to intercept the culprits heading out of the mountains. I was glad Alfredo didn't try to confront the poachers himself.

When he drove away, it was a little disturbing to think there was someone out there with a rifle. I walked Pedro on patrol until it was almost completely dark, and took comfort from his playful unconcern.

The trees are randomly scattered through the forest like the stars in the sky. But with a godlike imagination it is easy to group them together in constellations—and it's always easy to find crosses!

By being close to Penny and Pedro and sharing our lives so intimately I felt as if I were also nearer to my God. To paraphrase Voltaire—"If dogs did not exist, God would have to invent them." I can blame such thoughts on being so close to my God in one of the finest Edens on this earth.

A plague and political unrest led to Sor Juana's harassment and the suppression of her free thinking scientific and literary enquiries. She capitulated to this pressure by selling her library, the most extensive in Mexico, and renewing her vows. In her own blood, she signed a statement of self-condemnation, and then turned to a life of penance and self-sacrifice. Within two years Sor Juana fell victim to an epidemic while nursing her sisters. [Sounds like the comet foretold with great accuracy the calamities in store for Mexico and Sor Juana.]

Once, Pedro jumped up on Penny and went through the motions of copulating; I wanted to discourage that so I shouted, "PEDRO, COME, COME." He looked very confused, unsure what I meant.

After 9-11, I was hit by a sense of loneliness that no person could ameliorate. It was too deep for that.

The Harvard Center for Risk Analysis has calculated the chances of falling victim to some unlikely non-terrorist events. The odds of dying in a motor-vehicle accident are about 1 in 6,745; in a fire, 1 in 82,977; on a bicycle, 1 in 376,165; by a lightning strike, 1 in 4,468,159. Death through an act of terrorism is less likely than any of these.

Fighting over the basket, my guys were like a belligerent Romulus and Remus—Mars would approve.

Holy Cow! The Hindu may have it wrong. It is more likely to be a dog harboring the soul of your parents, grandparents, or distant ancestors. No doubt, this is what Hamlet was driving at when he said, "For in that sleep of death what dreams may come, when we have shuffled off this mortal coil, must give us paws."

How we treat our dogs is how God will treat us.

Bibliography

Into a Desert Place – Graham Mackintosh, W.W. Norton, 1995

Journey With a Baja Burro – Graham Mackintosh, Sunbelt Publications, 2001

Camping and Climbing in Baja – John Robinson, La Siesta Press, 1967

How to be Your Dog's Best Friend – The Monks of New Skete, Little, Brown and Company, 1978

Dogs – Raymond and Lorna Coppinger, Scribner, 2001

Parque Nacional San Pedro Martir – Map by Jerry Schad, Centra Publications, 1988

Rim of Christendom – Herbert Bolton, Russell and Russell, 1960

Camp and Camino in Lower California – Arthur North, Rio Grande Press, 1977

Natural History of Southern California – Ancinec, Radford and Schwenkmeyer. Ginn Press, 1992

In the Company of Mushrooms – Elio Schaechter, Harvard University Press, 1997

Mushrooms Demystified – David Arora, Ten Speed Press, 1986

Soma, Divine Mushroom of Immortality – R. Gordon Wasson, Harcourt, Brace, Jovanovich, 1968

The Sacred Mushroom and the Cross – John Allegro, Hodder and Stoughton, 1973

Strange Fruit: Alchemy, Religion and Magical Foods, Clark Heinrich, Bloomsbury, 1995

Mountains of California – John Muir, Natural History Library, 1961

The Other Side: Journeys in Baja California – Judy Goldstein Botello, Sunbelt Publications, 1998

Baja California Plant Field Guide – Norman Roberts, La Jolla: Natural History Publishing Company, 1989

Baja – Joe Cummings, Moon Publications Handbook, 2002

Baja California – Lonely Planet Guides, 2001

The Baja Adventure Book – Walt Peterson, Wilderness Press, 1999

Loreto, Baja California: First Mission and Capital of Spanish California – Ann and Don O'Neil, Tio Press, 2001

Miraculous Air – C.M. Mayo, University of Utah Press, 2002

Baja Legends – Greg Niemann, Sunbelt Publications, 2002

Torrey Pines: Landscape and Legacy – Bill Evarts, Torrey Pines, 1995

Acknowledgements

Muchisimas gracias to the staff of the *Parque Nacional Sierra de San Pedro Mártir*, especially Alfredo Madriles and his family, Ruben Góngora, and Federico Godinez Leal. Muchisimas gracias also to Armando García and the hospitable folks at the San Pedro Mártir Observatory. And many, many thanks to Sunny Benedict and all the dedicated workers at the Baja Animal Sanctuary in Rosarito Beach.

Special thanks also to Gwyn Enright, Bill Evarts, Laurie Gibson, Ellen Goodwin, Gene Kira, Tom Klare, C. M. Mayo, Scott McMillan, Ann O'Neil, Suzy Orlofski, Jennifer Redmond, Elio Schaechter, Dick Schwenkmeyer, and Judy Webster for their valuable editorial and content assistance...and to Paul Anderson, Juan Pedro Arce, Elizabeth Ah Nee, Tomas Campbell, Juan Tintos Funke, Ann Hazard, Hugh and Carol Kramer, Andrew Miller, David Richardson, Dick Van Bree, and Sandy Yurmonovich, for helping out in other vital ways.

And last, but by no means least, a huge hug of gratitude to my ever tolerant and understanding wife, Bonni, who did so much to help make my sojourn in the mountains and this book possible.